FOR THE
WORLD
TO HEAR

FOR THE WORLD TO HEAR

A Biography of
HOWARD P. HOUSE, M.D.
by Sidney Hyman
Foreword by President Ronald Reagan

HOPE
Publishing House

Pasadena, California

For the World to Hear © 1990 Hope Publishing House

All rights reserved.

For information address Hope Publishing House
P.O.Box 60008, Pasadena, CA 91116

Printed in the United States of America

First edition

Manuscript Editor: Faith Annette Sand

Cover Design: Michael McClary/The Workshop

Library of Congress Cataloging-in-Publication Data

Hyman, Sidney R.
    For the world to hear : a biography of Dr. Howard P. House /
by Sidney Hyman ; with a foreword by President Ronald Reagan.
      p.   cm.
    ISBN 0-932727-31-X : $19.95
    1. House, Howard P. (Howard Payne), 1908-   .
    2. Otolaryngologists—United States—Biography. I. Title.
RF38.H6H96 1990
617.5'1'0092—dc20   89-15615
[B]   CIP

Dedicated by Howard P. House to the memory of his beloved wife Helen.

Table of Contents

To Howard House
With best wishes,

Ronald Reagan

Table of Contents

Acknowledgements

Emerson once laid it down as a rule that when old friends meet after a time apart they should greet each other by asking one question: "Has anything become clear to you since we were last together?" This biography comes under the writ of that rule. As an "old friend" for a number of years my work on it was broken into by the distractions known to most writers of books that deal with the lives of individuals. But now that I have come together with a manuscript that is ready for publication, I here state that one thing above all is clear to me—it is the extent of the depth of gratitude I owe to countless individuals for the different kinds of help they generously gave me.

They include members of the House family, surgeons, associates and trustees of the House Ear Institute and other benefactors. They include as well friends of mine on the faculties of the medical schools at the Universities of Harvard, Chicago, Northwestern, Illinois, USC, UCLA and the Rush Medical Center. All these in combination served as a very deep well to which I regularly returned for the information and perspective I needed.

On a plane apart from other sources of help, I owe an immense debt to three individuals in particular. The first is Nanette Fabray who was in a fundamental sense my editor-in-chief. Aside from her unique knowledge of the world of otology—and of Howard House personally—she brought to what was originally an oversized manuscript, her keen sense of stagecraft, governing, diction, highlights, cuts, sequences and juxtaposition of episodes. In my own experiences as an author of more than a dozen books and as a regular contributor to major magazines—besides being an editor in my own right—I have never encountered an editor whose judgment I respected more than I came to respect Nan's.

The second of the three individuals to whom I am particularly indebted is Ruth Barnes who has served four decades as the incomparable secretary to Howard House. I depended on her as my personalized traffic manager for the flow of contacts with Howard House and for the to and fro transmittal of documents and manuscript drafts. She was also the source of a much needed cooling hand pressed against my forehead when I was overheated by frustrations on one or another count. The third individual to whom I am particularly indebted is Janet Doak, executive vice-president of the House Ear Institute, who has played a major role in the development of the institute. A calm and judicious woman, she was burdened with the responsibility for bringing the biography of Howard House to a publication stage.

—*Sidney Hyman*, Chicago, Illinois

To Howard House
With best wishes,

Ronald Reagan

Foreword

One of the reasons I am proud to be an American is because our country is so full of wonderful men and women who, through diligent effort and creative drive, have made a tremendous difference in our world and brought to pass amazing scientific discoveries that have helped countless people everywhere. I love to hear these stories and that's why I enjoyed reading this fine book about my good friend, Dr. Howard P. House.

Dr. House is an outstanding example of what has made America great and it is important that others learn from his experience. I am especially pleased that during the eight years we spent in Washington, we were able to create a new Private Sector Initiatives Department. This department gathers information and records what splendid things are being done in community projects and programs all over our land. It has been my experience that the best way to solve problems is when people get together and figure out a solution through their own initiative. So this department has been able to provide a remarkable service, putting people with a question or a problem in touch with others who have faced the same difficulty. And all over the country there are people making a tremendous difference in their own communities by using their God-given talents to help one another.

I'm gratified to say that this department was so successful that the news got out. One day we got a phone call from Paris, France asking if we could assist them in setting up a similar department in their own country. And this idea of a Private Sector Initiatives Department spread around the world so that by the time we left Washington we had seen similar agencies developed worldwide—making it easier for people to solve their problems and learn from others who have done the same.

Personally I am grateful to one of these private initiative ventures—the work of the Drs. House—because I have benefited from the remarkable accomplishments of this great team of doctors at the Otologic Medical Group and the Research Institute they established. Everyone of us faces difficulties and problems at one point or another in our lives, and when you need help it is satisfying to find someone who has devoted a lifetime to assisting people just like you.

Years ago when I was on a movie set, a gunshot exploded too close to my right ear for comfort. Over the years I began having a progressively harder time hearing in that ear. Finally the day came, in the middle of my presidency, when it was obvious I needed help. Am I glad I knew where to turn!

I had long known about Dr. Howard P. House and all the brilliant work being done at the House Ear Institute for those experiencing hearing loss, but now it was my turn. It wasn't long before they had fitted me with a hearing aid that has made a tremendous difference in my own life.

This story, then, is an impressive account of how the world-renowned Otologic Medical Group and the House Ear Institute came about. This biography is packed full of humor, pathos, struggle, human helpfulness and a wonderful tale of great achievement. It is a delightful description of American ingenuity and free enterprise at its best.

—President Ronald Reagan

1

The Hinge of Fate

The trap was sprung at the end of the meeting on a Los Angeles day in June 1961. Admissions Committee members had already picked, from among thousands of applicants, the 85 students who would be offered places in the fall class of the University of Southern California's School of Medicine (USC). At this last session of the academic year, they agreed on the "wait list" for places in the class that might open up during the summer months. "Well," said Dr. Peter V. Lee, chair of the committee, after the names on the list had been ranked, "that wraps up our work."

The scrape of chairs and the buzz of small talk—the usual sounds of a meeting that is over—were broken into by a voice saying, "Just a minute. I'm not through yet." Dr. Howard Payne House, called "Dr. Howard" by his friends to distinguish him from his brother, Dr. William House, was speaking.

The committee members promptly paid Howard the respect of silence for reasons beyond the fact that he had chaired the successful fund-raising drive for the new medical school building they were in, named after Dean Paul S. McKibben. Howard had been on the school's faculty since 1939 and had served since 1951 as clinical professor and chair of the Department of Ear, Nose and Throat (ENT). By 1961, at the age of 53, he had founded two private institutions—the Los Angeles Foundation of Otology (now

1

the House Ear Institute) and the Otologic Medical Group (OMG)—both of which were gaining international attention among veteran and novitiate ear surgeons. In addition, he had already won a firm place for himself in the front rank of pioneering ear surgeons around the world and was a leader in several major professional organizations devoted to the study and treatment of hearing and balance disorders.

Howard had asked for "just a minute" in order to mount a last attack on what he believed was a wrong-headed aspect of admissions to medical schools. He would, if he could, reverse the existing rule where grades were the decisive criterion for choosing applicants, while judgments of their character and motivations based on personal interviews were often of slight importance. The trap to be sprung in order to drive home the point of his argument was initially masked by the oblique way he chose to unfold his case. His remarks, as recalled by Dr. Peter Lee, were framed as a request for help in a personal matter.

"As you know," Howard began, "I am resigning from this committee after a decade of service. Since I will not be with you next year, I want to call your attention to a young man I've known since childhood. I've watched him mature as a well-rounded young man with many interests. In college, he was on the tennis team, manager of the football team and a member of the debating team. These activities cut into the time he spent on his studies, but in my view he has all the qualities of mind and character that make for a good doctor."

Howard continued, "This young man wants to apply to the USC Medical School as a candidate for the fall class starting a year from now. I don't want to encourage him to apply only to see him rebuffed by next year's committee. So I need your opinion regarding the young man's prospects. I've made copies of his undergraduate academic record and deleted his name from the transcript because it might affect your judgment."

There was a rustle of anticipation as copies of the transcript were passed around the conference table, while Howard awaited the reaction of the committee members with what Mark Twain would call "the serenity of a Christian holding four aces."

The transcript itself traced the nameless young person's four-year undergraduate career at three institutions. At William Jewel College in Missouri, where the young man spent his freshman year, he earned two Ds in chemistry and an F in German, for a grade point average of 2.18. He transferred to USC for the first semester of his sophomore year where he earned a D in chemistry and a D in psychology—in reward for which he was placed on probation.

At Whittier College, to which he had transferred for the second semester, he earned another D in chemistry, a D in German and a D in "Introduction to Literature." It was a disastrous year and his overall grade point average dropped to 1.35. The young person's junior year was marked by an F in American government, another D in German and a D in "Biblical Introduction," for a grade point average of 2.26. There was an improvement in his senior year, with no Ds and a grade point average of 2.8, but his four years in college showed a record of ten Ds and two Fs. His only As were in tennis, public speaking and a mysterious course called "Minor Problems."

A wave of laughter rolled over the length of the conference table. "Howard," one of the members at last said, "you really can't be serious about this. Your own years of service on this committee should tell you that we wouldn't even consider applicants with a grade point average less than 3.0 and your young man has an overall average of 2.15."

Other voices cut in with their own variations on the

theme, *"Impossible,"* until the hubbub was checked by the gavel of the chair and by the question he put to Howard. Did he want a vote on whether or not the young man should apply to the USC medical school?

"Absolutely," Howard replied.

In the show of hands that followed, nine votes were in the negative; the only affirmative vote was Howard's.

With that, Howard passed around copies of the very same transcript, but this one had *his* name on it. The committee members were stunned. "Yes," said Howard, *"I* am the young man none of you would have allowed to enter this medical school. The transcript you saw was *my* undergraduate record when I applied in the Spring of 1930. Yet I was admitted by Dean Paul S. McKibben and I am sure I was admitted largely on the basis of my personal interview with him."

Howard then bore down on the moral of the story. "During the ten years I've been on this committee," he said, "I've often wondered how many applicants might have made major contributions to medicine, but for the fact that committees such as this cannot look closely at the qualities comprising their character, but automatically deny them admission to medical schools mainly due to their low grade averages in college."

Later, when the committee members gathered in the home of Dr. Lee for the traditional dinner that marked the end of a year's work, the trap Howard had sprung had lost its sharp bite and the ruse was on its way to becoming another item in the fund of comic anecdotes about him in the medical profession. As for Howard, he often wondered aloud why many good things came his way which were denied to very deserving people. In particular, he never ceased to wonder why, despite his checkered academic record, he was nonetheless admitted to the USC medical school.

Whenever he focused his thoughts on who and what shaped the main bent of his life, Howard invariably dwelt on the influence of his father, Dr. Milus Marion House—a major figure in 20th century dentistry. In some families, as time goes by, the memory of a deceased father tends to lose its clarity of line. Milus, even in death, remained a vivid presence in the life of his sons.

He influenced his four sons in matters of character, medical research and determination to excel—and inspired them as much by his hand stretching out from the grave, as when he was alive. In fact, unless the figure of Milus House is seen first and his sons afterward, the mainsprings of *their* actions will remain half-hidden. In Howard's specific case, there is a striking symmetry between the career of his father and certain stages of his *own* development, in his *own* time, within his *own* metier.

2

Young Milus

Milus Marion House was born on April Fools' Day, 1879, in Paxton, Illinois. In later life he talked of his formative years as though he had plucked himself out of the nameless army of waifs and strays fated to go nowhere. He was, in fact, part of an extended family that contributed more than its ordinary share to America's Midwestern rural aristocracy—comprised of teachers, preachers, editors and doctors.

Milus' mother, Clara Logan House, born on a farm near Chicago, was a niece of General John A. Logan of Civil War celebrity, as well as the original developer of what is now Logan Square in Chicago. His father, Howard Everett House, born in southern Illinois and a farmer by vocation, was a very literate man in an era when the fourth grade marked the end of formal education for most rural boys. He was an author of homespun poetry and conducted a "singing school," a centerpiece of social life in rural areas. Milus' aunt, Mrs. Sarah K. Hunney, his mother's sister, was a "degreed" physician—a rarity for that time. She was engaged in general practice first in Concordia, Kansas and later in Mankato, where her husband published the local newspaper.

In 1894, the reports which Howard Everett House and his wife Clara received about the "bright prospects" of life in Kansas induced them to leave Illinois and buy 160 acres of

6

land a few miles west of Concordia, Kansas. With the relocation, Milus and his sister Mabel, his senior by 18 months, were enrolled in the same one-room school. Mabel, the excellent student, shone in the class but was forced to suffer the presence of a brother who, as she later recalled, "would not recite and paid no attention to what was going on around him except to look at the teacher in open-mouthed amazement. He would not do anything—just the dumbest thing you ever saw. I was so ashamed of him I did not know what to do."

To such a boy, a release from compulsory attendance when he turned 13 amounted to a Jubilee. His sense of freedom was reinforced when he was allowed to keep whatever money he earned by "hiring out" to neighbors for menial and irksome farm tasks. In the winter months he worked as a driver for his aunt, Dr. Sarah Hunney, as she made the rounds of farm houses in her winterized buggy. The excursions with his aunt stirred the youth's general interest in medicine, but something else pointed him specifically toward dentistry.

One time when his mother had a toothache, Milus took her to see a Concordia dentist where the dentist had placed a gold crown on her tooth—a five-hour ordeal. What, he asked, after examining the shining addition, had the dentist charged? When he heard the answer—five dollars—Milus quickly figured out how long it would take him to earn five dollars on the farm. Days later he announced to his parents that he planned to head for Indianapolis to enroll in the Indiana Dental College, now the Indiana University School of Dentistry.

On arriving in Indianapolis by train in the late summer of 1899, Milus' net worth, he recalled in later life, consisted of "twelve dollars and a bicycle." He encamped in the Indianapolis home of his married cousin, Maude Le May, until he lined up jobs to cover his living expenses elsewhere as well as pay his school fees. His aspirations were derailed when he presented himself to Dean George E. Hunt of the Indiana Dental College as a prospective dental student and learned that a precondition for admission to the college was a high school diploma or its "equivalent"—a word whose meaning was left to the discretion of the dean. The youth, now out of school for five years, was not one to be defeated by a dictionary. He enrolled in high school.

A year later Milus again called on Dean Hunt—a meeting which prefigured by three decades an encounter between the Dean of the USC School of Medicine and young Howard P. House. Dean Hunt apparently saw within Milus a driving ambition that went far beyond his skimpy academic record, so he agreed that Milus now had the "equivalent" of a high school diploma and admitted him to the dental school. Nothing about the youth at the age of 21 hinted that he would one day be a major figure in the history of modern dentistry.

Milus had been reared in a home whose religious tone had been set by his mother, a devout Protestant "fundamentalist." When he began his studies at Indiana Dental College his choice of a church to attend on Sunday mornings depended on where he found himself in "downtown" Indianapolis. One Sunday morning, he wandered into the First Christian Church where his ears presently led him to focus his eyes on a young soloist in the choir. Concluding that both she and her singing voice were beautiful, he investigated and learned that her name was Jesse Payne and that she had studied at the Boston Conservatory of Music. He presently contrived an introduction and was encouraged by her response. With that, he was treated to the agreeable revelation that his natural spiritual home was the First Christian Church.

Jesse, the oldest of the four children of Dorsey and Ann Payne, was followed in age by Floyd, Dorothy and Harold.

Dorsey Payne, the head of the family, was in some respects a transcript of Milus' own father—both a farmer and a music teacher who taught vocalists and conducted "singing lessons." Jesse herself, a gentle soul, had a promising voice which sustained the hope that she might one day be an opera singer of note. In her relationship with Milus, a point was reached where they spoke of coupling their lives for a common destiny, but marriage was not an immediate prospect. Milus was hard pressed merely to meet the costs of his dental training without adding the financial responsibility of providing for a wife.

The profession of dentistry for which Milus prepared himself developed independently of medicine, for the medical profession assigned it the déclassé status of a craft. Ironically, however, the basis for major advances in all kinds of surgery were made not by members of the regular medical profession but by a dentist, Dr. William Morton, who proved in 1846 that the inhalation of a little-known chemical compound—ether—could anesthetize patients during surgical operations. Without anesthetics, the surgeon had to be able to ignore the shrieks of the patients and finish the ghastly business quickly.

Basic research was at a bare bone level of performance in 1903 when Milus completed his dental training. No postgraduate training courses were available; however, progress had been made in prosthetics ranging from gold fillings and amalgams to porcelain dentures. New style articulators, though flawed as a device for duplicating the natural movement of the lower jaw, were becoming available to set arrangements of artificial teeth.

All such developments in the opening years of the 20th century brought the world of dentistry alive with promising prospects—just as the world of otology was alive with promising prospects after Howard House began his practice in the late 1930s and again when Bill House began his

9

residency in otology in the early 1950s. Yet if there were many things to be understood and done, the difference, starting with Milus House, and duplicated by two of his sons in their day, was that he would actually do what others seemed merely to talk about. Virtually every aspect of dentistry—research, education, technique, professional organizations—was to benefit from his inventive mind and awesome power of concentration. This would be true of his sons as well in their respective medical careers.

Milus began to make his mark on the technology of dentistry during the two years he spent in a Boston dental laboratory following his graduation from Indiana Dental College. When his innovative work came to the attention of a rival company based in Pittsburgh, the terms offered for his service drew him back to Indianapolis long enough to marry Jesse in April 1906, followed by a move to Pittsburgh.

In December that year, however, the pattern of their new life was altered by a report from Indianapolis. Jesse's father had suffered a fatal concussion when he slipped and fell on the ice. He died shortly before Christmas. It was plain to Jesse, the oldest child in the family, and to Milus, the oldest male in what was now his family by marriage, that their continual presence in Indianapolis was needed to help Jesse's mother Ann cope with the radically changed circumstances she now faced. Floyd dropped out of the Indiana University and went to work in a grocery store to supplement the family income, for Dorothy and Harold were still in grammar school. Milus, now 27, detached himself from the promising work he had underway in Pittsburgh, and the young couple packed their few possessions and returned to Indianapolis to make their home and start his practice.

Milus' reputation for skill in prosthetics (artificial dentures) cast a welcome shadow before it. The first dental office he opened with the help of a $5,000 bank loan was in a two-story house near 17th and College Streets. The four members of the Payne family moved in along with Milus and Jesse, so Milus, for his own professional needs, divided a large upstairs front room where one part served as a waiting room and the other as an operatory. The vital center of the set-up was the attic where he had his laboratory—and where Milus did his research and made prosthetic appliances not only for his own patients, but on order from other Indianapolis dentists—an important source of income before his own private practice became firmly established.

It was in the attic laboratory where Milus began to focus on the relationship between general health and dental health. The disinterest of the physicians he contacted for help compounded Milus' frustration because his own lack of medical training limited what he could personally do to get at the primary cause of oral diseases, and not merely to treat their effects. The frustration would have consequences for his son Howard.

In the fall of 1907 Jesse became pregnant. There was much discussion within the family about what the infant should be named if it turned out to be a boy. Jesse and Milus favored the name Henry but Floyd was adamantly opposed saying, "Don't name him Henry, because sure as hell, when he grows up he will be called "Hen House." It was agreed in the end that the infant, if a boy, should be called Howard, the first name of his paternal grandfather and that his middle name should be Payne, after his mother's family. On June 29, 1908 Howard Payne House was duly born into the name that preceded his arrival.

Floyd's help notwithstanding, as time went by, Howard found his name to be problematic. In high school he was given the name "Out," for "Outhouse." Later in college he was called "Back," for "Backhouse." Then in medical school, the "Payne" came to be spelled "Pain," hardly an attractive identity for a doctor. To shorten the "Payne" to "P" inevitably invited the name "Pee House." His personal stationery would simply read "Howard House."

With the extended family living under the same roof, from the time of his birth the infant did not "belong" to Jesse and Milus alone. Strong claims were made on him by his Grandmother Payne, his Uncle Floyd, his Aunt Dorothy and even his Uncle Harold who was only five years old and was fated to live only until the age of ten. Howard was cooed over, caressed and sung to by every member of the family. He was enveloped by love and, as he recalled years later, he was also "spoiled" from the start. With each birthday and with each Christmas, as well as the times in between, he was showered with gifts. But an iron law of compensation was also at work in his young life. He was presently denied the most fundamental of all his needs.

3

Death in the Family

Parents stand to children like two covers of a book which hold together the pages in-between. When one cover drops off, the remaining one must do double duty for the bereft children, though the task is sometimes shared by others if they live as part of an extended family. Things turned out that way in the House and Payne families.

In Howard's early childhood, an erratic turn in his mother's health forced her to curtail her normal activities. No one could diagnose her condition. As Milus' concern mounted, he insisted that Jesse have an examination by her uncle, Dr. Allergic Payne, who recommended the removal of her infected tonsils. But Jesse wavered because she feared it might impair her voice and thus end her dream of being an opera singer. She soon succumbed to pneumonia following acute tonsillitis and died in 1912 at the age of 30.

The impact of her death seemed to break off Milus' capacity for emotional attachments to other human beings. He had always shown the traits of what is now called a "workaholic." With Jesse's death, he "lost" himself in work to numb the pain of what had disappeared from his life.

Though Howard was only four years old when his mother died, of all the impressions he retained of the event, one in particular dominated the rest. He could never forget the sight of his mother as she lay in an open coffin in their home and the cold sensation of her face upon his lips when someone picked him up and made him kiss her good-bye. In future years Howard's son, Kenneth, who is a psychoanalyst, saw a direct connection between the experiences of the four-year-old Howard at his mother's bier and the nature of his complex relationship with women when he was a mature man. His affections, though real, always seemed subject to an invisible barrier limit as to what could be given or taken—because the cherished woman might "suddenly go away."

The trauma of the young child who touched death for the first time did not stop at the bier of his mother. Within the year of Jesse's death, ten-year-old Harold Payne succumbed to rheumatic fever. This young uncle had been like an older brother to Howard. The latest death in the family snapped Milus' capacity to concentrate on his professional work. He concluded that a trip to Europe with his family—meaning Howard, Ann, Dorothy, Floyd and his wife to be, Mary Lier—would help revive his spirits and brace the shaken morale of the other members of the family.

The European trip was made in mid-1913 against the background of rising tensions among the major European powers, fated to erupt a year later as "the Guns of August" ushered in the carnage of the First World War.

At one point on the German leg of the train trip, Milus excitedly called attention to a zeppelin flying nearby. Then, in his eagerness to catch a better view of this lighter-than-air novelty, he lunged toward the train window. The window was closed and the impact shattered the glass. The cuts on Milus' face, though not serious, were enough to terrify young Howard when he saw the trickles of blood. He imagined his father might die as his mother had already died.

Even after Milus reappeared, freshly cleaned and the cuts on his face neatly patched over, the child remembered ever afterward the face which had seemed to be a geyser of

14

blood. The memory, lodged deep in his psyche, lived on in the form of a conviction that he must never do anything that might result in the "loss" of his father.

After returning from abroad, Milus resumed his dental practice, research and teaching with renewed enthusiasm. His family vied for the chance to help in the care of young Howard. The grandmother was the first to protest when Milus' disciplinary hand seemed to bear down needlessly hard on young Howard, while Floyd looked upon the child as though he were his own son.

Howard had an almost painfully close relationship with his father, yet he would later say, "I can't recall Dad ever going fishing with me, to a ball game, taking me to the theater or ever watching me play tennis. It was my Uncle Floyd who always filled Dad's role in matters not directly related to plans for work. It was Floyd, and not Dad, who introduced me to sports and to much else."

The traits Howard himself eventually showed as a mature man—a mixture of impenetrable reserve and unbuttoned friendliness—may owe much to the fact that during his formative years he was shaped in roughly equal measure by his stern, self-absorbed father who found his best holiday in work, and by his Uncle Floyd who, though a master in his own line of work, found his holiday in life itself.

Floyd had entered the restaurant business in Indianapolis with a loan of $500 from his mother and $500 from Milus. He used the money to launch what he called the Busy Bee Restaurant featuring his invention—the first steam table where prepared food could be served warm and quickly to people in a hurry. The innovation caught the eye of the Indianapolis press and the free publicity helped make the Busy Bee Restaurant an instant success—and the mother of a chain of 21 restaurants bearing the same trade name, a development that won Floyd a place in the inner circle of the most prominent business people in the community. One of these was Harry Stutz, the automobile manufacturer, from whom Floyd bought a Stutz sports roadster as a gift for his wife Mary—to the delight of Howard who enjoyed riding in the car.

Floyd secured the food concessions at the Indianapolis speedway auto races on Memorial Day. The family helped make thousands of sandwiches for delivery to the speedway to be sold for five cents each. In Floyd's new open Cadillac touring car, Howard would visit with the race drivers in the pits and ride in the car alongside a driver and police officer to collect buckets full of nickels from each concessionaire's stand. The money would be deposited in a nearby bank and the trio would then return to the speedway to repeat the collection process while the races were going on.

The chain of 21 restaurants generated a small mountain of garbage. It occurred to Floyd that garbage should not be wasted, so he bought 200 acres of farm land some 30 minutes from Indianapolis and turned it into a pig farm, reserving a ten-acre stand of locust trees with a stream as a home site. The pigs and the farm became a thriving secondary business.

The beautiful home Floyd constructed in the setting of locust trees was used as a holiday retreat. He built a large log cabin for entertainment next to the swimming pool and developed an artificial lake amid the trees. Each Sunday during the summer months, Floyd's prominent business friends with their families—usually between 50 and 60 people in all—would appear in the early afternoon to enjoy the swimming facilities, the farm and a dinner served either in the log cabin or in the open among the trees. Howard always looked forward to these happy gatherings, just as he also welcomed any chance to be in Floyd's company. When a municipal ruling eventually barred Floyd from using his own garbage to feed his own pigs, he liquidated the "pig business," subdivided the farm, but kept the home and ten acres for the enjoyment of his friends and family. Meanwhile, the extended family living arrangements enabled Milus to concentrate not only on the growth of his private practice, but on dental research and the dissemination of information to other dentists about what he was learning and doing. Within Indianapolis itself, for example, he organized what came to be known as the Milus House Study Group which met twice a month in his office to discuss problems in dental research and practice. Among these were the use of innovations such as X-rays and novocaine which were altering the practice of dentistry. In 1914 he designed an articulator that could reproduce all the movements of the lower jaw which is still used by the dental profession today.

As his own work became better known, he was increasingly called to universities and other cities to give lectures and offer practical demonstrations on complete denture prostheses, as Howard would do in his work later on.

4

Young Howard

At the age of six, Howard was enrolled in grammar school. Milus would drive Howard to and from school, yet it would be impossible to overstate the importance to Howard of the support he gained from the members of the Payne family—his grandmother, Dorothy, as well as from his Uncle Floyd, his "new" Aunt Mary, together with her two beautiful daughters by a previous marriage, Mamie and Burnice. His relationships with them were sunlit and happy. It was through Floyd in particular that he absorbed the spirit of a man who combined within himself a joyous exuberance for the pleasure of life and a keen head for business as well.

They all lived in Floyd's new large home. After the entire family had supper together, Milus would read a story to Howard, tuck him into bed and then head straight for his laboratory where he would work well into the night. On Saturdays the child was permitted into the laboratory where his father showed him how various machine tools were used and called his attention to interesting features in the skulls he was accumulating for dental study. Sundays meant church in the morning and a large noon-day family dinner, often at the farm with friends.

Young Howard had an eccentric musical career in school, starting with Milus' conclusion that his son's front teeth were protruding to an excessive degree. His solution was to buy Howard a trumpet and soon the youth was playing it as a member of the school orchestra. Within two years Milus concluded that the constant pressure of the trumpet mouthpiece had pushed the boy's teeth too far back, so he substituted a clarinet and the outward pressure of the mouthpiece straightened out Howard's teeth without resorting to wires and rubber bands. That put an end to the clarinet or to any other instrument entailing the use of a mouthpiece. Milus gave him a banjo as a concession to the child's interest in music. There was no place in the school orchestra for banjo players, yet the music teacher never understood Howard's explanation that he had to drop out of the orchestra because of his teeth!

Floyd was the force behind the child's first deliberate show of animal courage. As a beloved orphan, Howard had no need to be a street fighter—he got whatever he asked for. However, the fact that he was showered with every plaything a child could want made him a target for envy, especially when he was given his first two-wheeler bicycle at a time when other boys on the block either had none or old ones at best. The many times Howard was shoved off his new bicycle without resistance came to Floyd's worried attention. Acting as a punching bag, he showed his nephew how to feign toward the stomach with his left fist and when the uncle dropped his guard, Howard was to hit him in the jaw with his right fist. The drill was practiced until the child was pronounced ready for battle.

The enemy materialized in the form of young Fred Nash, a member of the Nash automobile family who was a next door neighbor and just a year older than Howard. Nash regularly ran out of the house to knock Howard off the bicycle each time he saw him ride by. It happened again while Floyd watched from a second story window.

The battle plan was followed to the letter—up to a point. Howard, after scrambling to his feet, made a feign toward

Fred's stomach, then hit him in the face so hard he fell to the ground. But what was to be done next? The uncle and the nephew had not planned that far ahead. Howard could only improvise. He jumped on top of Fred and continued to pound him until the dazed youth managed to squirm out from under Howard and run screaming into his house. The best part of the contest, in Howard's own eyes, was the fact that he won his uncle's enthusiastic approval. Of course, when the other boys in the neighborhood heard what happened to Fred, Howard's reputation as a combatant enabled him to ride the streets unabused and unafraid.

The happy outcome of this event was offset by a fatal bicycle episode which was burned into Howard's memory along with the memory of the cold touch of his mother's skin in death and his father's blood-covered face.

Across the street from where Howard lived were two brothers his age whom he counted among the close friends of his childhood. The threesome often cruised around on their bikes testing their speed and skill. The station house for the town's horse-drawn fire engines was nearby, and whenever the three heard the fire engine clang its way out on a rescue mission, the boys would speed after it, trying to keep up with it on their bicycles. On one such chase during a winter day they fell far behind the fire engine and gave up the pursuit, ending up next to Fall Creek.

Howard had been repeatedly warned by his father to steer clear of that creek, and with good reason, for scarcely a year passed when someone didn't drown in it, especially in winter. The two brothers got off their bicycles, ran toward Fall Creek and called to Howard to join them. "I'm not allowed to," he shouted back. "My dad says the creek is too dangerous!"

"Your dad isn't around. Come on," they hollered, "let's take a slide on that big sheet of ice."

Howard watched the brothers head for the ice and then decided to join them. The younger of the brothers was the first to run, but he couldn't check his momentum and slid off the edge of the ice into the water. He failed to surface and his terrified older brother dived in after him. Seconds passed and Howard saw matched yellow tassels on two stocking caps rise to break the water line and then two pairs of hands grasping for the edge of the ice. He started running toward them when a man on a nearby bridge yelled at him, "Get away from there! They'll pull you in too! You can't save them!"

Howard was sickened by the sight of the fingers slipping from the ice into the water, followed by the matched yellow tassels on the stocking caps. He ran to his bicycle and pedaled home, hardly able to see because of the tears streaming down his cheeks. His family awaited news about the fate of the two brothers. When their drowning was confirmed, Milus took a trembling Howard across the street so he could tell their parents exactly what happened.

Even veteran doctors dread informing a family that one of its members has died. It is not hard to imagine the crushing burden carried by a child who had to detail every aspect of the event, with its final scene of the hands and caps sinking out of sight. When the ordeal with the distraught parents was over and Milus and Howard were back home, the father sat the sobbing son on his lap to administer a soft rebuke: "Remember I told you not to go near the creek. You must believe, Howard, that fathers know some things better than their sons."

A psychologist might see in this doleful experience the seeds of a sensitive child's resolve to engage one day in some form of the healing arts as an expiation for his own survival while his young friends' lives were snuffed out.

In the fall of 1916 when Howard was eight years old Alta Mae Fouts, a young woman related to the Paynes, appeared on the Indianapolis scene. Her father, a very successful farmer near Deer Creek, Indiana, worked closely with people at Purdue University in developing the soybean business. Her mother was the sister of Ann Payne which made Floyd, Dorothy and the lately deceased Jesse her first cousins.

Alta came to Indianapolis to enter Teacher's College, which was near Floyd's home. There was a warm bond among all these kinfolk and Alta was a welcome presence in their midst. She soon became attached to another member of the Payne household—young Howard House. So it went from season to season, while Alta completed successive courses that would qualify her for a teacher's certificate.

One evening after Alta finished reading a story to Howard, Milus, who was hovering nearby, told him that Alta would soon be his new mother. A week after Alta graduated in June of 1918, she and Milus were married at the Fouts' country home. Howard, now ten, helped several other pranksters jack up the hind wheel of Milus' car so that it wouldn't go when the newlyweds got ready to say their good-byes. Howard himself went along on their honeymoon and years later he was heard to say with mock seriousness that he may have been the first child ever to go on the honeymoon of his parents.

When the threesome returned to Indianapolis the orderly world Howard had known collapsed in a sea of confusion. The first blow came when he was moved some distance away from the Paynes into a new home Milus bought. He painfully missed the familiar and predictable embrace of his grandmother, uncle and aunts, with their gaiety and games as well as the companionship of the boys in the neighborhood left behind. Worse, where he once had the exclusive attention of his father during the days Milus was in town, he now found that he had to share that attention with Alta. Too young to understand the mainsprings of his sudden resentment of Alta's presence, or the link between it and his vengeful behavior toward her, Howard systematically set out to make life miserable for the woman who had taken his father away from him. Alta, a robust and accommodating woman, understood what was going on in the child's teeming brain.

If Alta said yes, he said no. If she said no, he said yes. If she had just washed the kitchen floor, he deliberately walked over it with muddy shoes. When he learned that harmless garden snakes frightened her, he brought as many as he could find into the house and released them to slither slowly across her path. This cruel behavior toward Alta continued for about a year while she suffered its effects in understanding silence. But there had to be an end to the matter, and it came literally with a bang.

Howard and a friend named Lawton often roamed the nearby State Fairgrounds, rummaging through leftover debris in search for hidden treasures. Once, coming upon a can of carbide used for lighting, they agreed it was just what they needed for an experiment, and rushed back with their find to their "laboratory" —a little "clubhouse" located between two garages in the rear of Howard's home. They knew that carbide when mixed with water formed gas, and the object of the experiment was to see what happened if a match was thrown into the mixture. The effect of the experiment was an explosion that partly burned both garages.

Howard, whose eyelashes and hair were singed and right hand burned, explained the disastrous experiment to a surprised Alta when she returned home from shopping, but he was in a sweat over what he would say to his father who was due home that weekend from one of his working trips. When Milus saw the havoc, he said laconically, "I'll have to get somebody out here to rebuild the garages."

Howard spent a sleepless Saturday night. He persuaded himself that he would disclose all to his father the next day. He did nothing of the sort—not at breakfast, not on the way to church nor on the way home again.

When the three were having their usual Sunday meal, there was a knock on the front door. Milus opened it to reveal the figure of a police officer. "Is this the home of Howard House?" asked the uniformed man. "I have a warrant for his arrest on a charge of arson."

Milus acted shocked. Howard was scared out of his wits. Under the stern prompting of his father, he told the full story of what had happened.

"I'll have to take the boy in," the officer solemnly said. Milus volunteered to drive everyone to the police station.

At the station, while Howard was being escorted to the captain's desk, he passed down a row of jail cells whose inmates looked to him like a mixed bag of cutthroats. He quaked at their sight. His father asked the captain if Howard would have to stay in the cell block that night.

"Well, Dr. House," replied the captain, "you understand that your son has committed a very serious crime, but recognizing your standing in the community, I will allow you to take your son home overnight providing you return him to court tomorrow afternoon at four."

The following day after school, they went to court. Lawton was also there with his father. The judge explained they were too young to be taken away from their families and forced to spend time in jail. He would put both on probation for a year.

At this point the judge looked directly at Milus and said, "I am only going to give him probation if you, Dr. House, realize that you are responsible for your son and will have to go to jail with Howard if a similar incident occurs in the future."

With that, Milus put his hand gently on Howard's shoulder and said, "You know I am responsible for you and I will stand by you." He then turned to the judge and thanked him for his compassion.

It was not until years later that Howard learned Milus had prearranged the encounter with the criminal justice system. Yet the contrived episode, in its immediate affect on Howard, marked a fundamental change in his relationship with Alta. He began to embrace her warmly, as she had always tried to embrace him. Years afterwards, when she recalled the stormy episodes of the past, she laughingly would say she never was able to understand how such a rascal became so fine a doctor.

As Howard passed through adolescence, some things went wrong for him even when he meant for them to go right. One of his chores at harvest time was to be in charge of a water cart pulled by a pony which brought water to the hot and thirsty field hands. One summer day when a thrashing machine and combine—owned by the farmer's cooperative—was working in the Fouts' field, young Howard was granted a cherished "promotion." He was relieved from duty with the water cart and was invited to come aboard a large hay wagon for a new task. As other farmers in the cooperative pitchforked sheaves of wheat from the ground onto the wagon, young Howard was to scoop up the sheaves with his own pitchfork and hurl them onto a conveyor belt that fed the combine.

Howard was thrilled with this grown-up responsibility. On his first scoop, the pitchfork slipped from his hand onto the moving conveyor belt along with the hay. As steel hit steel, there was a piercing, grinding halt. The combine stammered, choked and ground to a halt. Almost two full days were lost in a race against the time and weather before repairs were made. Howard went back to the same job but was advised: "Hold the handle tightly next time."

Unknown to himself, the youth had embarked on a stream of experiences which his associate, Dr. James Sheehy, in later years grouped under the general heading: *"The Hazards of being Howard."*

Another time Howard and several farm boys made experimental cigarettes out of corn silks and strips of paper. Sitting lined up in a row along a fence they were puffing away only to be surprised by the sudden appearance of Milus. Instead of the lightning bolt Howard expected, he was treated to a display of his father's genial manner.

Taking in the scene Milus said, "Oh, I didn't realize you fellows were old enough to smoke." Then pulling some cigars from his vest pocket he said, "Let's enjoy a real smoke together," and passed them among the boys. Carefully showing them how to bite off the end, Milus lit his own and used it to light the cigars the boys had clutched in their teeth before sitting down next to Howard.

He had them draw deeply on the cigars repeatedly and he made a special point of blowing his own smoke straight into Howard's face so he would not miss the pleasures of its aroma. Before long Howard, along with the others, became dizzy and nauseated. Back at the Fouts' home, Howard headed for the refuge of his bed. The next morning when he returned to the world of the living his father laid out the terms of a conditional offer. "Howard," he said, "I know you want a car of your own. If you promise not to smoke until you are 21, you will have the car at that time."

The promise was made. Milus and Howard drove to a little bank in Camden where Milus opened an account with $400, to be withdrawn when Howard was 21 for the purchase of a car. On the day of the deposit, Howard was confident that he would respect to the letter the terms of his promise.

Meanwhile, Howard's complete change of heart toward Alta was consolidated irrevocably when she presented him with the brothers he always wanted. First came Warren, born in 1922, followed by Bill in 1923 and Jim in 1925.

5

Change of Venue

Milus and John J. Deaner had been Indiana Dental College students together. Deaner was a stranger to the ways of sober habits, hard work and a thrifty style of life. If it had not been for Milus' tutoring, he would never have graduated with a D.D.S. degree for his drinking bouts and gambling instincts would have been his undoing.

After Deaner's graduation from dental college, when en route to Texas, he stepped off the train in a small dusty town called Okmulgee, Oklahoma, to refresh himself briefly in a saloon. One drink led to another and the train, with his luggage, left without him. Awaking the next morning, fully clothed on a small bed in a hotel room, he saw another of his drinking companions from the night before on the other bed. As the two were attempting to face the new day Deaner explained that he had just graduated from dental school and was en route to Texas where he meant to start a practice. The other young man, son of the local banker, remarked that Okmulgee lacked a dentist. If Deaner would stay, the young man added, he would urge his own father to grant him a bank loan to cover the start-up costs of a dental office. Matters worked out that way.

Deaner's first patient needed a full set of dentures, but every cent the patient had was tied up in a lease on land upon which he hoped oil would be found. In payment for the dental work to be done, he offered to give Deaner a percentage of the lease where drilling would soon begin. Deaner, a sporting type, accepted the gamble. A gusher was struck. When the wildcatter honored the terms of his agreement, Deaner used his share of the revenue to speculate in more oil leases. Within a year he was a millionaire and gave up his dental practice. He readily admitted he was absurdly lucky in the topsy-turvy way his fortune was made and years later he decided to do something wonderful for American dentistry. He would establish a Deaner Institute in Kansas City to provide the finest of dental care. A special fund would provide care free of charge to poor children. In Deaner's view, only one man could bring his plans to fruition: his friend and helpmate of long ago—Dr. Milus Marion House.

In 1922 Milus was 43 and, as would be true of his son Howard at the same age, his private practice had expanded to a degree that it was necessary to bring several associates into his office to help care for the patients and give him more time for his research. He was also recognized nationally as a leader in his profession and was in constant demand throughout the country to conduct seminars on his technique to make artificial dentures. The unique molds and the carved teeth he made not only were prototypes but would remain in continuous use within the dental profession so that 90 percent of teeth manufactured in the United States today are from these molds.

Milus was excited about the challenge because he believed the Deaner Institute could advance dentistry simultaneously on all fronts: patient care, research and dental education. With that vision, he accepted the directorship, effective January 1, 1923.

Howard was 14 years old when he, Alta and the six month old Warren moved with Milus to Kansas City, Missouri. The usual problems of adjustment to a new city neighborhood and high school were aggravated by the fact that Howard was seized by an affliction of boils, boils and more boils on his face and neck—which persisted in spite of medical treatment. The physical discomfort was bad enough, but it was nothing compared to his painful self-consciousness about how his appearance was disfigured by the boils. He tried to conceal his plight by using high collars in all types of weather and sitting in the last row of a classroom so there would be no one behind him whose stare would be focused like a magnifying glass on his plague.

Boys in high school are stirred by a prurient interest in girls, but how could any girl overlook the boils? He hesitated to ask any girl out on a date, fearing she would rebuff him, and then when he managed to get a girlfriend in high school, after he introduced her to a good-looking friend of his who had no boils, she dropped Howard.

His one reliable source of pleasure was confined to the summer months when he could play tennis with his new friend, John Callan. They won most of the local doubles tournaments for their age group, but neither had any social life with girls unless it revolved around tennis. The second of the only two girlfriends Howard had in high school was a tennis player and she went the way of the first.

A more elaborate sex-related episode in Howard's high school years occurred the summer he turned 16. While he was dressing for another hot, sticky day on the city's clay courts, his father came into his room and said, "Instead of spending the summer hitting tennis balls, you ought to take some drawing lessons at the Art Institute. It will help you in college."

Howard persuaded John Callan to join him but the drawing class was full, so they signed up for sculpting. They were the only boys in the class, along with four girls from their high school. During the first week everything went well. They all wore long smocks and made copies of a statue of David.

The second week, however, things started to fall apart. A live female model came to class, took off her silk robe and stood naked before them on a revolving pedestal in the middle of the room. John and Howard were mesmerized but embarrassed by what they saw.

"House," the instructor asked, "How do you want her to pose, standing or sitting?"

He mumbled, "Have her sit down," but then John poked him in the ribs. "Or stand up. I don't care."

She was beautiful and both John and Howard were paralyzed. When the instructor saw how poorly they were doing, he took Howard's hand and placed it on the model's shoulder and then ran it down her body, past her buttocks. "Here, feel the form she has. That's what I want you to get out of your clay."

All Howard could feel was the flush in his face and he thanked God he was wearing a long smock! The giggles of the girls made matters even worse while he stumbled back to his glob of clay. At the end of that morning session, John and Howard went back to tennis for the rest of the summer. Sometime later Milus asked Howard how the sculpting class went and he truthfully answered, "I couldn't do anything with my clay."

There was a puzzling misfit between his obvious shyness and his ability to make himself popular in school when he put his mind to the task. In his senior year he won election as vice president of his class and it fell to him to arrange interclass dances with other schools, yet he never took a partner to those affairs in which he was a prime mover. He convinced himself that he had so much to do to keep the dance going that he would have no time to give to a date, even if a girl might go with him. The boils continued to plague him for years.

6

The Choice of Career

Howard's own perceptions of his father's work and status underwent a change with the move to Kansas City. As a child in Indianapolis, he stood in awe of his father's authority. When the family settled in Kansas City, Howard was old enough to appreciate what it meant for his father to be the head of an *institution* where leaders of the dental profession in the United States and abroad came to observe and learn from the work being done at the Deaner Institute. Decades later when the House Ear Institute was being founded, Howard's memories of how his father launched the Deaner Institute plainly influenced his own decisions to launch his own innovative research institute.

Howard's new perspective of his father's role was further enlarged as he watched the Deaner Institute Building—a five-story structure covering a city block—being built. Completed in 1924, the opening ceremonies were attended by the *Who's Who* of American dentistry as well as city and state officials. The more Howard learned about his father's work, the more he was convinced that dentistry was alive with different challenges and he resolved to be a dentist in his father's mold.

Milus himself had never talked "career" to Howard prior to a memorable summer evening in 1925 when he had just turned 17. The pair were seated on the swing of a screened-in porch of their home overlooking the lights of

Kansas City. The younger three children slept—Warren, just turned three, Bill, almost two and Jim, just six months old. Alta had retired for the night and neighbors, who had come over for a chat, had spoken their good-nights.

The moment was ripe for a unique father-son exchange of confidences. Howard had just completed his junior year at Westport High School and would soon be leaving for a two-month transcontinental motor trip with his Uncle Floyd, Aunt Mary and her daughter Burnice.

Suddenly Milus asked, "Have you decided, son, what you are going to do when you grow up?"

Startled, Howard replied, "I'm going to be a dentist—like you."

"That's wonderful, and I can be a lot of help to you," Milus said in a matter-of-fact way. "But if *I* had to do it over again, I would go to medical school *first*, and then go on to dentistry because I would have been a better dentist if I had had a thorough background in medicine. You just can't divorce the teeth from the rest of the body."

And so the logic of that short exchange won Howard's quick assent to study medicine prior to his pursuing a career in dentistry. At the same time, he believed he had entered into an irrevocable contract with his father which expressly *bound* him to study dentistry after medical school.

Shortly after this Floyd, Mary and Burnice arrived from Indianapolis to pick up Howard for the transcontinental trip. By the summer of 1925 the completion of successive legs of the "Lincoln Highway" was emblematic of the "end of remoteness" that went with the fast-developing Age of the Automobile. Areas of the country previously lost in rural isolation were opening up to travelers because of the growing network of all-weather highways, advances in the technology of automobiles as well as the spread of gasoline stations and garages for repairs.

Floyd was eager to explore parts of the country he had never seen. His flourishing Busy Bee restaurants no longer taxed his talents or imagination. Ripe for new ventures, he acquired a new Cadillac seven-passenger touring car equipped with gas tanks on the side above the running board, isinglass curtains and camping equipment. The family group was ready to see the natural wonders of the American continent and visit members of both the House and Payne families who had moved to Southern California.

The trip covered 13,000 miles and Howard, as the Homer of the Odyssey, kept a diary whose title page introduced the cast of characters by name and role: *Mary*—cook; *Burnice*—dishwasher; *Floyd*—eater and sleeper; *Howard*—good for nothing; *Extra Ballast*—Floyd's rifle, thermos bottle and Howard House.

The record listed 16 places under the heading, "Cities in Which We Camped or Had a Cottage," five under "Places Where We Froze Stiff," nine under "Where We Had Tough Luck," six "Where We Were Lucky" and 39 locales were "Cities in Which We Patronized the Hotels."

At first glance the diary reads like a serialized tale of woe. Aside from the youth's protest against what he believed were extortionist prices for food in out-of-the-way places—a foretaste of the grown man's frugality—the misfortunes were endless: flat tires, blowouts, new tires stolen, no gas in the tank, rock slides, the engine perilously overheating on steep mountain grades, an arrest and fine for speeding at 55 m.p.h., temperatures of 104 degrees in the shade (and no shade), two instances where the car veered off the road and landed in a ditch, a fender-bender in Canada when Howard backed the car into the only road sign within 50 miles, and a near catastrophe when the car stopped with its front wheels overhanging the edge of a precipice.

The essential element of the diary, however, is the record of Howard's celebration of his happy relationship with his Uncle Floyd. At least every other page contains another variation on the theme of laughter: "Floyd and I had a good laugh . . . Floyd and I lay on our cots laughing and talking until daybreak . . . Floyd and I keeled over laughing after he recovered from being hit on the head by the surf board . . . I couldn't stop laughing after I saw Floyd swing so hard at the baseball that he fell down . . . Floyd and I . . ."

Howard's trip diary concludes with six words set off in brackets: "The end of a perfect summer."

Floyd, the university drop-out who revolutionized the way the nation served food, returned home with a vision: the country obviously had a need for a better quality of food and lodging than he had encountered on this cross-country journey. He would do for the Age of the Automobile what his friend Fred Harvey had done for the Age of the Railroad and build a network of distinctively identified inns whose standard quality could be relied upon by motor vehicle travelers. He coined the word "motel" to describe what he had in mind and named his proposed network the Star Motels, each providing good food and entertainment. Land would be acquired a few miles from towns or cities 200 or 300 miles apart and identified by a tower with a revolving star. As the cities grew, the acquired land would increase in value. How could he miss?

Floyd was prepared to commit himself personally and financially to the project on the condition that his nephew Howard become his partner. Whether Howard joined him immediately after graduating from high school or did so after securing the semblance of a college education was secondary. The immediate point was whether plans for the future should be made on the assumption that Howard would eventually work by Floyd's side and be his heir-designate.

There was nothing fanciful about Floyd's idea. It anticipated by some years the realities that later materialized for travelers in the form of national chains bearing names such as Holiday Inn, Ramada Inn, Howard Johnson, Marriott and Hilton. As for Howard, he was enchanted by the prospect of working by the side of his uncle despite his previously expressed certainty that he eventually wanted to be a dentist.

Milus' response to the plan, when Floyd put it to him, was a flat No. "If Howard entered the business world," he explained, "he could lose his shirt when times turned bad. But if he prepared himself for a profession, he could always retain his knowledge and skill, no matter what happened to the economy." The No was final and Floyd never broached the subject again. As he had no son of his own, his grand design died for the want of anyone who could fill the place he had reserved for Howard.

The next June, a few days shy of his 18th birthday, Howard graduated from Westport High School. Although there was nothing dazzling about his academic record, no dark wind blew through it either, for it showed him to be an "average" student who ranked in the upper half of the class. At the time only four percent of all students went on to college after graduating from high school—as against the present figure of some 50 percent.

Howard was accepted at William Jewel College, an excellent small liberal arts school in Liberty, Missouri, 15 miles from Kansas City. But before classes started, Howard was treated to a trip to the East with his father. The details of this trip were again recorded in a diary, but the few references he made to his father in the first half of the diary—and none with any laughter in them—are in contrast to the frequent and joyous entries made the summer before about Floyd on the western trip. His father was simply *there*, a serious and solemn presence.

Howard's description of Washington, D.C. reflects his fascination with the statistics of "bigness": he recorded the number of bodies buried in the Arlington Cemetery, the number of people that could be seated in the amphitheater at the Unknown Soldier's Tomb, the amount of money that could be printed in a day by the Engraving Bureau, the construction costs for a bridge across the Potomac, the number of volumes in the Library of Congress and the size of a stuffed whale at the Smithsonian Institution. ("After seeing it, I am sure the whale swallowed Jonah.")

In Philadelphia where he and Milus attended a dental convention, he wrote, "I went to Dad's booth and attempted to demonstrate his new articulator and rotary grinder." This was followed by a cryptic reference to his father's upset stomach ascribed to the aftereffects of a seafood dinner.

The most pleasurable time, according to the entries, were the first days spent in New York—the excitement of traveling through the tunnel under the Hudson River, the skyscrapers "everywhere," a visit to Coney Island: "On a beach four miles long and 40 feet wide, 600,000 people were huddled in so great a tangle of arms and legs that it was impossible to tell where bodies ended and sand began." There was also a play on Broadway: " 'My Country!' and it sure was good. Tried to see 'Abie's Irish Rose,' but all the seats were sold out."

The New York junket, however, was marred by problems with Milus' health: "Dad wasn't feeling very well since he had been loaded up with the monoxide of the cars." After that: "Dad is feeling worse." The pair boarded a train for Boston where Milus had business with a dental supply company. His "upset stomach," with unrelenting diarrhea, made the time spent in Boston a grim ordeal. On the long train trip back to Kansas City, Milus shunned food and water and was denied even the temporary refuge of sleep. When the pair reached home, Milus immediately crawled into bed and called successive doctors to his side. He did what they prescribed, but he remained in the iron grip of a baffling, debilitating illness that made it impossible for him to return to work at the Deaner Institute.

7

Transitions

When classes were to start at William Jewel College, Howard feared that because of his boils no college fraternity would want him as a pledge. To Howard the very term "fraternity" was a synonym for "college." If he never "made" a fraternity, it would be as though the doors to college had been slammed shut in his face and he could never be a "success in life." His view was not uncommon to many college students in the 1920s.

All freshmen at William Jewel had to live in a dormitory, but those who were pledged to a fraternity could lounge around the fraternity house and share its social life. During the first months of the school year Howard was an envious outsider looking in on the freshmen who "made it."

When he was eventually asked to pledge to Kappa Sigma, he counted the invitation—which he snapped up—to be the greatest triumph of his young life. In the belief that he was accepted by the fraternity crowd mainly because of his fame as a tennis star in the Kansas City area, Howard dedicated himself to tennis for the glory of Kappa Sigma. Despite his local celebrity status as a tennis player, the college professors did not hesitate to pelt him with Ds and marginal Cs. Tennis accounted for the only A he would earn at William Jewel—though on his transcript the grade was recorded as given for Phys. Ed.

Still, in his first weeks as a Kappa Sigma pledge, Howard discovered the old truth that the problems of success can be as great as those of failure. High school episodes where girls were invariably "busy" when he asked them for a date occurred behind a curtain of privacy. As a fraternity pledge, his woes became public. "For the first fraternity dance I was eligible to attend," Howard later said, "I called Sadie Burke, a Kansas City friend, but she had already been invited to the dance by another fraternity brother. There was no one else I could think of asking. On the night of the dance I drove to a parking lot next to where the dance was held and listened to the music that came through the open windows—until I was driven away by my unbearable isolation."

In the year Howard spent at William Jewel, he never had a single date and he discouraged his fraternity brothers from arranging one for him. When social activities were set at the fraternity, he went into hiding. He saw a lot of movies and played tennis and poker with "the fellows." In their company he sometimes puffed on a pipe or a cigarette without inhaling the smoke—a legalistic difference designed to avoid a breach of the contract made with his father in order to be eligible for the promised new car by abstaining from smoking until he was 21.

Meanwhile, Milus, bedridden for three months, was in a depression of spirit as his baffling illness worsened. Since his condition made it impossible for him to be active at the Deaner Institute, rather than imperil its future by leaving its leadership in a vacuum while he battled the disease from which he was wasting away, Milus resigned from the enterprise in which he had placed such high hopes.

But that left another matter up in the air. How were his four sons to be educated? After discussing various alternatives with Alta he finally decided on a move to Southern California—to be near the members of his family in the event he never recovered from his malaise. Awaiting the possibility of death—which seemed more imminent than ever before—he would try to work with his waning strength at his beloved profession of dentistry.

In response to inquiries regarding the examination for a license, Milus was told by California's Board of Dental Examiners that because of his preeminence in the dental profession it would be ludicrous to force an examination on him. Rather it was he who could examine the examiners. All that was required was that he register for the examination and he would be granted a license. Milus, a stickler for rules, refused to accept the proposed shortcut.

Somehow Milus managed to get to Los Angeles where he prepared himself for the examination. While there, another physical examination revealed that he had amebic dysentery, a fatal disease usually caused by contaminated food or water. Fortunately a new medication had just become available and Milus began gradually to recover his health— coincident with his being granted a license to practice dentistry in California.

Howard, meanwhile, made plans to leave William Jewel College at the end of the academic year and transfer to a California-based school a few months before the rest of the family would be arriving in California. He blindly applied to three and was accepted at each as a transfer student—the University of Southern California (USC), Stanford University and the publicly supported University of California at Los Angeles (UCLA)—despite his dim academic record at William Jewel College. The reason his record full of Ds and Cs was no barrier to being accepted scarcely seems credible today, but at that time any student awarded a high school diploma was thought to be generally qualified for college work.

Howard noticed that it cost far less to attend UCLA than it did the other two and that its location made it easy to reach by streetcar from the nearby home of his Aunt Mabel, so he opted for UCLA on arrival in Los Angeles and moved in with his aunt and uncle who now held a Methodist pulpit there. Costs and propinquity decided the schooling issue.

During his first day on the UCLA campus Howard registered and paid his tuition and other fees by check. But there were complications: First, when he tried to register for a chemistry class he needed as a premed student, the class was full. Sorry. He then learned it was mandatory for male students at UCLA—a land grant college—to take part in the school's R.O.T.C. program. Howard, no enthusiast for any kind of drill, reported to the military supply room where the army sergeant issued him a uniform along with wraparound leggings and a pair of army shoes—all First World War surplus.

To dress properly in his uniform Howard got up an hour early, but then the leggings came apart during his streetcar ride to the campus. This was annoying, but the real difficulty was with the army issue shoes. They were too tight.

He complained to the supply sergeant, "My army shoes are the wrong size."

"You've got the only pair you're going to have," replied the sergeant.

"In that case I'll wear my own shoes during the drill," Howard announced.

The next day Howard came to the parade ground in his uniform with the disintegrating wraparound leggings, but wearing his own shoes. When the sergeant caught sight of the shoes he told Howard he couldn't go to school unless he took R.O.T.C. and he couldn't take R.O.T.C. unless he wore regulation army shoes.

Howard calmly went and changed to his civilian clothes and then gave the sergeant all the military gear he had been issued, down to the last shoelace.

"Wait a minute," the sergeant said uneasily when he grasped the radical implication of the gesture. "Maybe I can get you a pair of shoes that fit."

"Too late," Howard replied, as he turned his back on the sergeant and walked away. He proceeded to his bank where he canceled payment on the check for his tuition and then went across town to USC where classes began two weeks later than at UCLA and where he had already been accepted. No one there knew he had already been a three-day student at UCLA.

Soon he received a letter from UCLA's bursar concerning the canceled check and the tuition money he owed the school. The polite reply was that he owed nothing because he could not get the chemistry course he needed. The issue of shoes was not mentioned. The bursar responded with a threat. If Howard didn't pay the tuition due, he would never be allowed on the campus of any college in the California state system.

Years later when Howard appeared at UCLA as a lecturer, he enjoyed telling his experience as a three-day UCLA student and capped the account with a mock serious request to the students to keep his presence on the campus a secret from the institution's regulatory authorities.

When the rest of the family arrived in Southern California in late 1927 Milus preferred to settle in a small town which would provide a better atmosphere in which to rear his young boys. After he bought a citrus ranch in Whittier, near Los Angeles, Alta and the boys attended to their assigned chores while Milus began to transform the appearance of the ranch by working alongside some local "hammer and saw" men in his own role as architect, contractor, plumber, electrician and painter.

The two-story barn was remodeled so that a complete machine shop with a drill press, lathe and racks of small tools for research work was set up on the first floor while the second floor was altered to contain two dental chair treatment rooms, a reception area, an office and laboratory. Milus was sometimes questioned about the wisdom of assembling a layout where the patient's view from the dental office was a machine shop.

"I see nothing wrong with that," Milus would reply. "It should comfort patients to know that we have the equipment to make anything their case might require."

Howard joined his family in Whittier and commuted by car—an old Essex—to and from his classes at USC. Because of his boils, he did not make himself known to the Kappa Sigma chapter at USC and had little social life. His grades were balanced so precariously on the razor's edge of failure that he was placed on probation and could not join the school's tennis team. His first and only semester at USC came down to this—no girls, no fraternity, no tennis team; just boils, commuting, rotten grades, probation—the portrait of Job as a Young Man. To cut down on the wear and tear of commuting, he transferred from USC to Whittier College for the spring semester of his sophomore year.

In later life, however, he was honored as the Outstanding USC Alumnus of the Year, the Outstanding Medical School Alumnus of the Year and was also awarded an honorary degree of Doctor of Laws from the university. As he remarked at the time, "It is nice to receive roses while you can still smell them."

8

Challenge and Response

Howard received the remainder of his undergraduate education at Whittier College. His grades continued to be depressed, but in other respects he felt he was living the busy and gratifying life of a "college man." His energies were consumed by playing tennis and poker—his love—and by becoming a member of the debating team and the manager of the football team. Of greater importance, the boils began to clear—though by means of an appalling remedy.

A classified ad in a Los Angeles newspaper promised a cure for acne and boils at a center located in an old white house on Alvarado Street near Third, close to the present site of the Otologic Medical Group and the House Ear Institute. The elderly doctor who examined him said, "Young fellow, X-ray treatments will fix up your boils."

Howard urged him to go to work at once and returned to the center for treatments twice a week for a number of weeks. The effects dried some of the boils, tightened the skin and made his face feel better, but the day came when the old doctor said, "Young fellow, that's all the X-ray treatments I can safely give you."

It was not all the young fellow craved and when he saw another newspaper ad like the first, he presented himself to the new doctor without telling him he had already undergone similar treatments. In later years he realized the immense risks he had desperately taken and he thanked a kind providence that the duplicated treatment did not produce radiation cancer. Giddy with delight because the treatments reduced his disfiguring boils, Howard found the courage to ask a few girls to go out with him and some actually agreed to do so.

Ever ready to use any means to get in the good graces of girls, should they want to use his Essex car, Howard would eagerly give them the keys and ride his bicycle to school. He kept looking and hoping for a durable romance—which seemed within the realm of probability as his boils began to clear.

On the first day of a Bible course at Whittier he noticed a beautiful blond seated three rows away who appeared to know everything about the Bible. She seemed to be pretty smart, but what attracted Howard to her was a dizzy incident. The second day of class she moved back and sat two rows away. On the third day, she sat closer, directly in front of him. So far they had not exchanged a single word. Suddenly she turned around and asked if he had a watch. Pulling out an Ingersol pocket watch he handed it to her.

For the remainder of the class she kept the watch and methodically took it apart: dial, back, wheels, springs. When the bell rang, with no apologies, she said, "I don't have time to put the pieces back together again. Here they are." There was nothing to do except put the pieces in his pocket. And in this strange way Howard met his future wife, Helen May Zenz.

John Zenz, Helen's father, made custom-built wagons for ice and bakery companies, in addition to buggies and carriages. Eventually he switched over to custom-built truck bodies, but sold out when the automobile companies started to make their own truck bodies. For years afterward motion picture companies engaged his services to make special wheels, and perhaps his best known wheels were on the chariots that were used in "Ben Hur." Helen was the only child of his marriage to his wife Bertie Muff.

Howard and Helen eventually began to "go steady" when they were in Whittier, but it would be dead wrong to suggest their relationship en route to marriage eight years later was radiant with ineffable bliss. On more than a few occasions Howard seemed poised to dismantle his link to Helen as methodically as she had dismantled his Ingersol watch.

When Howard completed his junior year, he obtained an appointment with Dr. Paul S. McKibben of the newly revived USC School of Medicine. The school had opened in 1886, but closed during the sharp depression of 1919-1921. It reopened in 1928, operating on the shoestring budget of $360,000 annually (the current budget is in excess of $50,000,000 with 138 students in each class). The reopened establishment admitted 52 students for each entering class, but the medical faculty had no building of their own, so the school's courses were sandwiched into the science building. Since they lacked hospital facilities, the first two classes had no choice but to complete their last two years of clinical work at other medical schools.

Howard's introductory interview with Dr. McKibben came at a time when his grade point average stood at 1.8 after three years of college work. What transpired at the interview embedded itself so deeply in Howard's psyche that he always reconstructed it in exactly the same way, syllable for syllable:

McKibben: Mr. House, I understand you are interested in going to medical school here.

Howard: Yes, sir, and I've brought my transcript with me.

McKibben (glancing at the transcript): Mr. House, you're not serious about wanting to be a doctor!

Howard: Yes, sir, I am.

McKibben: Our classes are very small. The courses are very hard and we don't want to admit anyone unless they've got a chance of getting through. Why do you think you've made such terrible grades?

Howard: I've had a lot of outside activities—tennis team, manager of the football team, member of the debating team.

McKibben: Do you like girls and date a lot?

Howard: Yes.

McKibben (after a long puff on his pipe): Mr. House, when you go back to Whittier in the fall, give up some of your activities and dates, and if you make better grades your senior year, I'll have a place for you in the next year's fall class.

Howard's summer months were spent working in the oil fields of Santa Fe Springs. On June 29, 1929—his 21st birthday—he returned from work, covered as usual with oil, but walked into a surprise birthday party. His surviving grandparents, aunts and uncles had all come to Whittier to join the rest of the House family in celebrating Howard's majority. After he cleaned up, presents were unwrapped except the largest of all—the one that depended on the agreement made long ago in Deer Creek when Milus promised to buy Howard a new Ford car if he abstained from smoking until the age of 21. Milus held up a certified check from the Camden Bank. "Howard," he asked, "have you ever smoked since the time I deposited this money to your account?"

Howard swallowed hard but did not stammer. "Now and again when I was with the fellows," he replied, "I puffed on a pipe or cigarette—but I never inhaled."

Waving the distinction aside, Milus folded and pocketed the certified check. "Even if you didn't inhale, you smoked. There will be no new car for you."

"Milus!" Grandmother Payne shouted. "You know Howard doesn't smoke! You are not being fair!"

"I am being fair," Milus said to his ex-mother-in-law. Turning to Howard he explained: "Son, you won't get the new car you've always wanted. But you'll get something better. You've demonstrated that you have the quality above all others that is indispensable in a doctor—integrity. Therefore, I will give you the entire costs of your medical education."

With that unexpected gift added to the "iffy" encouragement from Dr. McKibben, Howard spent his senior year at Whittier in an academic sweatshop. He gave up his activities and sharply reduced the time he spent with Helen Zenz to concentrate on his studies as never before. His instructors, fully supportive and aware of the conditions upon which he held a fighting chance to gain admission to medical school, gave him special attention. His efforts paid off and he managed to raise his academic performance to the level of B grades. Later in life Howard was honored as Whittier's Outstanding Alumnus of the year, was awarded an honorary degree of science and would serve as a member of Whittier's Board of Trustees.

Howard's father was in New York on business and in order to be present at Whittier College on Howard's graduation, he made one of the first transcontinental flights on a Ford tri-motor aluminum airplane. Twelve passengers flew by day and before darkness fell transferred to a train for nighttime travel. The next morning they were picked up by another tri-motor plane that proceeded on the next daylight leg of the trip. In this way, he arrived in Whittier just in time for Howard's great day.

Immediately after graduation and buoyed by his achievement in improving his grades as required, Howard returned to the office of Dr. McKibben. "I remember you," Dr. McKibben said in greeting. "I recall telling you that if you came back with better grades, I would have a place for you this fall." He glanced at Howard's transcript. "I see," he said, "you've made better grades. Unfortunately, the class is full." Saying that, he looked directly into Howard's eyes and asked, "What are you going to do now?"

The actual practice of medicine requires doctors employ no small amount of make-believe to mask their true feelings about patients or the actual state of their health. Howard rose to the challenge and showed his ability at play-acting. Without flinching, and despite his bitter disappointment, he met Dr. McKibben's searching look and said, "What I do now, Dr. McKibben, is up to you. You tell me what to do and I'll do it. I'll go back to college next year, and the next, and the year after that if necessary, because one of these days, I am going to be a doctor."

Dr. McKibben silently puffed on his pipe for a moment, but then said, "I'll take your case up with the admissions committee and we will decide on what you should do this next year and, if necessary, the year following."

That was the end of the interview. Howard thanked Dr. McKibben and left, sagging under the leaden weight of his defeat. He was unaware that the medical school was so new in its born-again state that Dr. McKibben was just about everything rolled into one. In addition to teaching, he was the acting dean, the admissions committee, the curriculum committee and the budget committee.

Howard spent the next two weeks wavering between the listlessness of despondency and the feverish expectations with each mail delivery. When suddenly a letter arrived from the Office of the Dean, The University of Southern California School of Medicine, he ripped open the envelope and gave a joyous whoop.

"There has been a vacancy in the September class and we have a place for you," it said. Howard grabbed his checkbook, jumped into his old car and straightened out all the curves on the road from Whittier to the administrative office of the USC School of Medicine. There would be no stopping payment on the check he wrote for his tuition and fees. With a 2.15 grade point average on his undergraduate work he was a first-year medical student!

Why did he get in? Howard often speculated about the question in later years. Many factors contributed to his opportunity. Since incoming students were required to transfer to other medical schools to finish their clinical work, those who could preferred to start at a school where they could remain for the full four years. Another factor was the growing depression which made the costs of attending a private medical school prohibitive, so that the competition for a place in the entering USC class in 1930 may not have been as fierce as it appeared on the surface.

In Howard's view, however, the decisive factor was the depths of his commitment to a career in medicine. Dr. McKibben must have appraised this not so much on the evidence that he had worked hard to improve his grades, but rather on the way Howard reacted to the news that the promised place in the entering class was no longer available. Years later Howard learned from Dr. McKibben that all along there had been a place for him in the class. The no-vacancy fable had been invented in order to assess how Howard would react to the crisis and the bitter disappointment inherent in it.

9

The Medical Student

As a new medical student in need of lodgings near the USC campus, Howard found a small house in back of another house which contained two bedrooms, a bathroom, a living room, and a kitchen—at $20 a month. He rented the place, then looked for someone to split the costs. A roommate materialized in the person of another first-year medical student, Merle Swanson of Claremont Falls, Oregon. Swanson took the second bedroom and shared cooking chores, although Howard's knowledge of cuisine (to judge the past from the present) may have been confined to toast, fried eggs and ice cream.

Swanson was a pleasant young man but his personality lacked the seasoning of humor and the mysterious elements of "charm" that had begun to mark Howard's manner as he matured. However, he was far better placed to survive in medical school than Howard, for he had been thoroughly prepared in basic undergraduate science courses of critical importance to a first-year medical student. In fact, Swanson could race through a week's assignments and then take the weekend off. Howard, who was never able to do that, had in his roommate a generous source of help for his own studies.

The prevalent rule among medical schools in Howard's time was that if students failed more than one examination in a course the ax fell. The place they vacated was thus open for someone else to fill. This fact had been explained to the 52 first-year students by Dr. McKibben during his opening lecture in anatomy. "I suggest," he began, "that you take a good look at the person seated on your right, then on your left, because next year, one of you may not be here. The faculty will do all it can to help prepare you for the examinations you will take, but your prospects for success will depend on your own efforts in trying to master the subjects required of you."

Howard's problem of survival was more acute than for the majority of his classmates. Besides his load of regular medical school courses, he had to master the many background subjects such as chemistry which had slipped through his fingers in college. His problem of survival was further complicated by a fact unknown to him at the time: he was red-green color blind.

This was a crucial lapse since a capacity to distinguish between different colors held the key to the answers expected of him in subjects such as quantitative analysis and differentiation of bacteria seen under the microscope. Some of the answers which he gave, based on the way he saw things, differed so radically from how his professors and fellow students perceived them as to excite their wonder about what went on in his mind. Fortunately, because classes were small, his professors were always accessible when Howard needed extra help and he was further helped by students in the Nu Sigma Nu medical fraternity he joined. On top of all else, he engaged an assistant professor as a tutor for many of the science courses.

In later life, Howard spoke of his experiences as a first-year medical student as a nightmare he would never wish on anybody. He studied day and night, through the regular schedule of classes and straight through weekends and breaks for holidays. Helen Zenz, who had been his steady date since his junior year at Whittier, was now working in the office of a doctor. Except for quick dinners Howard was rarely with her, and even then he was always glancing at his wristwatch as if he meant to ration his time. This tended also to be true when he made hasty trips home to visit with his father and Alta, drop off his soiled laundry, stock up on fruits and food supplies, romp briefly with his growing half-brothers and then speed back to his studies.

First-year medical courses were in large measure tests of memory—a reality that inspired the acid comment among the students themselves that "if an ape could memorize, he could pass the first two years in medical school." Howard chained himself to a monastic routine in order to absorb the mass of details he might be required to know on the examinations.

To the same end, he used all the hallowed aides to memory familiar to generations of medical students. Medical names for the bones of the wrist, for example, start with the letters N, L, T, P, M, M, C and H. An old saw translated this into the ditty, "Never Lift Tillie's Pants, Mother Might Come Home." In the same way the names of the cranial nerves were brought to mind by the saying, "On Old Olympus' Towering Tops, A Finn and German Picked Some Hops."

The tensions surrounding his examinations remained a great presence in Howard's memory. Years later he could vividly recall specific examination questions asked that year and how he answered them. For instance, in McKibben's final anatomy examination, Howard answered all questions correctly except one concerning the location of a particular vein that crosses the spinal column. Over a half century later Howard stood in front of McKibben's photograph hanging on a wall of his office reserved for the pictures of those who meant so much in his life and addressed the photograph as though he were a student again—to acknowledge the mistake he had made and answer the question correctly.

Dr. McKibben's prediction regarding the fate of the first-year students materialized in a failure rate of ten percent. The casualties drifted off after an embarrassed round of good-byes and expressions of good luck. Howard, fortunately among the jubilant survivors, later recalled that along with other survivors in his medical fraternity, he marked the end of the first year with a celebration that violated not only the prohibition laws, but some of the cardinal rules of health taught to medical students. The fraternity brothers secured a five-gallon tin of alcohol from a bootlegger, made a bathtub full of gin and proceeded to drink the tub dry.

Returning home to Whittier for summer break, Howard was a happy young man. Not only could he spend a little more time with Helen Zenz but he would have more time with his half-brothers. He could be for them what his Uncle Floyd had been for him—a surrogate father who could join them in the games and horseplay not engaged in by Milus either for temperamental reasons or because he was too busy. Of greater importance, as a successful first-year medical student, he began to equalize the distance between himself and his father and to speak with him knowledgeably about scientific matters of common interest.

10

A Taste of Clinical Medicine

During his second year in medical school, Howard still needed help in his basic science courses. Moreover, he still was not aware that he was red-green color-blind—which complicated his grasp of bacteriology just as it had bothered him the year before in the quantitative analysis of chemistry. His self confidence had improved, however, for having survived the first year's ordeal. Beside, his introductory taste of clinical medicine was heady and stimulating. It meant direct contact with patients at the county hospital where USC had established an affiliation so that its students no longer had to transfer to other facilities for their hospital experience.

In those days doctors had neither antibiotics nor the battery of new machines available now. The practice of medicine generally entailed direct, intimate, one-on-one exchanges between a single doctor and a patient—the kind of approach where a compassionate grasp of a patient's psychological needs held a place of importance often coequal with medication and surgery. Compassion, of course, cannot be taught. It is a habit of the heart which works best when unaware of itself. In a medical school, however, with its highly charged context for discipleship, the compassionate manner of a teacher can mold the bearing of those students who cluster around to hear every word, to watch every gesture and to sort out and retain in memory much of what was said and done.

Though Howard's initial encounter with clinical medicine as a second-year student was limited in scope, he found that unlike the first year, clinical medicine was profoundly compatible with his temperament. He no longer learned only with his eye and mind merely to get a passing grade in a course. He fell in love with clinical medicine and would never fall out of it. It would have a central place in the roll and cadences of his life.

In clinical medicine he prepared his first detailed medical history of a patient's case—while a knot of fellow students stood nearby. The patient was a large black woman. Howard, who had panicked at his art instructor's invitation to feel the contours of a model's body in a sculpture class, tried to be sensitive to the questions he must ask bearing on intimate details of her bodily functions and so launched his questions in a soft, confidential voice, only to learn that the patient was very hard of hearing.

The only way to communicate was to shout his questions. She, keeping the rhythm, shouted back her answers. Finally he asked, "Do you have any children?" "No sir," she gleefully shouted in reply, "but, sonny, I sure had lots of fun trying." The laughter from the patients in the ward and his fellow students made it hard for Howard to remain composed during the rest of the first test of his bedside manner.

One day during his second year, Howard was called to Dean McKibben's office, ostensibly for a discussion of his academic standing. The dean remarked that his prior doubts about Howard's ability to make the grade as a medical student accounted for the close attention he had paid to the young student's work. He was pleased to report that Howard now ranked in the upper third of his class.

There was another issue McKibben wanted to raise. He recalled that as an undergraduate, Howard had been a tennis whiz. If it did not interfere with his studies, could they play a game some Saturday? Howard was delighted by the invitation, but remarked that he had not held a tennis racquet in his hand in three years. He might not be much of a match for the dean.

McKibben picked Howard up the next Saturday morning. In the course of the warm-up vollies, Howard realized that McKibben, then in his mid-50s, would run him ragged. After several sets during which a rusty Howard was demolished, McKibben waved aside his apologies, saying: "You have good basic strokes. Why don't we play again?" They played some Saturday mornings and Howard slowly regained his old form. He cherished the intimacy the game invited and yet he also respected the invisible net strung as a dividing line between his own and McKibben's status.

At different stages in the course of his life, Howard had many "fathers" besides his natural one, to whom he owed an immense debt of gratitude for the roles each played in shaping his career. His Uncle Floyd was the first. Dr. Paul S. McKibben was the second and in one sense, the most important. If not for McKibben, Howard would never have had a chance at a medical career. He would never forget what he owed to Dean McKibben. In the 1960s Howard served as chair of a fund-raising drive to provide the USC Medical School with its own home adjacent to the Los Angeles County Hospital and had the satisfaction of seeing the building named in memory of Paul S. McKibben. To this day Howard never mentions McKibben's name without adding the words, "Bless him."

During the third and fourth years of medical school when Howard was introduced to many branches of medicine, he realized that being a "good doctor" was essentially a solitary, personal enterprise requiring a finely tuned balance between intuitive judgment and empirical data, between observation and manipulative skill. It also required a capacity to listen to patients in order to determine what they did not know about themselves, namely the key factors which accounted for their condition.

The deeper Howard penetrated the province of clinical medicine during these third and fourth years, the more he sorted out impressions that went beyond the data of textbook medicine. Many of these impressions he would retain and use to advantage from the start of his private practice as a surgeon. Such was the case when Howard chose the nurses who became regular members of his personal surgical team. Even as a student he seemed to have clearly fixed in his mind for future reference the qualities of the nurses who would comprise his extra eyes, hands, fingers—and heart—as a surgeon. He particularly admired those who moved with grace in an operating room, who ministered not only to the bodily needs of patients but to their emotional needs as well, whether by a hand clasped on a wrist to reassure the frightened or by a word spoken in place of a "friend" or "family member" when none visited a patient.

The Georgia Street City Receiving Hospital in Los Angeles provided emergency treatment for people involved in traffic accidents, gunshot wounds, burns and about everything else that puts life at hazard. It also dispensed emergency treatment to the battered figures of the sporting world and regular care that covered all the medical and surgical needs of the Los Angeles Police and Fire Departments.

During his third year in medical school Howard became well acquainted with the doctors who worked at Georgia Street in addition to their private practice and teaching at USC. He learned from the chief surgeon, Dr. Wallace Dodge, that the hospital's busiest nights were Saturdays,

Christmas and New Year's Eve. The latter two holidays in particular were the nights of the highest suicide attempts and the most traffic accidents. Howard asked if he could come to the hospital on those nights to observe the work done on people brought in for emergency treatment.

"No," Dr. Dodge replied, "but you can come down to help without salary any time your schedule will allow you to do so."

Howard began to take advantage of this opportunity. To Helen's disappointment—but quiet pride—he often showed up at the hospital on Saturday nights, Christmas and New Year's Eve. It was a great moment when the fledgling doctor was allowed to sew up some of the injured people who were brought in.

It was in his third year as a medical student that the great 1933 earthquake struck Southern California at 6:00 p.m. At its onset Howard happened to be standing in the yard of his parents' home in Whittier. As the quake eased, Howard jumped into his car and drove as fast as he could to Georgia Street. The effects of the quake were visible along the route: trees and telephone poles down, roofs caved in, broken windows and walls of buildings sliced off. The greatest devastation had occurred in Long Beach which, according to a shortwave radio report, was a city on fire.

When Howard reached the Georgia Street Hospital it was already swamped by an incoming tide of earthquake victims. He joined many volunteer nurses and doctors who went with two ambulances and several trucks loaded with medical supplies to the train station. Here they were transferred to a special train destined for Long Beach, but were turned back because a huge water tank had been toppled astride the tracks.

Due to various delays the caravan did not reach Long Beach until four in the morning—only to discover that the earlier reports about how "Long Beach was on fire" were untrue, even though the devastation was extensive. Had the quake hit earlier while school was in session, thousands of children would have been killed because all the brick school buildings had been destroyed. Amid this sea of destruction, Howard was deeply moved by how people responded spontaneously to ease the common distress as best they could. Countless volunteers, doctors and nurses set up "curbside" aid stations assisting those whose injuries did not require hospitalization.

During his senior year, Howard had more free time to visit his family and young brothers in Whittier. It was 1934 and the blight of the depression remained a devastating reality, but Milus did not lack work. Other dentists continued to send him their difficult cases. Milus never wanted to become directly associated with a university, because he feared it would stifle his freedom to work as he saw fit. He did, however, conduct many seminars at university-affiliated dental schools around the country and fellow dentists began urging him to duplicate these courses at his Whittier ranch. In the avocado and citrus grove a suitable facility was built which contained twelve dental chairs, a lecture hall and a laboratory where Milus could make his own porcelain teeth.

Requests for instruction grew until four classes, each with twelve dentists, met monthly in the new building. Howard saw at close range the evolution of these aspects of his father's work and appreciated the value of such advanced educational programs. As in the case of his father's prior work at the Deaner Institute, the example of the classes his father formed in Whittier would later flower in Howard's design for what is now the House Ear Institute.

Milus believed that children should learn the responsibility of caring for animals. His younger sons—Warren, Bill and Jim—who grew up on the Whittier property learned their lessons well. First there were chickens, cats and dogs; then came burros, goats, ponies and, last of all, calves. The ponies, hitched to a two-wheeled cart, were trained to negotiate a track through the citrus grove, with each boy imagining himself to be Ben Hur in the Coliseum. When the calves grew up and became cows, there was a surplus of milk which drastically cut into the time allotted for chariot races.

The boys began selling the surplus milk to the neighbors and Milus required them to keep careful records of the transactions. He agreed to furnish the feed for the cows, in return for which the boys were to spread manure from the dairy barn in the citrus and avocado groves. The income from the milk business was divided equally among the three and deposited in their individual savings accounts. This arrangement was the source of the question Milus often asked his guests, "Which do you want to drink, milk or champagne? They both cost me the same."

In later life each of the younger three sons remembered differently how they complied with their father's decrees. Warren, the oldest, was expected to perform ranching and farming chores—which he liked. Bill, with an adversity to farming, did only as much as was needed to stay out of trouble and later ambiguously referred to these experiences as being "instructive." Jim, the youngest, tried to play "catch up" to equal what Warren could do and later said the whole experience was depressing.

Bill, a "dreamer," was also the most adventuresome of the three boys. As was common with many their age, the three were fascinated with flying. At one point they constructed a parachute, but the only testing site available was the roof of one of the buildings on the ranch. By a vote of two to one, they decided Bill should have the honor of making history. The fateful day came with all the equipment at "Go." As Bill teetered on the edge not quite confident of his equipment, Warren launched his brother into space with a push.

The crash left Bill with a broken ankle but it was to be to humanity's good fortune that his parents' ban against risky tests did not stop Bill in future years from pursuing his extraordinary adventures in the world of ear surgery.

Meanwhile it was forcefully brought home to Howard as a fourth year student that clinical medicine also had its cruel costs. During the spring of 1934 a polio epidemic struck Los Angeles that exceeded the capacity of county hospital physicians to care for the staggering case load. A proposal was made to five seniors that they would be exempt from final examinations if they agreed to drop out of school and go to work prematurely—as interns in the county hospital. Howard and the others who accepted the offer were assigned to the admitting room.

This was no academic drill and two of the five student-interns came down with polio. Several of the regular physicians and nurses were also permanently crippled. "The setup," Howard recalled in after years, "was scary as hell. You never knew how long it would take before you may become one of the polio victims."

In this setting where tensions were high and perils great, there was a moment marked by a comedy of errors due to a quick judgment Howard made. When patients were wheeled into the admitting room with a backache and headache—among the symptoms of oncoming polio—a red blanket was tossed over them and they were promptly sent to the Contagious Disease (CD) Unit.

At one point a heavyset woman was brought into the admitting room on a stretcher. As if to escape the intense pain in her back, she rocked from side to side, while the sounds she emitted were a medley of moans, screams and sobs. To Howard it was obvious the poor woman was in the grip of polio. He quickly tossed a red blanket over her and had an orderly rush her to CD. A bit later Howard got a call from the chief resident at CD.

"Look," he said in a matter-of-fact way, "we are pretty busy here and you sent us a woman in labor. We've just delivered a fine baby boy. In the future," he growled, "send those cases to the OB department."

An embarrassed Howard stammered his apologies, but there was a long-distance gain in the blunder. After that he was careful not to assume that similar external symptoms had the same internal causes.

11

The Intern

When Howard completed his four years in medical school in 1934 because of his exposure to his father's lifelong studies, his interests were already tilted toward ear, nose and throat work (ENT). The pressure of his "understanding" with Milus back in Kansas City was undoubtedly a factor as well. A firm grounding in ENT would be an excellent preparation for a career in dentistry because, as Milus had said, "teeth could not be divorced from the rest of the body."

Although Howard wanted to spend his internship year at Los Angeles County Hospital, hundreds of applicants from across the country competed for some 200 appointments. Even were he accepted as an intern, to get the package he wanted—which included a six-weeks' service on ENT—he needed a number rating of under 40. In the pessimistic belief that he had only a slim chance to get a number that low, he drove to San Diego to apply for an internship at San Diego County Hospital—a relatively small institution where the interns passed through all the specialty services instead of competing for a package that included their particular interest. Howard was accepted on the spot and signed a contract binding him for his internship year.

Several weeks later he received word from Dr. Phoebus Berman, Medical Director of the Los Angeles County Hospital, that his application for an internship had been accepted with the very low number of nine which meant he would easily obtain the package of his choice. By trading with other interns, he might even be able to secure two more six-week ENT services.

His contract with the San Diego County Hospital, however, was the fly in the ointment. Howard doubled back to San Diego and explained to the hospital director the surprising development in Los Angeles and its advantages. Was there any way he could be released from his contract? The director said yes if Howard could find someone to take his place in San Diego. Back in Los Angeles, Howard checked the names of the applicants for internships at Los Angeles County which were listed according to their number rating and approached a classmate who had been given a high number. This classmate was delighted to accept an internship in San Diego and could not thank Howard enough for his "thoughtfulness."

In July the new group of interns, including Howard, reported for duty. The hospital contained a joint organization of interns and residents, with an intern chosen to serve as its president for one year while a resident served the following year. To Howard's surprise, he was elected president and was immediately caught up in a crisis sparked by a decision of the county board of supervisors.

The board, which controlled the hospital's budget, had decreed an austerity program for the institution. Dr. Berman sent a memorandum to all interns and residents stating that in view of the cut in funds, no one would get more than two bath towels a week in their rooms. Howard, as the group's president, was pressured to confront Dr. Berman with their protests.

Traditionally when problems arose Dr. Berman was known to say, "You must understand, this is a very big institution." Howard was treated to the same words when he called on the medical director to raise the issue of the towel allowance. Dr. Berman stood firm. Howard then convened a meeting of the interns and residents to report on Dr. Berman's reaction.

Someone suggested they use a tactic that had proven successful in a confrontation between the residents and the administration several years before—they would simply not discharge any patients from the hospital for 24 hours.

Howard returned to Dr. Berman with this new information. Unless the voluntary faculty assumed the work load in the discharge process, the hospital would run out of vacant beds before the day was over. Dr. Berman relented, "Tell the interns and residents they can have their towels."

On the grand scale of history, the victory amounted to little more than an air bubble on the surface of the Pacific, but that did not detract from its immediate satisfaction on the overworked interns and residents.

Contemporary stage plays, films and television series—when projected against the background of a hospital—almost always feature comic characters. If there were such in the hospital when Howard was there, none seemed to figure in his recollections. Quiet inside jokes, however, helped ease the tensions within the hospital. On some evenings, for example, the operator of the public address system would announce, "Calling Dr. Wapp, Calling Dr. Wapp. Room 960." "Dr. Wapp" did not exist within the hospital. It was a code name announcing that a poker game was being arranged in Room 960 and that interns or residents could report there if they were interested in joining the game.

The public address system—and the operating rooms—also figured in Howard's arrangement to give his half-brothers, who were in grade school, the thrill of their young lives. One or the other would be invited to spend a day or night with him at the hospital and on occasion they would hear themselves summoned over the public address system: "Calling Dr. Warren House," "Calling Dr. William House,"

or "Calling Dr. James House." Howard would also dress the
visiting brother in a surgical mask and gown and take him
into the operating room to "supervise surgery firsthand."
After one such visit, Jim returned to Whittier to report with
immense satisfaction, "Today we did six tonsillectomies."

Milus, strangely enough, never came to the hospital to
witness his son making rounds or observe him perform in
the operating room. Howard's Uncle Floyd, however,
cherished a photograph of himself at the hospital in
surgeon's attire as he proudly observed his intern-nephew
operate.

This man who had shaped "half" of Howard's character,
unlike other bold entrepreneurs, was not flattened by the
Great Crash of October 1929. The year before the crash
Floyd, believing the profits from his restaurants were as
"unreal" as the booming economy, had welcomed a chance
to sell his business to the Child's Restaurant chain and had
proceeded to convert the money from this sale into gold
certificates. Then, in the very trough of the Great
Depression, he purchased blocks of property in Miami,
Florida, betting on a future day when the properties would
prove very valuable. He did not, however, live to see that
day for he died of cancer of the breast complicated by a
heart attack during Howard's intern year.

Looking back on this time as an intern and resident,
Howard counted them among "the greatest years" of his
"entire experience in medicine." Though his chief interest
lay in ENT work, it became known that he would stand in
for his colleagues on other services when they wanted to be
away in the evening. Helen continued working for Dr.
Townsend and, when possible, would join Howard for
dinner. Saturday nights when he was not at Georgia Street,
Howard and Helen would drive to Whittier for dinner with
his family—which always included horseplay with his half-
brothers.

The true center of his life, however, remained with the interns and residents. Unlike today, most were unmarried and lived in the hospital bound together in a special league. Even when they were not on duty they were still around, ready to lend an extra hand in case of need. After their meals together they would often sit around the dining table to talk of interesting cases, other services, other emergencies, appraising the merits of decisions made and offering possible alternatives. Often they would marvel at the skill of a particular doctor or mutter about the dubious technique of another. Later as they made their rounds, they would make time to chat.

The hospital was also a topnotch institution for training student nurses and provided them with dormitory quarters and a separate dining room. It could not, however, endow all student nurses with fail-safe common sense. This was impressed on Howard when he had to help resolve the confusion caused by a student nurse on the ENT service who had been told to remove and clean the false teeth of patients with dentures. She promptly collected the dentures from all the patients, put them in a large washbasin and proceeded to scrub them with praiseworthy thoroughness. When she attempted to return them, she discovered the scrambled problem she had created for herself and for the staff in the ward. Howard, along with the other interns, residents and regular nurses on duty, could only proceed by trial and error to get the proper dentures fitted back into the right mouths.

One of the more memorable characters Howard met as an intern was a Dr. Percy who specialized in desperate cancer cases. He had a spectacular, domineering personality and was addicted to outlandish theatrical devices in order to drive home his commonsense approach to cancer problems. Because he never used a cold knife when operating on cancer patients, he had been nicknamed "Hot

Point." His argument was that the extensive bleeding common to surgery with a cold knife contributed to the spread of cancer cells and he maintained that he curbed the spread by using different shaped, long-handled blades which were kept at a cherry-red heat. If someone came into his office with a lip or skin cancer, Hot Point would excise the cancer with a scoop of one of his cherry-red knives. The heat from the blades served immediately to anesthetize the skin and cauterize the blood vessels so there was no pain or bleeding.

On one of his trips home to Whittier, Howard noticed a black spot on the bald head of his father appeared to be growing rapidly. He kept his worst fears to himself but managed to persuade Milus to come to the hospital so that Dr. Percy could examine the spot. One look and Hot Point declared, "This is a melanoma—the most malignant of all cancers!" He promptly marched Milus into the operating room and without anesthetics, used his famous knives to cut a circle a half-inch away from the rim of the black spot and at a depth right down to the bare bone of the skull.

"How else," he asked when the operation was over, "can you know that you got it all out?" Analysis afterward showed that this was indeed a melanoma. Milus at the time was in his 50s, but was spared a premature death and lived into his 80s.

This event, coupled with Milus' post-operative care, served to bring Howard and Hot Point together in a close mentor-student relationship. Percy was anxious to help Howard "get off to a good start" once he finished his training. In offering advice he made no bones about the value of his own "showmanship."

When he arrived in Illinois to establish a practice, he recalled for Howard's benefit, the first thing he did to make himself known was buy two beautiful white horses and a fine black carriage. When he drove down the street with his white hair flowing, people would ask, "Who's that?" Soon "the new doctor in town" was known to the populace. To become acquainted with the medical profession, he joined the staff of all the hospitals, had breakfast in a different one on successive days, made an effort to discuss his cases with the doctors and members of the hospital staffs, and tried to schedule his operations in various hospitals. Above all, he explained, he was careful in how he dealt with patients.

"When patients say they've got something wrong," Percy exclaimed to Howard, "never lose the faith of those patients by saying, 'I don't know what's wrong.' Even if you don't know, be positive with your answers. Your guess is better than theirs! Give them sympathy, reassurance and hope and do something for them, even if you do nothing more than give them a pill!"

What proved to be the most harrowing period of Howard's internship began in a fairly routine manner. One morning a wide-eyed, terrified four-year-old boy was carried into the admitting room by his parents. He had a litile fever, but his parents offered the only clue to what might be wrong with him: any time he was offered a glass of water he went into convulsions. Howard had read only a little about rabies, but he knew the term "hydrophobia" meant "fear of water." He himself at 14 had been bitten by a rabid dog in Kansas City and subsequently had undergone daily antirabies shots (given in the belly) on 21 consecutive days.

With only this to go on, Howard asked whether the boy had been bitten by any animals. Yes, the parents replied, the month before he had been "nipped" by a dog. Taking a glass of water Howard extended it to the child, who promptly went into convulsions. Convinced he was dealing with a case of human rabies complicated by the month-long lapse since the child was bitten Howard was sure there was no hope. He had the child placed in a crib and telephoned Dr. Chester Bowers, Chief of Communicable Disease Services.

Upon hearing the details of Howard's report, Bowers doubted that they indicated a rare case of rabies. He was wrong, for a spinal tap confirmed that the boy had rabies, presenting Howard with his first test of having to convey grim information to a family that their child was beyond rescue. Howard's own anguish was not to be compared with the shock of the parents when they realized that their own failure to act promptly had sealed their boy's fate.

To chart the course of the disease in detail Howard took a spinal tap on the child every six hours. Soon the boy went into a coma from pressure on the brain, but throughout the rest of the day and during the night, Howard continued to take spinal taps at regular intervals which showed the spinal fluid was getting thicker. At dawn a nurse called to say the child had expired. Although it was not necessary for Howard to take another spinal tap, he wanted to complete the record so put on his rubber gloves and proceeded to insert the needle for a last spinal tap. His weariness from the night's work and loss of sleep made him careless. When he withdrew the needle, it pierced his rubber glove and went into his finger, resulting in a direct inoculation of rabies. He tore the glove off his hand, made a tourniquet around his forearm, then raced down to the admitting room where Dr. Paula Horne was in charge. She grabbed a knife and made a large "V" incision at the point of the inoculation so that the blood would flow out freely. After a while she bandaged his hand.

Howard could do no more work that day. He went to the hospital library where he began to read all the available literature about rabies. The medical history told of instances where dogcatchers had been bitten and then treated with shots. One dogcatcher, bitten a second time and given another antirabies series, had died instantly from anaphylactic shock (when the body rejects a foreign protein or other substance). The records also cited another dogcatcher who was bitten by a rabid dog twelve years after having received the antirabies injection. He elected not to repeat the injection a second time and did not develop rabies. No one was certain how long antirabies shots remained effective.

In Howard's case, 13 years had elapsed since the episode in Kansas City but he had no way of knowing whether or not the danger of anaphylactic shock was behind him. All he knew was that he had 21 days in which to decide whether to take a series of antirabies shots, with their potentially fatal risk, or do nothing in the hope that his earlier treatment would still prevent the development of rabies.

Howard was ethically bound to call on Dr. Berman to tell him what had happened and the dilemma it posed. Berman urged Howard to take the antirabies treatment. If he did not, he would have to forfeit the $5,000 life-insurance policy he carried with the hospital. Howard decided against the treatment and accepted the forfeit of his insurance policy.

Time passed slowly. The medical literature indicated there was a known case where the onset of rabies did not occur until four months after the victim was bitten. What would be the waiting period in his case? The first symptom of rabies is a slight headache. Each morning Howard shook his head to determine its condition. Once in a while, when he did in fact have a little headache, he counted the minutes and hours to see if it would become more intense or would ebb and vanish.

Aside from Dr. Berman, Howard told no one else about what he was going through, not even Helen or his father. He continued his work as an intern from one week to the next, wondering whether there would be a "next week."

After the stretched-out four months deadline had passed, Howard disclosed to Helen and his father the terrifying ordeal he had gone through. At a happy family dinner in celebration of his "recovery," Milus assured Howard that he would much rather have him alive than have the insurance money that had been forfeited.

Howard was 27 in June 1935 when his internship was over and he was scheduled to receive his M.D. degree. With his performance in clinical medicine that marked him as a "comer," he had forged to the top of his class, yet in his mind he continued to be subordinate to the will of his impressive father. He spent restless nights wondering how he could bring up the subject of the understanding reached on the swing in Kansas City. Finally he drove to Whittier to tell Milus of his decision to remain in medicine and not go on to dental school. He hoped to ease his father's displeasure by explaining that oral surgery and problems of the jaw were a part of the training program of an ENT specialist and throughout his future career in medicine he would deal with the same matters that had engrossed his father's lifelong interest.

In Whittier itself, Howard chatted before dinner with his father and family about hospital-related episodes. During the meal there was pleasant general conversation around the table. After dinner more generalities were discussed. Finally the boys and Alta went to bed, but still Howard could not bring himself to talk to his father about his decision. Around eleven o'clock when Howard knew he must soon return to the hospital, in a nervous sweat he blurted out the reasons why he wanted to continue on in medicine by taking a residency in ENT which would give him extensive training in oral surgery.

Milus' reaction to the cascade of words was unexpected. "Howard," he said with a broad smile, "that night on the swing in Kansas City when I suggested you go into medicine first and then take dentistry—do you know why I said that? Medicine is a much broader field with many more opportunities than dentistry. If I had told you I wanted you to be an M.D.—you, as the admiring son, would have felt duty bound to say, 'No, Dad, I want to be a dentist like you!' I am delighted that you will pursue a career in medicine."

With a warm embrace Milus sent a buoyant Howard back to the hospital with his blessing. The son marveled anew at the father's psychological insights.

12

Shock

At his graduation when Howard received his M.D. degree, his father asked if he knew what the diploma really meant. Before he could respond Milus answered his own question. "Howard," he said, "it represents nothing more than a license to begin to learn."

The truth of that remark would be brought home to Howard with full force. He had reason to feel confident on the eve of the licensure examination given by the California State Board of Medical Examiners. He was one of the abler young interns and his technical style and temperament had favorably impressed the various ENT faculty members. After interviewing at County Hospital along with 14 other applicants for the single ENT residency, the post was given to Howard effective July 1st. There were three ENT residents in all, with Drs. John Bullis and Ross Goodcell being second year or "senior" residents. Under the system, Howard would become the senior resident the following year, with two junior residents under him.

The state licensure board examination was held over three successive days. To pass, one had to have an overall average grade of 72, though a candidate could still fail if his grade in any subject was 60 or below.

The first day of the boards focused on general medicine and surgery and Howard swiftly answered the questions with ease. He duplicated the performance on the second day when the questions focused on other general subjects. During the morning of the third day he missed one question: What is the most common cause of hearing impairment, and give its treatment? Howard wrote a long essay on otosclerosis, the most common cause of progressive hearing loss in young adults. The conventional answer would be to cite wax as a cause and washing it out as its treatment.

The afternoon session of the third and final day included the subject of public health, with ten questions each counting for ten percent of the final grade. Howard glanced at the questions and knew he was in very deep trouble. The first five questions dealt with California's narcotics laws. Howard had not reviewed them. Which "soft" narcotics, for example, require prescriptions? Which require triplicate forms? If physicians knew a patient was a drug addict, what was their responsibility?

In after years, Howard remarked that in his ignorance, "I chased the addict all the way to San Quentin prison."

Howard knew he had failed when he reached the sixth question: "Discuss industrial plumbism." What was "plumbism?" He hoped the question might have something to do with industrial plumbing as related to sanitation. There were only two things he could think of in that connection. Drinking fountains should be slanted to prevent individuals from slobbering their saliva over the spigot. He also knew that at county hospital, as in prison cells, there were no toilet seats on the toilets. The user merely sat down on the cold ceramic bowl. Howard believed this was unsanitary and in his answer to the question about "plumbism" he urged the use of toilet seats throughout industry.

Howard left the examination room deeply depressed and made his way to the office of Dr. Raulston, then dean of the medical school. "Dean," he blurted out, "I have failed the California State Boards!"

"What makes you think so?" Raulston asked. "No one in the history of the USC Medical School has ever failed the boards. And you? Never! Don't worry. Wait until you hear from the state board."

Howard explained that he had been unprepared for the questions on narcotic laws.

The interns held a party that night to celebrate taking the boards. Howard was present to drown his private sorrows. A week later he was informed by letter that he had failed, but could retake the examination on a future date. All the other interns had passed. Howard again called on Dean Raulston. What should he do next? He could not start his residency on July 1st without a state license. Raulston advised Howard to see Dr. Maloney who had been one of his teachers and was president of the board of medical examiners.

"I know you failed the boards," Maloney began after Howard was seated in his inner office. "Now do you know California's narcotic laws?"

"Yes," Howard fervently answered. "Backwards and forwards."

"But the question about industrial plumbism," Maloney continued, "none of us on the board could figure it out, with all that rigmarole about drinking fountains and toilet seats. You got a 98 in surgery, a 96 in medicine, and a 94 on the general average of medical specialties, but you came up with a 49 in public health. What on earth did you have in mind in connection with plumbism?"

Howard explained that he knew he had failed the first five questions and was so crestfallen that he totally forgot that plumbism was lead poisoning. He assumed instead the term had something to do with plumbing. Maloney began to laugh and phoned the secretary of the state board in Sacramento to share the joke with him at Howard's expense. There was much more bemused talk back and forth over the telephone, while Howard thought of the great difference between his own circumstance and the way Maloney could be indifferent to the mounting cost of the long-distance call. If and when he ever began work as a resident, he would get room, board, uniforms and $9.09 a month during his first year and $75 a month during his second. The leisurely gossip with the secretary finally came to an end.

Dr. Maloney said the board would meet in three months and review his examination. On that day Howard was to be in his room in the hospital at 4 p.m. Dr. Maloney would call and let him know the board's decision. He might have to leave at once for Sacramento to retake the public health part of the examination. Howard pointed out the serious problem he faced. The date for the next board would come well after July 1 when he was to start the ENT residency. Dr. Maloney assured him he could start provided he didn't write any prescriptions for narcotics.

When Howard alerted Dean Raulston as to what was in prospect, his fame as the advocate of toilet seats had already preceded him and the dean greeted Howard with a peal of laughter. It was agreed Howard could start his residency.

At no time did Howard tell his family he had failed the boards. Shame and self-pride sealed his tongue, though there was a moment when he came perilously close to being unmasked by a newspaper Milus read. In glancing over the list of those who passed, he noticed his son's name was missing. Why? "Quite a few names were left out," Howard said. "But everything is just fine. Just fine."

He could not withhold the truth from Helen, his "steady girl" since their senior year together in Whittier. For the past six years she had been a loyal Penelope, waiting for Howard to make his Ulysses-like passage through medical school, internship and residency. Howard suggested she date other men, but she never seriously looked elsewhere, accepting the price of his drive to be a doctor. When he disclosed the reasons why he might have to go to Sacramento, he added that he didn't have the money to pay for the overnight train trip, but couldn't ask his father to help without explaining what lay behind the request. Helen agreed to loan him what he needed. The round trip was $24, all Howard had was five dollars.

Three months later Howard was waiting in his room when the prearranged call came, at exactly four o'clock.

"The full board reviewed your paper on public health," Dr. Maloney began in an official voice. "We discovered some errors in the way your answers were graded. With the correction of those errors, your grade of 49 in public health has been raised to 61. So congratulations!" His voice then shifted from the impersonal to the intimate. "I have the pleasure to tell you that though you only got a 61 in public health, your overall average is now 89, which places you in the upper third of all who took the boards. Better yet, your 98 in surgery and 96 in medicine, were the highest grades of anyone in the two areas which we consider to be the most important."

Chancellor Bismarck's comment that, "One ought not to inquire into the way laws and sausages are made," might have been amended by Howard: "One ought not ask how a failure on an examination is converted into a passing grade because errors in the marking were discovered and corrected."

He let the case stand in the version passed on to him by Dr. Maloney. The $25 Helen had loaned Howard was partially spent that night on what was, for them, a luxurious dinner. During the celebration they reviewed again, as they had often done in the past, what still "had to happen" before they could be married.

13

The Resident

When Howard became a resident in ENT, "specialization" had advanced a considerable distance since the start of the 1900s when the country was filled with "specialists" who asserted a claim to whatever they said they were. At best, their background, starting in a general practice of medicine, might consist of a six-week trip to Europe to see what was going on, especially in Vienna. It was difficult for the public to know who really was a specialist and who wasn't.

The case was changed when the American Boards was founded to approve training regimens and give examinations to physicians who had completed approved programs in the various specialties. At the time of Howard's ENT residency, the program took two years after the internship. Today, because of the complexity of diagnostic, medical and surgical techniques, the programs require five or six years before the physician can take the American Boards and become a certified specialist.

Howard's work as an ENT resident is known as otolaryngology—head and neck surgery—and is limited to medical and surgical problems, including various types of cancer that affect the face, ear, nose, throat and neck. In the years between 1900 and 1936 the field of otolaryngology advanced slowly, with few innovations. Professional relations in the field were fixed in ways that limited ear surgeons to a narrow sphere of activity. Only neurosurgeons, for example, did operations for tumors on the hearing nerve. Plastic surgeons, who often had degrees in dentistry as well as medicine, claimed the sole right to correct virtually anything wrong that happened to the human face. Not only were they opposed to any role by ENT surgeons in matters relating to the human face, but many of them would not even allow ENT doctors to observe plastic operations.

Beyond this, at the time of Howard's training, because most ENT specialists believed that sinus symptoms were due to infections, operations were regularly performed on patients showing these symptoms. Most ENT specialists failed to understand that in some such cases they were dealing with allergies, not infections. Mastoid surgery was performed by using a mallet, gouge and curettes to remove infection from the ear. The prime object was to save a life; preserving hearing was of secondary importance. Attempts to treat deafness through surgery began at the end of the 19th century, as well as the ear-related tinnitus—a sensation of ringing ears—and Ménière's disease—which is marked by attacks of vertigo. The surgical procedures risked the serious dangers of infection, meningitis and death, so were soon discarded and conventional wisdom tended to dismiss the possibility that surgery could ever restore hearing.

When antibiotics later became available, many ENT specialists thought these drugs would eliminate the need for many surgical procedures traditionally used to get at infections, but they did not foresee how antibiotics would permit the reconstruction of the hearing mechanism after the infected bone was removed surgically.

During Howard's residency, Dr. J. Mackenzie Brown, volunteer chief of the ENT department at the USC medical school and County Hospital, became another figure among those who filled the role of surrogate father to Howard. Other members of the ENT faculty included Peter Viole, a pioneer in facial nerve surgery, Frank Detling, a loving and understanding teacher and Simon Jesberg, an innovator in his specialty. The three ENT residents, in combination with the voluntary faculty, cared for a very busy and large department.

Before antibiotics, epidemics of colds frequently caused acute mastoid infections and as many as six emergency mastoid operations would be performed in one night—which meant the team would go on working into the small hours of the morning. Only then could the volunteer faculty doctor return to his home for a few hours sleep before resuming his regular practice the next day. Prior to the advent of the operating microscope, ear surgery depended on naked eye observation and the surgeon's manual dexterity with hammer and gouge. Howard performed over 360 mastoid operations as a resident and subsequently in private practice, he was to perform over 32,000 ear operations.

The residency was filled with unforgettable experiences. One night a man was brought into the ENT service complaining of a fierce pain on the top of his head in an area the size of a silver dollar. Howard had never seen a case of acute sphenoid sinusitis, but the symptoms corresponded to a textbook description of the disease.

The first step in the treatment called for inserting a canula (a tiny metal tube) into the opening of the sinus. Due to the swelling, however, Howard couldn't find the natural opening, so he took a long needle and placed it exactly where the opening should be and then pushed the needle into the sinus and drained it. The patient cried out, "Doctor! I'm cured! The pain is gone!"

Howard had him remain in the hospital overnight so he could present this rare case to the senior surgeons, Drs. J. Mackenzie Brown and Frank Detling. When the pair examined the patient the next morning, they complimented Howard on "the great job" he had done.

Suddenly the patient joined the bedside talk. "Before you leave," he said, "you should know that when I sit up in bed like this, clear moisture drops from my nose."

The three doctors looked at each other in stunned silence, for the drop of clear fluid meant that Howard, by the thrust of the spinal needle, had caused a leak in the spinal fluid surrounding the brain. X-rays shed a startling light on the source of the leak. The patient had a cancerous brain tumor, totally unrelated to the sinus infection which had eroded the back wall of the sinus and the fluid was seeping through the eroded wall into the nose.

In the absence of antibiotics the patient was doomed to die from meningitis, so Howard was left with the sad role of compiling one of the most detailed daily descriptive accounts of the stages by which a patient, stricken with meningitis, finally succumbs. The dying man tried to console Howard. "I know," he said, "you did everything you could to help me." An autopsy revealed that the needle went where it should have gone and had nothing to do with the patient's death. When the sinus was drained, the pressure that had previously held back the cancerous wall was eased and the wall collapsed.

Relief from the tensions of the intense hospital chores came to the residents through a contact at Paramount Pictures. When motion picture crews were on location, the studios kept a licensed physician in attendance who was paid $15 a day in addition to room, board and transportation. The residents were delighted to take turns going on these filming junkets, enjoying the company of actors, actresses and directors. A complete emergency medical bag was provided by the studio.

One of Howard's experiences as a motion picture physician involved Joan Bennett, the star of a picture called

"Dirigible." One scene, shot in an airport hanger, was supposed to be the Arctic where the dirigible had crashed. As Joan emerged from the make-believe crash while the cameras rolled, she stepped on a nail hidden by the artificial snow and was hustled to her dressing room. Howard asked if she would remove her shoe and stocking so that he could examine her foot. He was amazed to hear her answer. "I must wait," she said, "for my maid to do that for me."

After a delay of 15 minutes, the maid was located. The shoe and stocking, when removed, revealed a small puncture wound on the sole of her foot. Howard cleaned the area, covered it with a band-aid and was getting ready to inject Joan with an anti-tetanus vaccine when she suddenly announced she needed a real doctor and demanded to be taken to her private physician.

This was Howard's first encounter with an imperious star, but the studio people seemed accustomed to such events which stopped the cameras for the rest of the day.

A more flattering experience for Howard happened with another star—the beautiful, young Virginia Mayo—during the filming of a picture on Catalina Island. To Howard's delight she seemed to go out of her way to become better acquainted, even though it was difficult to believe she would be the least bit interested in him. At one point in their conversations she asked if he had a "steady girl friend." "Oh yes," he blurted out, "I'm getting married soon." His conversations with Virginia rapidly diminished for the remainder of the shooting.

If Howard was awed by his early encounters with these stars, he would later become their friend and one of their favorite doctors. They, in turn, would be of incalculable help in building the House Ear Institute.

As a junior resident, Howard's $9.09 monthly check helped cover the cost of his entertainment outside the hospital. He particularly favored the Coconut Grove in Los Angeles' Ambassador Hotel. At a cost of $3.95 for a pitcher of punch, he and Helen could have a table, listen to Bing Crosby sing and dance to Phil Harris' band. On one such evening, when the waiter presented the $3.95 tab, Howard asked if he would accept his monthly paycheck from the County Hospital. The waiter answered, "If it's not too large." One glance at the $9.09 check and he simply said, "I believe we can handle your check. Thank you." The waiter's sensitive tableside manner was equal to any doctor's best bedside manner.

Other diversions for the residents came when they served as ambulance doctors for an undertaker named Overholtzer who had a contract to remove casualties at sporting events. The pay was $15 a night which Howard and his roommate, Bob Kennedy, would split. At wrestling and boxing matches they were given ringside seats where they sat with their medical and oxygen supplies.

One night they were eye-witnesses to a world championship wrestling match between Man Mountain Dean, a 400-pound monster and the current champion, Jim Lundis. Man Mountain's wrestling strategy was to get his opponent on the canvas with a strangle hold and keep him there until he was about to pass out. He would then jump, bottom first, on the prone figure and crush him. This was about to happen, but the groggy Jim Lundis managed to move just as Man Mountain came at him with a flying leap. He missed his target and crashed on the canvas floor flat on his back. As he lay injured, Lundis still groggy, rolled on top of him, was declared the winner and retained his world championship.

The white-clad Howard and Bob climbed into the ring with their small fold-up stretcher. Dean was writhing on the mat and to ease his back pain, Howard gave him a large injection of morphine. But nothing they did could get Man

Mountain onto the stretcher. One leg they could lift, but not both. Besides, his enormous torso was too huge for the narrow stretcher. Waves of laughter swept over the packed crowd which had stayed to watch. Howard and Bob realized there was no way Dean could be carried out, so the referee removed the ropes from one side of the ring and Howard and Bob helped by some volunteers—managed to get him on his feet and into the nearby ambulance.

Howard had always thought wrestling matches were make-believe, but as the ambulance, tilting to one side with its cargo, sped toward the hospital, Man Mountain Dean began to sob. Howard asked if he were in pain. "Yes," he said, "but it's nothing a doctor can fix. I had that match won, but now I've lost my chance to be the world champion." Because of this back injury, Dean never wrestled again.

Another night, the two young doctors settled in their ringside seats with their stretcher and medical bag to watch a boxing match. Kennedy was particularly interested in one of the boxers, a heavyweight named Lee Ramage known for his power as a "counterpuncher." His opponent that night was an unknown young black man.

At the gong for the first round, the boxers came out of their corners. Gloves touched, followed by several feints, some weaving and bobbing, a sudden flurry of leather and one lightning short punch. There had been no chance for a counterpunch, for the match was over before three minutes had elapsed. Ramage was on the canvas, knocked senseless. The residents would remember this moment, for the black man with his arms held up in victory was Joe Louis, the Brown Bomber, who would go on to become the world heavyweight boxing champion.

These were the temporary diversions from the rhythm of Howard's life as a. resident where life-and-death decisions and mounting tensions made for the seriousness of the hospital's business.

A bleak task assigned Howard by a young attending physician, Dr. Alden Miller, whom Howard had met as an intern when Miller was the chief resident on the ENT service, concerned people who were admitted to the hospital with tuberculosis of the throat. In this period before tuberculosis could be successfully treated, Howard's duty was to enter the wards of the tuberculosis patients in the morning, pull their tongues forward and inject their larynx with chamugral oil which temporarily eased their pain. He would repeat the same procedure at night.

The patients would invariably cough in his face. So Howard obtained a welder's mask for protection, hoping he could get out of the hospital without tuberculosis, as in the case of some of the nurses, interns and residents who had contracted the disease from the patients they treated. In spite of the hazards of the assignment, Miller and Howard remained life-long friends. In later years, Howard regularly accused Miller of exposing him to tuberculous patients in order to avoid future competition from Howard in acquiring patients, playing poker, tennis or on the golf course.

A sense of time depends not only on a clock but on psychological attitudes. In Howard's case, the first year of his residency seemed suddenly to be over. For the second year, he would be the senior resident in charge of the ENT service and teach medical students, interns and his two new junior residents. His salary would increase from $9.09 to $75 a month—a heady jump in income for the young doctor.

14

Turns and Returns

Helen did not accept financial help from her father, but she lived with her parents and saved most of the modest salary paid her by Dr. Kenneth Townsend. Were they to pool her income with Howard's senior resident salary, they would have combined earnings of $200 a month—more than most young couples could count on during the Depression. The year was now 1936 and they were both 28. After seven years of "going together," they set August 15 as their wedding day.

Helen had wished for a "nice church wedding" and reception. What happened instead on the final approach to the marriage ceremony, if told in a mid-18th century novel, would be captioned: "A Chapter in Which Our Hero Doth Not Appear in a Good Light."

Strangely enough, Howard had never intimated to his father that he was seriously "interested" in Helen. In later years, looking back on his puzzling behavior, Howard could only explain that he was not sure Milus would approve of Helen, partly because her family were Christian Scientists. A more complex hypothesis has been suggested by Howard's son, Kenneth, a psychoanalyst. "Remember," he said, "my father had suffered a great deal as a boy when his mother died and grieved a great deal when Alta Fouts entered his life and seemed—so he thought—to take his father away from him. Howard would never do anything to displease his father and he wasn't sure that Milus would approve of any woman for his son."

In any case, Howard was the Great Agonizer. Several times he tried to tell his father what his plans were, only to suffer a failure of nerve at each opportunity. At the end of July, Milus was due to join Alta and the three boys in Indiana. Howard volunteered to drive him to the station with the intent, so he thought, to reveal his plans to be married.

The words never came out. When he helped settle his father on the train, he made another attempt at a confession. To gain time, he invented a story about seeing a colleague in San Bernardino and rode the train until that stop an hour later. Still Howard could not gather courage to disclose his marriage plans, so he left Milus at the San Bernardino stop, wished him a pleasant trip and took the bus back to Los Angeles.

The date for the wedding still stood and Howard and Helen agreed they would be married in Riverside by Howard's Uncle Ben, a minister. With not a word to anyone, on August 15, the couple got into Howard's car, a slightly used Buick given him by his father, and set off for the hour's drive to Riverside. It was Howard's worst moment and he was beside himself with alarm. Helen watched his developing tremors and his ashen face streaked with sweat, and finally blurted out, "Oh Howard, if you don't want to get married, say so and we won't be."

Howard could only assure her that he meant to "go through with it." Arriving at the Riverside home of his relatives, they rang the doorbell, and were greeted by an astonished Uncle Ben and Aunt Mabel. Howard announced their intentions to be married, adding that his father was still in Indiana, knew nothing of these plans. Aunt Mabel suggested it might be nice to have someone from the family in attendance. Grandma Payne was no longer alive, but

Howard at once offered to drive to Long Beach, 50 miles away, and pick up his surviving grandparents, Grandfather and Grandmother House.

A telephone call to Long Beach revealed they were too feeble to make the trip, so there was nothing left to do but mobilize some local witnesses and go through with the wedding ceremony. With little fanfare, Howard and Helen were shortly husband and wife under the laws of the State of California.

Their honeymoon was but an extension of the slap-stick comedy that marked their wedding. Howard had made no advance arrangements about anything, so Aunt Mabel and Uncle Ben came to the rescue and took the newlyweds to the Mission Inn in Riverside for a nuptial dinner. After that, what? Howard suggested they drive up to Lake Arrowhead, but when they arrived after midnight, they found there were no vacancies. The newlyweds drove back down the mountain to the Mission Inn, but again all the rooms were booked. In the small hours of the morning they were referred to a hotel located over a drug store. It was tacky, but it had an available room and that is where they spent their wedding night.

The next day the couple headed for Los Angeles where they planned to spend a night in the beautiful Bel Air Hotel. En route rain began to fall and to avoid being smashed by a skidding oncoming car, Howard drove into the ditch, ripping up fence posts in the process. After much commotion, Howard's banged up car was pulled out of the ditch, still in working order. They arrived at the Bel Air without further incident.

Trouble, however, continued to trail them as they headed north up the coast. In Monterey, Helen pointed out to the fascinated Howard the home of California's first governor. With his eyes averted, Howard managed to plow into the rear of a car that had stopped for a traffic light. Helen was thrown hard against the dash board and Howard was shaken up, but both were mobile.

The couple in the other car, both in their mid-60s, fortunately were not injured. What ensued was a colloquy that would not have seemed credible to the occupants of the other cars now edging their way around the accident. Howard explained how very sorry he was that he had not stopped. He was on his honeymoon with Helen and had been looking around at the sights. The victims smiled cordially and offered to give the newlyweds a wedding present. They would not only forget the damages but provided the honeymooners with a list of places to see in Monterey.

Not until Milus returned from Indiana to Whittier was he apprised of his son's marriage. Its clandestine nature must have been puzzling, and it certainly was difficult for Helen to be presented before Milus as though he alone could judge whether she was worthy to be the wife of his son.

Howard's marriage did not alter his relationship with his father. It continued to rank first in importance among his human loyalties. Fortunately, Helen was warmly welcomed into the House family. By this time the young couple had rented a one-bedroom duplex near the hospital for $35 a month. Helen continued her work and Howard was much absorbed by the hospital. On duty every third night, he always remained on call, so his evenings at home were often interrupted.

The transition from courtship to the realities of marriage are seldom free of strain under any circumstances, but during the first two years of their marriage Howard was not at liberty, or perhaps not of a mind, to give Helen more than minimal attention. His second year of residency unfolded in a series of episodes whose nature ceaselessly changed.

One day a girl of three was brought into the hospital by her mother who reported that her daughter had been coughing and choking. X-rays revealed to the astonished Howard that the child had three straight needles and two open safety pins in her stomach. It turned out they had been forced into her mouth by a jealous older sister. Once in the stomach, an open safety pin generally passes in the stool without difficulty, but needles seem to have a mind of their own.

Howard called Dr. Simon Jesberg, the hospital's expert in regard to foreign bodies, who told him no attempt should be made to remove the needles. He explained that the stomach wall, intestines and lungs were in constant motion and would slowly push the needles through the moving tissues which would seal themselves. Eventually the needles would show up as red spots on various parts of the skin where they could be grasped and removed. The child was hospitalized and her body was x-rayed often to observe the progress of the needles which were removed one by one. After three months, the third needle was finally removed and the child was released in good health.

During this second year of residency Howard was led by his curiosity to establish what came to be known as the "stuffy nose clinic"—the place where he made his first significant contribution to ENT surgery. Each Saturday the clinic was opened with several volunteer student nurses—who also had stuffy nose problems—helping out. Having noticed that many people had trouble breathing through their nose for causes that varied from person to person, Howard was determined to analyze the problem and try various treatments.

The nasal airway is guarded by three turbinates (small bone projections covered by mucous membrane on the inside of the nose) which are capable of swelling. Any swelling of the largest of the turbinates, which is called the inferior turbinate, narrows the airway and leads to "the stuffy nose syndrome." Swelling normally occurs in the presence of a common cold, infections, climatic changes, allergies or various other irritants. Patients who have had cosmetic surgery on the nose also often developed breathing difficulties.

The more Howard investigated this difficulty, the more he was convinced that by removing the tiny bone within the inferior turbinate, he could reduce its size and create a more adequate airway without disturbing the covering mucosa. He developed the necessary instruments and worked out the surgical procedure on cadavers before he was ready to apply what he had learned to his "stuffy nose patients."

After performing a number of these operations which he called "submucous resection of the inferior turbinate," he demonstrated the procedure and presented the patients to Dr. J. Mackenzie Brown, his chief. When Brown observed the favorable results, he enthusiastically urged Howard to publish a paper on the new operation, but Howard demurred. He wanted to wait until he had a larger series of cases over a longer period of time to be assured that the results would be permanent. In 1951 he published the details in a medical journal, *The Laryngoscope*, and today the method is universally used where indicated for the "stuffy nose syndrome." In its summary the journal wrote, "This is an important contribution to rhinology by a physician who is usually thought of as an otologist. Clearly and concisely, a surgical technique is described that should be well-known to every practitioner of rhinology. Its indications are many, its effectiveness is impressive, its simplicity and safety are notable. Undesirable changes in nasal physiology are avoided."

When Howard finished his residency his father asked him what he was going to do. The obvious option, in Howard's opinion, was to open an office and try to make a living. Milus then asked if there was anyone in the United States or abroad who knew more than Howard did about ear, nose and throat work. Howard rattled off the names of some of the giants in the field, and his father then said, "There will never be a better time than right now to visit them all. You need to get into their offices, operating rooms and clinics to see how they take care of their patients and study what motivates them, what their personalities are like and what makes them the success they are. You should also study their interests outside of medicine and try to get into their homes to see how their families have promoted their success. Whether it takes six months or two years, now is the time."

Howard liked the idea but reminded his father that the proposed venture would cost a tidy sum of money. Milus responded that money would never be spent for a better purpose. He would put $5,000 into a checking account and Howard could repay him when he got into practice. That sum was to sustain Howard for a year-and-a-half of post-residency training.

To start the process he spent three weeks with Dr. Arthur Smith, a well-known Los Angeles plastic surgeon and one of Milus' close friends. His time with Dr. Smith convinced Howard that though plastic surgeons knew how to correct the external appearances of the nose, they did not fully understand its internal functions. There was an obvious need for surgeons who could skillfully handle both the aesthetic aspects and the breathing functions of the nose. Howard was convinced this would be his future.

Leaving Los Angeles, Howard carried letters of introduction from his father addressed to friends among the nation's leading plastic surgeons, who were often doctors of both dentistry and medicine. His first stop was the University of Iowa Medical School where Dr. Dean Lierle, though relatively young, headed the ENT department. The stay was an eye-opener. The department had an animal research laboratory—something not true in Los Angeles. What is more, the doctors had their subspecialties, one in the ear, another the nose, one in facial plastics and another in throat and neck work.

In Los Angeles all ENT doctors did everything in their field, but the new organizational structure had obvious implications for the future. With the right volume of patients it would be possible to concentrate on one phase of ENT work rather than try to be the expert on everything, and it would be possible to be a sub-specialist within the broad specialty of ENT, just as his father had specialized in artificial dentures.

This time spent at the Iowa Medical School marked the onset of a life-long friendship between Lierle and Howard. Lierle was later to become secretary of the American Board of Otolaryngology and a major figure in the American Academy of Ophthalmology and Otolaryngology, along with other national associations of ENT specialists. Throughout these years he helped Howard in his rise to places of national leadership in medical specialty organizations.

The next stop for Howard was Washington University in St. Louis where the head of the ENT department was Dr. Lee Wallace Dean, an exceptionally able administrator and well-known ENT specialist. The school had become the center for plastic surgery in the United States under the able leadership of Dr. Vilbray P. Blair, another of Milus' intimate friends.

On meeting Howard, Dr. Blair announced, "I want to do everything I can for you. Come into my surgery and my office and examine my patients before and after surgery. See how we do things."

No such "open door policy" applied to other members of the ENT faculty school and many, not knowing he was

"Milus' son" were amazed at Howard's easy access. When Howard examined the effects of Blair's work on patients, he again encountered the hard truth that though many patients emerged from surgery with "fine looking noses," some had difficulty breathing. His conviction was growing that he could have a bright future if he combined what he was learning about plastic surgery with what he knew about the inside of the nose and how it functioned.

During the three months Howard remained in St. Louis, his only contacts with Helen were occasional telephone calls and the frequent letters he wrote. His long stay in St. Louis was due not only to what he was learning about plastic surgery, but also his fascination with the work of Drs. French Hansel and Dorothy Wolff.

Dr. Hansel was interested in "nasal allergies"—a subject that amounted to a dark continent as far as Howard was concerned. The faculty at the school was leery of Hansel's work because the general belief was that nasal allergies had no place in the world of reality. Howard became a convert when he was exposed directly to Hansel's work.

Doubting that all drainage from the nose was due to sinus infection, Hansel observed, with the help of a microscope, that laboratory specimens from patients were often loaded with cells characteristic of allergies known as eosinophils. Hansel invited Howard to attend a two-week course in allergies. When he showed up, he found he was the only student in it. This did not diminish Hansel's pride in having at least one student who took his work seriously.

Hansel was a terrible teacher; however, his incoherence would vanish when they would walk from his office to a nearby bar known as the Coal Hole. The remarkable thing was that despite the many drinks, or perhaps because of them, his "lectures" about allergies were clear, incisive and compelling. He went on to publish a textbook on nasal allergy, still widely used today, and was also the founder of the American Otolaryngological Allergy Society.

Dorothy Wolff, a Ph.D., was studying the histopathology of the temporal bone, which is an integral part of the base and lateral wall of the skull. The temporal bone, a dazzling piece of engineering, contains the mechanism for human hearing and balance, houses the ear canal, the eardrum and the middle ear with its three bones—the malleus (hammer), incus (anvil) and stapes (stirrup). The inner ear, which contains the delicate balance and hearing mechanisms as well as the nerves that move the face, provide taste to the tongue and carry balance and hearing sensations to the brain, is also located in the temporal bone.

The middle ear is the size of the eraser on a lead pencil while the entire inner ear can be placed on the surface of a dime. Sound waves strike the eardrum which vibrates the three little bones. They, in turn, move the fluid in the inner ear which stimulates the endings of the hearing nerve and the electrical currents they create which are then transmitted to the brain where they are interpreted as understandable sound. Motions of the head also move the same inner ear fluid, stimulating the endings of the balance nerve; these create the electric impulses which tell the brain the position of the head. Both the hearing and balance nerves are slightly larger than the lead in a lead pencil and contain thousands of nerve fibers, each of which transmits an electric impulse.

Before Dr. Dorothy Wolff introduced Howard to her work he had never seen a temporal bone slide. Although Howard's preoccupation with medicine for several years had given him little time to appreciate painting, ballet, drama or symphonies, his aesthetic sensibilities were not dull and he responded with passionate enthusiasm to what he perceived as "elegant" in surgery—the single stroke that achieved its aim with precise grace and efficiency. He responded with the same enthusiasm to the wondrous things he saw in Dr. Dorothy Wolff's laboratory. In later years, when speaking of her slides, he still exploded with his original excitement, saying; "My God, it was beautiful! How I loved it!"

He suggested and Dorothy Wolff agreed, that scientific benefits from the study would be multiplied if it were possible to match the medical records of a deceased patient with the study of their respective temporal bones. The insight he had gained with Dr. Dorothy Wolff as his guide would later result in the creation at the House Ear Institute of the Eccles Temporal Bone Laboratory, now one of the foremost laboratories of its kind, having been made so by the work of two eminent doctors, George Kelemen and Fred Linthicum, Jr.

From St. Louis Howard moved on to Chicago for a visit with Dr. George Shambaugh, Sr., an authority on otosclerosis, the chair of the ENT department of the Rush Medical School and one of the organizers of the American Board of Otolaryngology that certifies otolaryngologists. During his residency Howard had never diagnosed a patient with otosclerosis. He thought their hearing problems were due to the obstruction of the eustachian tube (which connects the middle ear with the back of the nose and equalizes the air pressure on both sides of the eardrum) when he inflated a tube to remove an obstruction, the result was only a temporary improvement in hearing.

Otosclerosis, the most common cause of progressive hearing impairment in young adults, is hereditary in origin, although it may skip generations and is twice as common in females as it is in males. The hearing loss gradually increases as the little bone known as the stapes, or stirrup, becomes fixed due to bony growth. Otosclerosis patients can usually hear with properly fitted hearing aids and only rarely does the hearing loss progress to total deafness.

Numerous surgical attempts had been made over the years to deal with otosclerosis. One English Lord in the 1800s who experienced difficulty hearing the debates in Parliament had treated himself with a small silver rod whose tip he placed on his eardrum. By jiggling the rod vigorously he managed to loosen the fixed stapes (stirrup) causing it to vibrate. This form of self-mobilization enabled him to hear for a spell until the bone refixed and prompted him to repeat the process. All his doctors could see was the scar on his eardrum where he used the rod.

In 1877 a Dr. Kessel had published in a German medical journal the story of a young man who, after a skull fracture, regained his lost hearing. Kessel outlived the young man and obtained his temporal bone. He found that a crack in the bone had allowed sound vibrations to create waves in the inner ear fluid, which in turn activated the hearing nerve. Kessel tried through surgery to duplicate such a crack on patients with otosclerosis, but the operation was not a success. Much the same fate haunted other attempts at stapes mobilization reported from France in 1888 by Dr. Bouheron, from Berlin in 1890 by Dr. Miot, and from Boston in 1893 by Drs. Jack and Blake. The failures were largely due to the lack of adequate magnification and antibiotics.

However, the principle of loosening the fixed stapes was reaffirmed in the opening years of the 20th century, again as the result of an accident. A travelling "patent medicine" man in Indiana attracted a crowd by offering five dollars to anyone who could stay in the ring with a boxer who was part of the medicine man's routine. A hard-of-hearing farm boy who accepted the challenge, got into the ring and was knocked out. In falling, he banged his head against one of the posts that held the ropes, and when he regained his senses, his first words were, "By God, I can hear!" From that time on the patent medicine man, in the course of his travels, would announce to a crowd, "If you have a hearing loss, your deafness may be helped by having my boxing man strike you in the ear!"

The one-shot miracle was never duplicated, but the episode, when brought to the attention of otologists, helped to rivet their thoughts on the problem of fixed stapes.

In 1937 Dr. Shambaugh, Sr. was suffering from Parkinson's disease, so Howard could not see him at work in the operating room. He was, however, mesmerized by what the latter told him about otosclerosis. Though Shambaugh, Sr. was a pioneer in the diagnosis of otosclerosis, he was initially skeptical of its treatment through "fenestration surgery," as developed by Dr. Julius Lempert of New York City. Nevertheless, in his role as editor of the *Archives*, he bravely published Lempert's first article in defiance of some of the doctors on his editorial board who threatened to resign should he print Lempert's description of a new technique for a mastoid operation through the ear canal, in contrast to the traditional approach behind the ear.

The care of George Shambaugh, Sr.'s patients passed into the skilled hands of his son, George Shambaugh, Jr., who, like his father, would later become internationally known for his many contributions to otology, especially in connection with otosclerosis and for his textbook titled, *Surgery of the Ear*. It is still used the world over and regarded as the finest book available on this subject.

Howard's introductory meeting with George, Jr., five years his senior, would mark the onset of their life-long friendship. Not only were both among the earliest converts to the works of French Hansel in allergy and to Julius Lempert in fenestration surgery, they also shared the same birthday and regularly exchanged the same greeting, "Congratulations, you made it another year!"

In Chicago Howard also called on several other ENT pioneers who were coming to the front in their fields. Dr. Francis Lederer, the head of the ENT department at the University of Illinois, was at the time writing a textbook that would later be in universal use. Dr. Paul Hollinger, who had just begun his practice limited to problems of the larynx, esophagus and the trachea, would later not only develop a motion picture camera which provided spectacular pictures for teaching purposes but would also publish a fine textbook on his specialty. Dr. John Lindsay of the University of Chicago Medical School and chief of its ENT service was also in the highly specialized field of temporal bone histopathology. All three of these young Chicagoans would become world renowned in their specialties and be counted among Howard's close friends.

From Chicago Howard went to Ann Arbor to take a course on osteomyelitis of the skull from Dr. Artie O. Furstenberg, then dean of the University of Michigan Medical School and head of its ENT department. Through the example of Furstenberg, Howard learned that it was possible to so arrange one's day as to be able simultaneously to do extensive teaching and still carry on a large private practice.

After finishing the Furstenberg course, Howard remained in Ann Arbor for a week's instruction by Dr. James Maxwell in surgical techniques related to the facial nerve. He, in turn, demonstrated for Furstenberg and Maxwell, at their request, his submucous resection of the inferior turbinate operation. Both were impressed and later spoke of the operation many times at different meetings throughout the country.

Howard's next stop was New York where he called on two noted authorities in the ENT field, each the author of a major textbook on the ear and active in national societies: Dr. Samuel J. Kopetzky, who was also a general in the army, and Dr. Isadore Friesner, the chief of the ENT service at Mt. Sinai Hospital. After observing their surgery, Howard concluded that there was a gross disconnection between knowledge on one side and skill in the operating room on the other.

The stay in New York was rounded out with a visit to two plastic surgeons, Drs. Eastman and Alfrect. Both were friends of Milus House and Howard was allowed to witness their surgery and analyze the results. Again he noted that though the patients were provided with "fine looking noses," many had trouble breathing. By now Howard was anxious to start his private practice. He hoped to concentrate on nasal plastic surgery work.

At Temple University in Philadelphia he took a course offered by Dr. Chevalaire Jackson and his son on ways to remove foreign bodies from air passages, similar to the work of Dr. Jesberg. Due to Howard's previous experiences in treating patients suffering from tuberculosis, he had a strong distaste for these procedures, but he knew he might have to perform them at the onset of his practice, so it was best to learn the Jacksons' method also. As it turned out, during the second World War, he was one of three surgeons in the entire Los Angeles area capable of doing bronchoscopies.

In Baltimore Howard observed the work of Dr. Samuel Crowe, head of ENT at Johns Hopkins Medical School, who was promoting the use of radium on adenoid tissue in children—a practice then widely used but soon abandoned. Other specialists whom he met there included Dr. Stacy Guild, active in histopathology of the temporal bone, and Dr. John E. Boardley, later to be the head of the ENT department at Johns Hopkins.

In time, young Dr. George Nager, son and namesake of an eminent surgeon Howard was to meet in Zürich, Switzerland, would later spend a year with Howard in Los

Angeles and then move on to Baltimore where he would eventually replace Boardley as chair of the Johns Hopkins ENT department.

Shortly before Christmas Howard returned to Los Angeles for a brief reunion with Helen and his family, reflecting on what he had gained from this experience.

In advance of his cross-country trip he had read every published article he could find written by the doctors he was due to visit. In the process he had digested vast amounts of new knowledge and had seen new organizational structures for medical enterprises, gaining important insights into the problems of medical management, leadership and fund-raising. Not insignificantly, he had also put himself on display directly under the eyes of leading figures in the fields of plastic surgery and otolaryngology and he had come away from them with their compliments ringing in his ears. Also the trip had set in place the basis for his life-long friendship with many of them.

Yet the extraordinary phase in his post-residency education—and from the standpoint of his career, the most decisive phase—still lay ahead for him.

15

Between Mosher and Lempert

Dr. Harris P. Mosher, head of the ENT department at Harvard Medical School and the Massachusetts Eye and Ear Infirmary, was divided from within like two different men in the same body. In his time as the nation's foremost authority on head and neck surgery, he was a major force in the development of professional organizations of otolaryngologists to upgrade professional training and standards in the field. Besides being a founder of the American Board of Otolaryngology, he had served as president of all national societies in his medical specialty.

Mosher left his private practice early to devote himself to academic medicine, which was fortunate for if he had not done so, he might have "starved to death." His acerbic personality would have driven patients away. However, he could be a stickler for fair play—a terror to any doctor who, in reporting on a research project, did not give full credit to those on whose work he had drawn and he could do magnanimous deeds. Once while Clair M. Kos, who was to become one of Howard's closest friends and a major figure in modern otology—research, teaching, private practice, Executive Secretary of the Academy, and president of many national societies—was a resident under Mosher, financial adversity threatened to halt his training. With no fanfare, Mosher quietly came to his rescue.

While Mosher's tongue could wound, it could also make a meeting rock with laughter when it was trained on a subject—including himself. Even at the end of his career, his tart humor was in fine form. In his remarks "On Being a Professor Emeritus" at a dinner where he was the guest of honor, he said:

> Everything comes to an end except walking a dog. It has been the custom in universities when a professor reaches the age limit, to retire him with the title of Professor Emeritus. It is the kiss of death. Conferring the title is the academic form of execution. You and other victims of time are given a place of honor on the commencement platform like that of a corpse at a funeral. You rise when the president of the university comes to your name on his list and bow your white head, to all outward appearances, submissively. The title conferred, you are then legally and academically dead.

He then went on to lay down succinct rules of conduct for a retired chief of service in a hospital,

> Keep away from the hospital for a year until the new person is comfortably settled in his job. Expect improvements. Give advice only when asked. Don't expect to be asked. Make no comparisons, listen to none; they may be uncomplimentary to you. Don't feel openly hurt if your pet instruments, especially those you invented, are not used, but are put in the historical collection. Don't embarrass your hospital by leaving behind or giving it anything too personal. Sentiment hampers administration. Don't ask if you are missed. Out of politeness the answer will always be "yes," whether true or not. Should anyone voluntarily say that you are missed, it will be sweet music to your ears for that is what you long to hear. Of course, I have broken some of these rules. It was only human to do so, and I have been accused of being more human of late.

Howard, unaware of the harsh angles of Mosher's character, knew only that once a year Mosher gave a four-week postgraduate course to which he accepted only twelve students. The chance of being chosen from among a mass of competitors was slim, but Howard's application was supported by a strong letter of recommendation from Dr. Brown. Mosher wrote to Brown saying he would be pleased to have Howard in his class and that he should send a photograph of himself.

The course members were to convene on Sunday, January 8, 1938 for a get-together at four o'clock in Mosher's Boston home for tea so they could meet each other. Spouses were explicitly excluded for the duration of the course.

Determined to reduce the drain on his father's pocketbook and to save money on the transcontinental rail trip from California to Boston, Howard travelled by coach during the day, buying an upper berth only for the night time. During the day on the long trek east Howard had time to read through all the medical literature Mosher had published.

Arriving in Boston during a driving snowstorm delayed the train. Since he was already late, Howard told the cab driver to head straight for Mosher's home.

When Mosher opened the front door, Howard explained, "I'm Dr. House from Los Angeles."

"I know who you are," his host snapped back. "You're late!"

Howard tried to explain about the train, but was cut off. "No excuses," Mosher barked curtly. "You are late! Come into the house, but don't remove your overcoat. I'll take you around so you can meet the others. Then go to your hotel. Get some sleep, but be in the lecture room promptly at eight a.m. Not eight-oh-five, but eight o'clock sharp."

Too shaken by this strange reception to ask if he could use the phone to get a taxi, Howard picked up his bags and headed out the front door back into the snowstorm. Providentially, a cab drove up with a passenger who proved to be the twelfth member of the class. Howard got into the cab but asked the driver to wait and then watched a repeat performance of what had just happened to him.

"I know who you are," Mosher snapped at the tardy guest, "You are from Sydney, Australia. You are late. No excuses! Don't take off your coat," and so on through the rest of the litany.

When the Australian reemerged, he was grateful to see that Howard had kept the cab. Howard explained he had anticipated what would happen as he had just received the same treatment. The pair had reservations in the same hotel close to the school and became friends before the cab reached the place.

Howard rose early the next day, entered the lecture hall at seven-thirty and settled into a front row seat. Promptly at eight Mosher appeared, looked around and said, "I am certainly glad there are no front-row lackeys in this class."

Hearing these opening words Howard inwardly groaned and thought, Here I am causing one more infraction.

Mosher remarked that because of his imminent retirement, this was the second to the last course he would ever give. "You are," he said, "mighty lucky people," and then went on to explain that the course would cover the gamut of head and neck surgical anatomy. In the laboratory the class members would be provided with specimens to dissect and they would make plaster casts of the dissections, paint in the blood vessels and make drawings. Each noon, the class and Mosher would lunch together, but would daily rotate their places around the oval table so Mosher could get better acquainted. The laboratory would remain open at night so members of the class could return for work after dinner.

When the introductory session was over, Howard asked a redheaded man named David Braun what Mosher meant by "front-row boys?"

"Don't you know?" Braun asked. "He meant that there are no Jews in the class. 'Front-row boys' is his code word for 'Jews'."

"You mean," Howard asked incredulously, "he is anti-Semitic?"

The first afternoon Howard fell behind in his laboratory procedures because he repeatedly paused to photograph every stage of what he did so he would have a complete record of his work. That night he was the only member of the class to come back after dinner and was still there when Mosher walked in.

"Your name is House and you were the fellow who was late," Mosher said. "I noticed you were sitting in the front row." Looking around the empty laboratory he added, "Apparently I didn't give the others enough work to do." Then handing a specimen to Howard he continued, "Tomorrow morning I am going to talk about the facial nerve. I'd like you to take this and dissect out the facial nerve and all its branches. Put it on my lecture table with a damp cloth over it. I will use it for my lecture in the morning." Turning on his heels he abruptly left the lab.

Howard worked until three o'clock in the morning and then wrapped and left the prepared specimen as instructed. Proud of his achievement, he returned to his hotel for a few hours sleep.

The next morning Howard made sure he sat elsewhere than in the front row. Mosher talked for an hour on subjects unrelated to the facial nerve and never once glanced at the prepared specimen. Howard was at a loss to understand what was going on. At noon he joined the other members of the class for lunch. The first thing Mosher said in greeting was, "I want everyone except House to rotate their seats." Howard stayed put while everyone else moved.

That night after dinner he returned to the laboratory for further work. This time all the members of the class were on hand because word had gotten out that Mosher had been there the night before. Howard was at his bench when Dr. John Richardson, a young member of Mosher's staff, walked over and said, "You are House, aren't you? The chief is going to talk tomorrow on the external carotid artery. With this specimen he wants you to dissect out its branches and have it ready for him in the morning."

The task was even more complicated than the one involving the facial nerve. Howard knew something was seriously wrong, but could not figure out what. Promptly he went to work on the half-head, fearing even in an all-nighter he could not complete the dissection in time for Mosher's lecture, but at three a.m. he placed the wrapped specimen next to the dissection of the facial nerve from the previous evening.

After two nights without adequate sleep, Howard slumped into his lecture hall seat the next morning. Again he waited in vain for Mosher to make some reference to the facial nerve or external carotid artery. Never once did the professor glance at the specimens.

More insult was added to more injuries that noon at lunch when once again Mosher announced, "Everybody rotate their seats except House."

That afternoon Richardson approached Howard with a troubled look on his face. "The chief," he said in a whisper to avoid being overheard by others in the laboratory, "wants me to find out something, but I don't know how unless I ask you bluntly. He wants to know if you are Jewish."

By this time Howard's nerves were frayed from weariness, but he managed to say evenly, "Dr. Richardson, I am not

Jewish. You can also tell him that if I were Jewish, I'd be mighty proud of it."

Richardson was flustered. "No, no, no," he said, "I found out all I wanted to know."

The moment Richardson was out of the room, the redheaded Dr. Braun who had been at a worktable nearby, came close to Howard and said in a whisper: "I heard the question and your answer. Don't worry. Just get the most out of this course; I'm Jewish too."

Howard asked him what made him think he was Jewish. "Everything about you," Braun answered. "The intense way you do your work. The way you dress, do extra things. You are Jewish if ever I saw a Jewish person—but don't let the chief know."

Braun and Howard sealed their friendship on the spot but Howard was never able to convince him otherwise.

The effect of the information Richardson carried back to Mosher was visible the next morning. Mosher displayed the specimens Howard had prepared saying, "These dissections are the nicest I have seen done by a student. Howard, you have done a great job."

The thaw continued that noon at the Harvard Club when Mosher announced, "No one is to rotate at lunch. House, sit next to me."

More direct compliments followed the next morning when he called Howard to the front, gave him a roll of adhesive tape and asked him to outline, on a skeleton suspended in the room, the path the carotid artery takes. In breezing through the drill, Howard used the descriptive phrase "Lincoln Highway" in an allusion to the path of the artery.

"House," Mosher interrupted, "How did you know that passageway is called the 'Lincoln Highway'?"

Trying to conceal his sense of triumph, Howard replied, "Dr. Mosher, I read that in one of your publications."

The rest of the four-week course sped by happily. Traditionally, Mosher marked the end of the course by a ceremony staged in a hall before an invited audience that included members of the ENT faculty and their wives. On tables around the hall the students displayed the casts they had made of their dissections and of their drawings. Howard's display, besides casts and drawings, included the photographs he had taken and mounted in a book.

The high point of the ceremony was the awarding of a prize to the best student which consisted of a hand carving of the Harvard University seal done by Mosher himself. There had been much speculation among the students as to the likely winner in their class.

When the moment came for the winner to be announced, Mosher rapped for attention and asked his three ENT residents who were taking the course to stand up. While they were on their feet, he began tongue-lashing them, "I want you to know that you've disgraced us. This is the first time in the last three years this prize has not gone to one of my residents. Sit down!"

Having disposed of the three with this public humiliation, he called out with equal brusqueness: "The prize goes to a young man from the hinterlands of the far west. House, come up and get your prize!"

When the course was over Mosher asked Howard about his plans. Hearing the reply that he and Helen had reservations on the Queen Mary to go to Europe, Mosher took over. "It will surprise you when I tell you that this isn't going to happen. Get your wife on the phone and tell her you are not going. Monday morning Dr. Philip Meltzer of the Tuft Medical School is starting his two-week course in mastoid surgery here at Harvard."

Howard explained he had tried to get into the course, but had been advised it was full.

"You are in it!" Mosher insisted.

By telephone Howard explained the change of plans to Helen, went to the Cunard Line changing their reservation on the Queen Mary, and proceeded to enroll in Meltzer's course. He also moved into a rooming house.

When that session ended, Mosher asked Howard what he thought of the course now that it was completed. "Wasn't it great?"

To please Mosher, Howard said he had gained a great deal from the course, when in truth the main boon was the start of his lifelong friendship with Phil Meltzer. Otherwise he had learned little about mastoid surgery beyond what he already knew through extensive experience with mastoidectomies in Los Angeles and on his trip across the country.

There was more to the conversation than an evaluation of what had been learned in the previous two weeks. Howard later recalled, "Mosher again asked me what my plans were. I reminded him that I was due to meet my wife in New York and embark on the Queen Mary for the Atlantic crossing and the start of my work in Europe. Mosher nodded his head approvingly, volunteered to give me a stack of letters of introduction to his friends in Europe and then said, 'However, you are not going. Call your wife to say that the trip has been postponed again. I want you to work with me for a month in my research laboratory. You will learn from me and I'd like to work with you.' "

It was a great honor to be asked to work with Mosher, so again Howard called Helen to tell her what was afoot and then retraced his steps down to the Cunard office.

By this time, the Cunard representative had become sympathetic to Howard's plight. He arranged the cheapest fare—$500 per person, third class from New York and back, which also included the crossing to London, then on to Stockholm by a Swedish line, and by train from Stockholm to Berlin, Vienna, Zürich, Milan, Florence, Rome, Paris and return.

Howard explained to the agent his need to stay in London beyond the three days when the Swedish ship would leave for Stockholm. "In London," the representative said, "Cunard will pay for your hotel and meals until the ship leaves for Sweden. When it is time to leave, call the Cunard Line and report that your wife is ill and that you will have to wait until she recovers and can travel. In that way, you will not break the continuity of the trip covered by your ticket and won't have to pay an extra fare once you get ready to leave for Stockholm."

Howard's long absence had been hard on Helen back in Los Angeles. Now his successive change of plans cast a pall of uncertainty over her own. Repeatedly she had informed Dr. Townsend she would be leaving his office to join Howard for the European adventure, and then was forced to reverse herself and continue to work in order to add to her small savings.

Loneliness went hand in hand with uncertainty. She was conscious that her wishes regarding Howard were always subordinate to his father's judgments about what he should or should not do. In a particularly poignant letter to Howard, Helen once remarked that she "loved him more than he loved her," but added bravely, "I know, despite my unhappiness over this separation, that you are doing what you must do in order to be what you are destined to be—a great surgeon!"

The many letters she wrote Howard charted her own reactions to their separation for a half year. On February 24, 1938, she wrote, "I hope this long, long separation does us no harm. It is usually very bad for any couple to be separated for more than a week or so at a time, because both are apt to change so much that they can't get along together after that. I would just die if anything happened to our marriage, it means so much to me."

Three weeks later she penned the request, "When can I have a dog and baby? I am very interested in having several of each to keep me company when you are away. . . . What do you think of the European situation? Now that Herr Hitler has moved in Austria and the ENT specialists who are Jewish you wanted to study under are either being arrested or are running away, it might affect your visit to Vienna, or am I wrong? Do you think there will be a war very soon? It does not look so good, because Hitler is determined to carry out the plans the Kaiser had for expanding the German empire. It seems funny to me that the Germans should allow these nuts who are crazy with ambition to let them bring about so many wars."

On March 29, 1938 she said, "Isn't that a shame regarding 50 percent of the men teaching in Vienna being Jewish? What is happening to them certainly takes the heart right out of your stay there. I wish something could be done with Herr Hitler so that he would leave the Jews alone. Vienna held a lot more for you than other parts of Europe, didn't it? I am so sorry about it. It is a problem whether to go to Europe now and finish things in the East upon your return, or finish now and go to Europe later. I have my ideas of course, but you had better wait for your father. . . . You have been away for a long time and never a word about missing me, so I guess our love affair is one-sided."

The focus of Howard's added month with Mosher was on basic research, something Howard had never done before. Among other things, he studied chemical changes in the body, cellular structure and strictures of the esophagus. He also observed the work of the radiologist, Dr. Alexander MacMillan, who, to Howard's surprise, could identify nasal allergies by X-ray. In between his studies, Howard spent time with the innovative plastic surgeon, Dr. Kazangian.

When their time together was nearing an end, Mosher said, "By now you've observed the greats in plastic surgery." Then he warned, "but I hate to see you go into that field. You have diverse talents, don't limit them to the nose;" adding, "though I do want you to show me the operation you developed."

The next morning after Howard demonstrated the operation on a specimen of a cadaverous head, Mosher, as J. Mackenzie Brown had done before, urged him to publish a paper on his technique. At the end of this meeting, Mosher drew from his pocket another letter of introduction he had prepared, but had kept apart from the rest—as if he were quarantining a contagious disease.

In handing this to Howard, he explained its purpose. "House," he said, "there is a fellow in New York named Dr. Julius Lempert who is operating to restore hearing. He is a Jew. I have not allowed any of my faculty or residents to see him work. He is shoddy—not respected at all. However, I am very curious about what he is really doing. I am giving you this letter of introduction to him. Go observe what he is doing and tell me about it afterwards."

Howard agreed to follow through on the arrangement, without knowing that what lay in store for him would prove to be the strategic crossroad in his career.

The next morning, with his bags packed for the train trip from Boston to New York, Howard asked for the bill covering charges for his room and board. He was informed by the boarding house manager that "a gentleman came to the door yesterday and asked for Dr. House's bill and paid it." Under questioning, the "gentleman" described by the manager amounted to a portrait of Mosher—medium height, slightly heavy, with a bald head that was gray at the temples.

Howard rushed to Mosher's office and finding him in blurted out, "You shouldn't have paid my bill at the boarding house. You must let me reimburse you."

Mosher affected to be bewildered: "Me? I don't go around paying other people's bills. I have enough of my own to pay."

The intimate note on which the two men said their farewells served, through force of contrast, to make their raw collision nine months later all the more painful.

Dr. Julius Lempert and Dr. Harris P. Mosher stood in exact opposition to each other like placarded figures in a morality play. If Mosher was among the high priests of orthodox talent and respectability in medicine, Lempert, during the period when his talents were ignored, was condemned as a polluter of everything sacred in an idealized vision of medicine.

The view of Lempert as something odious was shared by Jewish doctors as well as WASP doctors. Dr. Isadore Friesner, for one, who was chief of the ENT service at Mt. Sinai Hospital in New York, forbade any junior members of his staff to visit Lempert's office in order to familiarize themselves with what he was doing. The few articles Lempert had so far contributed to medical literature, coupled with the growing rumors about his achievements, lay behind Mosher's own curiosity and the request he had put to Howard, but it was left to Howard to discover all the reasons for Lempert's difficulties with the leaders of the medical establishment—especially those based in the East.

Lempert was the last person central casting would pick for the role of a surgeon—and certainly the last the American Medical Association would choose to model for a poster featuring an ideal doctor. In his physical appearance he was short, had a large head framed by long hair and a small torso, with foreshortened arms and abnormally short legs. A needle-sharp pointed nose dominated his facial features, and he had a severe shoulder tick whose impulses were imparted to the rest of his head, as if by some sort of electrical short circuit.

Lempert affected very expensive clothes, rode about New York in an immense limousine driven by a man dressed up to resemble a Hollywood version of a chauffeur and when he walked his dog along Park Avenue, the limousine followed discreetly behind him along the edge of the curb. To add to this flamboyant image, Lempert married a "show girl," Flo, who had been in the chorus line of the Ziegfield Follies and the Rockettes of Radio City, and besides this he had made immensely profitable investments in "hit" Broadway productions, collected expensive art, had a table regularly reserved for his use at New York's 21 Club, and was a close friend of Damon Runyon.

All this was only peripheral to the more important reason why the guardians of medical respectability—Jews and gentiles alike—were offended by Lempert. He was ostracized because of the rankling manner in which he chose to press his own counterattack against his peers.

Born in a Jewish ghetto in Poland, Lempert and his parents miraculously escaped detection the year he was four years old when a Cossack troop swept down and killed every Jew they could find in their area. When the bloodbath ebbed, the Lemperts fled their village escaping through a North Sea port for a voyage that brought them to the teeming slums of the lower Eastside of New York where they joined in the common battle for survival. Julius had not yet lost his baby teeth when he went to work as a shoeshine boy, hawking apples on the side.

"My son, the doctor" was not a joking aspiration of Lempert's Jewish mother, but was in his case a driving personal ambition. His family could not pay for his upkeep in a well-regarded medical school and, given the prevailing quota system, he would not have been admitted to such a school had he been able to meet its financial costs. His only hope lay in the third-rate (classified as a "Class C" school by the American Medical Association) Long Island Medical College—which accepted him as a student.

With his school's infamous standing, when Lempert completed all his requirements for an M.D. degree and qualified for a license as well, he could not get a residency in a hospital where he could learn a medical specialty. His desire was to prepare himself for ENT work, but the door to residencies in the field were slammed shut in his face. What to do?

Devising one or another means, Lempert proceeded to get into clinics and operating rooms to watch ENT surgeons at work. But there was a disheartening, cyclical pattern to these visits. After he would hang around for a month or so, someone would learn that Lempert was not an "authorized" visiting spectator and would ask him to leave and not return. The process, begun at Bellevue Hospital, was repeated at other hospitals—Columbia, Cornell, Manhattan Eye and Ear and New York Eye and Ear.

As he later explained to Howard, "I thought that if that's the kind of treatment I'm going to get from people who govern the way things are done in organized medicine, then that's the way they are going to get it back from me."

When he managed to borrow enough money to establish a small hospital of his own on 57th Street—his first—with facilities for eight beds, he mailed announcements to all doctors in New York, stating boldly that if they would send him their ear, nose and throat surgical cases, he would return to them 50 percent of all the fees he collected.

With this kind of incentive, the lowliest practitioners in Brooklyn, the Bronx and the Lower East Side began to refer patients to him in droves. At the same time, the disapproval of more exalted physicians did not prevent them from stealthily coming to the small hospital to consult, for a handsome fee, on a difficult or complicated case.

Soon a tidal wave of patients from all over New York—and not from the depressed parts alone—swamped the facilities of the 57th Street hospital. By 1927 Lempert had performed 1,500 mastoid operations and hundreds of nose and throat surgeries. In 1928 George Shambaugh, Sr., editor of the *Archives* of otolaryngology, published the first article by Julius Lempert describing his new technique for performing mastoid surgery through the ear canal in contrast to the traditional approach behind the ear.

With a burgeoning practice, Lempert shifted his base of operations, moving to East 74th Street where he bought and converted a five-story building into a new medical institution which he called "Endaural Hospital." Everything he touched in the 1920s—whether in medicine or in the entertainment world—turned to gold, which he did not hesitate to flash publicly.

Suddenly, everything turned to ashes in Lempert's mouth. His 14-year-old son, who was to have been the conveyor of the father's intention to show organized medicine what a "real doctor" should be like, was stricken by leukemia and died. All that was left of Lempert's determination that this youth, with the kind of training that would make him a noted doctor earning—vicariously for Lempert—the respect of his peers, was his son's portrait, dominating Lempert's office.

Lempert grieved his son's death, despondently going home from work where he, joined by his wife, would tearfully sit for hours in silence—staring vacantly into space. A time came when he told his wife that he could not take it any longer. Closing his office and hospital, Lempert gave his wife all the money she would need for as long as he would be away (she returned to work for the Ziegfield

Follies in order to occupy her time) and he journeyed to Europe.

Reports concerning the work of Dr. Gunnar Holmgren of the famous Karolinska Institute drew Lempert to Stockholm. Holmgren was trying to perfect the fenestration operation he had introduced to relieve deafness due to otosclerosis surgically. Performed in three stages over a period of months, the operation was an attempt to construct a path or "window" to the hearing nerve that would bypass the stapes when it was "frozen" by otosclerosis. Since the hearing and balance centers in the inner ear are close together and contain the same fluid, Holmgren made a window—fenestra—in the wall of one of the three balance canals with hammer and gouge through which the sound vibrations could pass. Some patients heard but most were not successful—either due to infection or closure of the window due to bony regrowth.

Holmgren's current efforts were focused on the search for ways to keep the window permanently open. He knew nothing of Lempert's past and received him in a generous, unguarded way, showing him all the details of the three-stage operation and freely discussed its unresolved problems.

When Holmgren observed that if he only had certain instruments, he could do one or another thing, Lempert's response was, "Just tell me what you need and I'll buy it for you."

The pair quickly became close friends. Holmgren encouraged Lempert to continue his pilgrimage and go to Vienna where autopsies were mandatory. Given the ample supply of cadavers there Lempert could explore ways to improve on his fenestration technique.

During the months Lempert spent in Vienna he converted Holmgren's three-stage procedure into a one-stage operation which he was to call "fenestration nov-ovalis," a "new window." Among the unique features of his approach, he wore magnifying lenses to help him be precise in making a window measuring one by three millimeters and he also used a dental drill to make the opening rather than the hammer and gouge employed by Holmgren. Lempert believed the size of the fenestration and the use of the dental drill would reduce the incidence of bony closure.

Lempert came back to New York with a new lease on life. He resumed his married life and reopened his five-story hospital. The notice he sent to all doctors in New York reestablishing his practice no longer blared his willingness to split fees, rather Lempert discreetly announced he was limiting his practice to otology. Soon the word got around that he had developed an operation that restored hearing. Lempert did not claim his operation overcame every aspect of otosclerosis but he could, he published in a 1938 report, materially improve hearing in a small number of selected cases where the hearing nerve was in a healthy condition.

Howard, arriving in New York from Boston in the spring of 1938, checked into the Times Square Hotel—in the middle of the seediest part of the theatrical district where rooms were available for 75 cents a night—and proceeded to Lempert's office on East 74th Street.

After introducing himself to Lempert, who had no advance notice of his visit, Howard said "I'd very much like to observe your work," and then added, "and I have a letter of introduction to you."

Lempert opened the flap of the envelope, read the letter, and then peered intently at Howard. "You know Dr. Mosher?" he asked.

Howard explained he had just finished the four-week course Mosher gave plus an extra month working with him in his laboratory.

"Where are you staying?" Lempert asked.

"The Times Square Hotel," Howard replied.

To attract the attention of a staff member, Lempert always stomped his feet on the floor until the noise got the desired response. A nurse poked her head into the office and was told to get "John."

When John the chauffeur showed up, Lempert said "I want you to take Dr. House to his hotel. Pick up his luggage and drive him to the Waldorf Astoria where he is to check in." He turned to Howard, "You are my guest as long as you are here. We will have dinner at the 21 Club and take in some shows."

Howard, as naïve about what was happening here as he had been about Mosher's "front row boys," haltingly followed Lempert's instructions. Never having been driven around by a liveried chauffeur in a limousine left at his disposal, Howard tried to look the part and checked into the fine room waiting for him at the Waldorf—thinking all the while, "Wait till Helen hears about this."

Then the thought struck, having planned to stay in a rooming house which cost 75 cents a night, Howard realized this establishment would cause his pocketbook to hemorrhage. He casually approached the reservation desk where he put a question to the clerk, "How much?"

"Nothing," the clerk replied. "You are Dr. Lempert's guest and that includes whatever you want to charge to the room."

More mysteries.

Lempert's wife was with him when he picked Howard up for dinner at the 21 Club—where they were warmly greeted by captains, waiters and by diners who were identified as "stars" in different worlds. When the dinner was over, he was amazed to see Lempert hand out $5.00 bills to the staff as they lined up at the door to wish him a pleasant evening.

The next day, Howard saw a totally different side of this strange, nervous, flashy, over-eager, over-generous gnome of a man, because in the operating room Lempert's genius became apparent. Howard's eyes lit up and his concepts of everything he had been taught about ear surgery changed completely as he watched Lempert performance.

Lempert's brilliance outshone anyone else in the field. By his own tremendous strides, he carried all of otologic surgery forward with him. To the best of Howard's knowledge, everything Lempert did had never been done before. Instead of making an incision behind the ear, he made an endaural approach, going through the ear canal to open up—with elegant strokes—the mastoid, exposing the structures of the middle ear and laying it out in a textbook picture.

Howard had been taught to be especially careful in treating an infected ear because the facial nerve was often buried in a mass of infected tissue. The rule was, "Stay away from there." Lempert's concept was exactly the opposite. The first thing to do, he said, was to identify the facial nerve. Then you could take all the granulated tissue away without risk of injuring the nerve. He amplified saying that just as you would never drive down a street blindfolded—but would first identify where you wanted to turn, keeping your eyes open—so you must be familiar with the operating terrain.

He then proceeded to demonstrate for Howard every step of his ingenious "fenestration nov-ovalis" operation. Lempert was so far ahead of the rest of the profession that it was unbelievable how wide the gap was between what he was doing and all other practitioners in otology—including the "greats."

The fenestration operation which he had created had not yet overcome all the problems associated with it, but there was no doubt in Howard's mind that Lempert was moving in the right direction. His patients were regaining their hearing and their expression of love toward their "saviour who redeemed them from the world of impaired hearing" was profoundly stirring to witness.

During the days Howard spent with Lempert—before Helen arrived for the ocean voyage—he was treated like royalty. Belatedly he realized this care was due to the letter of introduction from Mosher—who to Lempert was like a demigod dwelling on Mt. Olympus. Since the letter Howard carried was the first sign that Lempert's mere existence was acknowledged by this idol, Lempert delighted in receiving Howard as though he were Mosher's emissary, and fortunately he did not know the original, dubious motive behind the visit.

Howard's previously held ambitions involving plastic surgery as his future specialty evaporated under this encounter with Lempert. Through him, Howard saw an exciting range of new possibilities in ear surgery and realized it was far more gratifying to restore a sense than to make a better-looking nose.

Howard would join George Shambaugh, Jr. and Philip Meltzer as one of Lempert's convinced disciples—not that Lempert was faultless—for he could be your devoted friend or implacable enemy, depending upon whether or not you performed the operations he pioneered exactly as he did them. In his own way Lempert could be as dogmatic as Mosher was in his.

16

Scenes in Europe

Early in April 1938 Howard and Helen sailed for England on the Queen Mary. On reaching London they spent three days in an old English hotel under the terms of the Cunard Line ticket, and then when it was time to leave for Sweden, as the American agent had suggested, Howard called the Cunard Line to say Helen was too ill to travel. He was told to contact the Cunard Line again when she recovered and they were able to continue their trip to Sweden. Having this settled, the couple moved to a better hotel near the center of London where it took "poor Helen" six weeks to recover from her nonexistent illness.

Howard had contrived the extended stay in London in order to study with a group of notable English doctors, starting with Sir Harold Gillies whose course in plastic surgery had been strongly recommended to him by Dr. Blair in St. Louis. Letters of introduction had been sent in advance of Howard's arrival in London to Gillies, chief of plastic surgery in the medical corps of the English armed forces and also the Queen's physician.

On calling at Gillies' office, Howard learned he would be the only student in his six-week course and that his teacher operated, not in a hospital, but in what appeared to be a private residence converted into a nursing home. During the day, Gillies talked only of plastic surgery—no small talk, no exchange of jokes—as in an American medical set-up.

The line drawn between his professional and his social life was underscored the day Howard returned to his hotel—having spent the entire day with Gillies—to find a handwritten note from Gillies' male secretary cordially inviting Howard and Helen to come to the Gillies' home for dinner at precisely 6:55 p.m. on a certain evening where dress would be "formal." Apparently it would have been in "bad form" had Gillies extended the invitation to Howard in person during the day.

The dinner was elegant, and the conversation among the other guests was, for the first time, not about plastic surgery—roaming over a wide range of subjects. When they were separated from the women at the end of the dinner and were gathered over their cigars and brandy, the men began to exchange somber views about recent incidents in Europe. Adolf Hitler had just declared his intention to absorb Austria into Greater Germany and all were concerned with how England would be affected by this. It never occurred to Howard that the United States could be caught up in these events that lined the road to war.

During these weeks whenever Howard was not engaged with Sir Harold Gillies he visited other leading ENT surgeons in London, all of whom received him in the grand style of professional collegiality. These included Sir Harold Negus, who had been knighted for his contribution to the surgical approach and technique involving problems of the larynx, airways and food passages and Terrence Cawthorne, another young ENT specialist, later to be knighted and the Queen's physician.

Cawthorne, destined to be a world renowned authority and lecturer on otological problems, was working in the area of balance disorders and was tentatively trying his hand at fenestration surgery. He was to become one of Howard's closest friends and their wives also became intimates as the two couples traveled throughout the world together while

Cawthorne and Howard gave lectures and demonstrated their respective surgical techniques.

As Cawthorne's guest at a lecture, Howard not only met Sir Alexander Fleming, the discoverer of penicillin, but heard him pronounce a maxim about the scientific process as it applied to his own discovery of penicillin, "It is not the observation but the application of that observation that matters." Howard paid several visits to the laboratory of this great man and later would often repeat this truism in his own talks to students.

The day came when Howard called the Cunard Lines to say that his wife had "recovered" and could continue with the Swedish leg of the scheduled trip. He was in luck, the Cunard people told Howard, because a Swedish ship was sailing the next day for Göteburg, Sweden. There was one catch. The only space left on the relatively small ship was the Royal Suite. Would that be acceptable if the Cunard Line absorbed the extra cost? Howard assented to the "inconvenience."

For the two nights and a day the voyage lasted, the honeymooning couple luxuriated in the Royal Suite, replete with grand piano and a fully stocked bar filled with fine wines and champagne. Rather than mixing with the other passengers, Howard and Helen elected to dine alone in their suite where they had the exclusive services of a steward who prepared wondrous meals for them—in a setting far removed from Howard's pinch-penny existence as a medical student, intern, and resident where hotels offering rooms for 75 cents a day was their norm. "Helen and I," he later recalled, "were willing to stay on that ship forever, as long as the Cunard Line picked up the tab."

When the ship docked in Göteburg, Howard briefly visited with Dr. Carl Axel Hamburger, head of the ENT department at the University of Göteburg whose special interest was the relief of pain in metastatic cancer. To get patients mobile again, Hamburger would remove—by means of an operation performed through the nose—the pituitary gland located deep in the head. Howard, previously unaware of the existence of any such treatment, was impressed by the favorable results achieved in the case of patients he was invited to question.

Stockholm, their next stop in Sweden, provided Howard a chance to visit Dr. Gunnar Holmgren at the Karolinska Institute. Arriving at the institute, Howard was introduced to a straight-backed, tall, slender man who no longer was young—but was, however, physically strong enough to live into his 90s and outlive four wives. Learning that Howard had come to see his work at the urging of Dr. Julius Lempert, Holmgren became incandescent with delight and announced he was currently engaged only in the "monkey business."

Howard laughed, but was embarrassed when this turned out to be true, for Holmgren, still struggling to perfect his three-stage fenestration operation, was no longer performing the operation on human beings. He had a cage full of operated monkeys, most of them with bandaged heads—the sign of the experiments he conducted in an attempt to solve the old problem of how to keep the fenestra he made from closing up.

Howard remained in Holmgren's company for two weeks and, though he savored his encounters with the originator of otosclerosis surgery, he was disappointed in what he learned—especially when Howard compared this with what he had seen of Lempert's work.

From Stockholm, Howard and Helen went by train to Berlin where he had no professional contacts and made none that were worthwhile. The city was covered with swastikas and was still electric with excitement over Hitler's latest coup in absorbing Austria into Greater Germany and with the tone of Hitler's strident polemics about the

Sudetenland. Military activity was visible everywhere, with columns of soldiers always on the march. The picture revived Howard's memories of his visit to Germany as a child on the eve of the First World War when his father had cut his face in his eagerness to see a dirigible flying in the distance.

After several days of sightseeing and visits to the University of Berlin, Howard and Helen boarded a local train traveling third class on wooden seats for a leisurely trip to Vienna. As the train passed through the Black Forest, because of his color blindness, Howard saw through the window a spectacle that escaped Helen's notice—because she had normal color vision. Concealed by miles of green and tawny camouflage netting, the Black Forest had been converted into a massive storage area for an arsenal of tanks, cannon, armored personnel carriers and planes with their wings off. All were lined up row upon row, poised for the fateful signal that would unleash their firepower.

The city of Vienna, which the Houses reached in the early summer of 1938, had always held a particular meaning for Howard who was in awe of being at this spot where world famous professors of medicine were engaged in full-time teaching and research in institutes organized along specialized lines, linked to the University of Vienna. Unfortunately, Howard was to be among the last group of young American doctors who caught a glimpse of Vienna before its preeminence in medicine was finally eclipsed by Nazi rule—as had already happened in Berlin.

In the 1930s the American Medical Association (AMA) of Vienna arranged for American doctors to take postgraduate courses in various specialties. The physical lay-out of the AMA headquarters consisted of a suite of offices with a public lounge located above a restaurant and opposite a large hospital complex.

From the second-floor lounge one had a sweeping view of Vienna's boulevard vistas, while the lounge itself provided a comfortable haven where sandwiches and snacks could be ordered from the first floor restaurant. But the place particularly throbbed with life in mid-afternoon when American doctors—often with Canadian, English, Scottish, Australian or Indian colleagues in tow—converged in the lounge for the Viennese mid-afternoon ritual of small talk, rumors and coffee *mit schlag*.

An American doctor with "seniority" was customarily elected president of the AMA setup. In 1938, however, the source of executive energy within the headquarters was Nancy Uloff, 25, blond, beautiful, engaging, witty, feline—a certified charmer. She organized the courses at the institutes, did the scheduling and posted notices. Her true identity and function would be learned only later.

Howard and Helen checked into the Pension America in Vienna. One morning while having breakfast alone in the large dining room, another couple entered and walked over to introduce themselves—Russell and Gina Fisher who with their year-old child "Skipper" had just arrived from the United States. Russell, a tenured professor of pathology on sabbatical leave from Philadelphia Medical School, had come to Vienna to work at the Institute of Pathology and was slated to be the last in the line of American doctors to serve as president of the American Medical Association in Vienna. This introductory meeting marked the start of a life-long friendship between the two couples.

Soon the Fishers had moved into an apartment they rented and the Houses also found comfortable quarters in a room where they shared kitchen facilities in the apartment of a congenial Frau Lehman.

At the AMA headquarters Howard signed up for all the ENT courses taught by the "greats" of Vienna, such as Professor Hans Brunner. Although he had never before studied the histopathology of the temporal bone beyond what he had learned from Dorothy Wolff, now he had an opportunity to do so under Brunner's tutelage—and with a poignant side-effect more than two decades later.

Since Austrian law required autopsies on bodies of deceased persons, this provided professors of medicine in Vienna with a wealth of readily accessible anatomical material. Howard soon learned that by paying the *diener* in charge of the hospital morgue two dollars, he would be granted a chance to work after-hours on an unclaimed body. Howard, in turn, would sell the other American doctors rights to their respective areas of interest in the body, such as orthopedic surgeons (extremities), thoracic surgeons (chest) and so on. In this way he not only got his "head" free but sometimes came out with a profit.

Howard's interest in perfecting his surgical skills often interfered with the social life of the Houses and the Fishers. Just when they would make plans together, Howard would often beg off because he had secured another specimen on which to practice, so the threesome would go off by themselves chanting the refrain, "Howard has a head!"

During these Vienna days Howard became well acquainted with the beautiful Nancy Uloff, manager of the AMA office. One day he asked her to write a letter to Miss Andrews who had worked so hard to teach him German at Whittier College. He then copied the letter which he had dictated in English and she obligingly had translated into German—which went something like this:

Dear Miss Andrews:
This finds me in Vienna, studying my specialty of ENT. How right you were to insist that I must know German because so much medical literature is in German. I want to thank you for helping me learn German which has been so extremely valuable to me. I hope this finds you enjoying good health.
—Howard House (Class of 1930)

Soon after, Howard received an ecstatic reply from Miss Andrews which read:

Dear Howard:

I remember you well, because of my efforts to keep you from failing. A failure would have harmed your chances of becoming a doctor. Would you mind my reading your wonderful letter to my class to encourage others and to recognize the importance of knowing the German language? I wish you every success and hope to see you on your return.

Howard's letter was no doubt well received by Miss Andrew's class and he assumed his little deception had brightened the day of a devoted teacher at Whittier College. For obvious reasons, he did not seek out Miss Andrews on his return. Fortunately most German medical literature was translated into English—which had virtually become the international scientific language.

The invisible "presence" of Julius Lempert followed Howard to Vienna. One day he walked into the Karl Reiner surgical instrument house, introduced himself to Reiner and explained he needed some instruments for ear work to use in a new fenestration operation. The word "fenestration" was no sooner out of his mouth than Reiner asked, "Do you know Dr. Julius Lempert?"

Enthusiastically Howard said, "yes;" whereupon Reiner recalled that when Lempert was working on his new technique he ordered many specially made instruments only to change his mind because he wanted something a little different. The instruments Lempert had bought, but found not quite right, were still on hand. By any chance did Howard want them? "Just carry them away!"

It was no easy thing to lug away the heavy box filled with top-grade instruments, but the price was right. When Helen learned how her husband obtained this treasure, she insisted that Reiner be a guest of the Houses for dinner.

Reiner's spontaneous generosity heightened the incongruity of what Howard and Helen observed of the Viennese delirium as the people hailed Adolf Hitler on one of his visits to the city. Along with the Fishers, they saw the processional entry from the vantage point of the American Medical Association headquarters.

First came squadrons of calvary—drummers, buglers and those who carried standards like the eagles of the Roman legions. Then came another honor guard on foot, hand-picked handsome young soldiers in snappy uniforms. Next in line were horse-drawn cannons, followed by truck-drawn cannons, followed by mile upon mile of troops whose jack-boots hit the pavement at the same precise instant, as though all were governed by the same brain.

The grand finale was Hitler himself, standing upright in an open Mercedes-Benz, acknowledging with a flick of his wrist the cheers of the rapidly fanaticized crowd. Loud speakers had been installed on the corners of the busy intersections and large crowds assembled at each location. Their Sig Heils were paeans of thanks for buildings that were painted, for streets that were paved, for jobs that were created.

The two American couples left their vantage point and joined the throngs that surged toward the Vienna Opera House where Hitler spoke from an outdoor balcony. Howard's German was terrible, but from the crowd's reaction to Hitler's speech—which was delivered extemporaneously by the hour—he concluded that the man was the most hypnotic speaker he had ever witnessed in action. Hitler promised whatever the crowd wanted to hear, whether on the side of hate or hope, vengeance or jobs.

When Howard had taken all ENT courses that were offered—though he still worked on specimen heads at night and on weekends—it occurred to him that when he returned home, he might open an office in a small town where he would treat eye as well as ENT cases. The consideration led him to Professor Ernst Fuchs—the world-famous authority on the histopathology of the eye. Howard took every one of Fuchs' courses as well as those offered by the other noted professors who specialized in problems of the eye.

By September 1938, while Russell Fisher was serving as president of the American Medical Association in Vienna, the intimate circle of the Houses and the Fishers had been enlarged by the addition of another young American doctor—Peter Arnold from Baltimore, unmarried, fluent in German and in Vienna for postgraduate work in ophthalmology.

However the winds of war were steadily on the rise as Hitler resolved to recover the Sudetenland from Czechoslovakia. The Czech response to his demands was to prepare for battle, while Prime Minister Chamberlain flew to Germany to meet with Hitler in an attempt to avoid the clash of arms. By the end of the month a continuous stream of troops, tanks and trucks loaded with military supplies passed through Vienna en route to the Czech border. A steady drove of American doctors informed the AMA headquarters in Vienna that they were returning home before they were caught by war in Europe.

When the dangers of staying in Vienna were discussed within their friendly circle, Howard argued that the United States would not be involved in any European war, so why run home? The rest of the group was won over to his view but also supported Fisher's contingency plan. Reasoning that if war broke out the German military would commandeer all autos and all gasoline, Fisher secured a horse and wagon which hopefully would escape the Nazi reach, at least for a while. They kept their lifeline hidden in a nearby stable so in an emergency the members of the group could travel by horse and wagon from Vienna to Innsbruck, then over to Switzerland or through the Brenner Pass into Italy if Italy stayed neutral.

Years later, Fisher recalled what they experienced during the days of the Munich Agreement:

> On the morning of September 28, it became apparent the Austrians were assuming the worst. The Institute of Pathology was shut down. Nearby hospitals were restricting their intake of new patients only to emergency cases. The American Medical Association headquarters was deserted. It seemed everyone had cleared out.
>
> We wondered what our group should do. The women decided to go off for what could be a last look at the shops. The men went to the Danube, rented a sailboat and spent the day, between ten in the morning and four in the afternoon, sailing up and down the river in an ideal breeze. What kind of world would they come back to? Two days later the false peace of the Munich Agreement gave Hitler what he wanted for the moment and Chamberlain returned to London to announce "Peace in our Time."

Seemingly oblivious to all the turmoil, Peter Arnold decided to visit a noted eye surgeon in Prague and Howard agreed to join him. That Sunday the pair boarded an almost-empty train to Bratislava, a short distance away on the Czech side of the border, from where they could transfer on to Prague. Arriving in the Bratislava station, the two young Americans were abruptly brought face-to-face with the facts of *realpolitik*.

Once the train ground to a halt, the conductor announced it could not proceed any further—the tracks were ripped up as far as the eye could see. The commander of the Czech army had ordered this chaos as a defensive war measure in anticipation of a German invasion. Added to this, at ten-minute intervals German military aircraft flew low overhead.

Even though they saw streams of people walking out of Bratislava carrying their worldly possessions in horse, dog or ox-drawn carts and wagons, they were still unaware that Hitler's plan for taking over the Sudetenland was set for the next day, Monday. As usual, Howard had his camera with him and took pictures of all he saw.

As they walked around trying to decide how to proceed, a man in civilian clothes approached them, identified himself as "Gestapo," took their passports and ordered Howard and Peter to accompany him. They walked by his side to the local police station and were brought before an officer wearing the uniform of a Nazi colonel. The Gestapo agent explained he had caught the pair taking pictures in town.

Arnold cut in to indicate that he was fluent in German, which made him the immediate object of the colonel's interrogation. He proceeded to explain that he and Howard were going to Prague in order to study with a famous eye doctor who had his clinic there.

The colonel was incredulous. Didn't the pair know there was going to be a war the next day? Didn't they read the newspaper? Didn't they listen to the radio?

Arnold explained that when they were in Vienna, they spent all their time studying and paid little attention to foreign or domestic politics.

A strip search down to the shorts followed. Everything prompted a question. What is this? What is that? The film was confiscated from their cameras.

At this point the conductor interrupted to announce the train was ready to return to Vienna. The colonel told him to go ahead without Howard and Arnold. It seemed that the pair were in deep trouble and they began to despair when they realized the train had left without them.

Fortunately, another Nazi officer who had hovered in the background of the police station before disappearing, returned to the interrogation room where the young doctors were being held. He had checked their statements. Yes, they were American medical students in Vienna. Yes, they had apartments at the addresses they gave. Yes, Howard was married (Helen had been contacted). Yes, there was a famous eye doctor in Prague.

The colonel apologized for his suspicions and said the pair could return to Vienna. Moreover, since they had missed the train, he would have them driven back in his service car—a large, camouflaged open car with a high back seat and huge wheels. The driver, a courteous soldier of about 18 who spoke English fluently, repeatedly had to pull over to the side of the road to allow troops to pass in the opposite direction. Howard often wondered whatever happened to the youth.

With the noted eye doctor in Prague proving beyond reach, Professor Fuchs—who wanted Howard to be an eye specialist—arranged for him to go to the small Hungarian town of Zambathay to do cataract surgery for a month.

Their rented quarters consisted of a room and a bath above a pub—memorable because the smell of urine permeated the place whether the window in their room was closed or open. A waitress in the pub provided Howard with a bicycle which carried him to and from the hospital, three miles away on the outskirts of the town.

On his first visit to the hospital, he was engulfed by peasants in need of medical care. The crush outside the place was matched by the confusion within the hospital proper. When Howard was ushered into the eye operating room, what he saw mocked everything he had ever learned about aseptic surgery: with every swirl of the wind coming from outside through the open windows, more dust settled on the inside where overflowing pails of surgical refuse stood in disarray.

The majority of the operations were for cataracts. Howard watched dumbfounded as the ophthalmologist would open the eye, tearing the capsule of the lens, before sticking a pipette into the lens and then orally sucking up the cataract material into the pipette, after which we would blow the material out on the floor. The surgeon would repeat this process as often as necessary to remove most of the lens material and then would replace the cornea and hold up three fingers to test the patients vision. A happy shout meant the patient could see, so the ophthalmologist would put a patch over the eye and send the patient home with instructions not to remove the patch for two days. The prohibitive costs meant no patients were later fitted with glasses.

Consigned to the role of a bystander, Howard watched this procedure which carried such a high risk of infection being performed for a week while he waited impatiently until he could perform the new technique for cataract surgery taught him by Fuchs—which entailed removing the entire lens without tearing the capsule so that no cataract material remained in the eye.

His chance finally came and Howard followed Fuch's procedure to the letter on a woman patient. Everything worked beautifully to the astonishment of the observing ophthalmologists for whom the procedure was altogether new, and when it was over the woman could see very clearly. She was kept in the hospital an extra day to be sure that everything was all right.

A week later the woman returned with a terrible eye infection. Howard had scrubbed long and hard and had personally sterilized all his instruments before the operation, taking every precaution available, including the use of the new antibiotics that had just become available. It was all to no avail and Howard was miserable because the results of his first and perfect eye operation was an eye that could not be saved.

Never again did the Hungarian ophthalmologist allow Howard to use the Fuch technique and for the remainder of his stay Howard was required to do things according to the Hungarian technique—with scissors and pipette and spitting the eye material sucked up through the pipette out on the floor. Eyes did occasionally get infected, but in far fewer numbers than Howard expected.

Despite the *NEIN*! of the ophthalmologist in Zambathay, Fuchs's technique eventually became the standard and universally used method throughout the world.

After a month Howard and Helen returned to Vienna. It was now late November 1938 and the Nazis had been in control of Austria for ten months. The exodus of imperiled persons who could escape was fully underway, as were pathetic meetings in the back alleys of Vienna late at night between Jews who turned over their marks to American doctors in exchange for future dollars. The transaction generally required little of the American doctor, who only had to give a name, address and telephone number in the United States to the intended refugee. If ever the latter actually reached the United States, the doctor contracted to forward the refugee an agreed-upon amount in dollars equal to the sum that had figured in the exchange in Vienna.

These transactions uncorked a grim surprise for it was belatedly learned that Nancy Uloff, the charmer who ran the AMA office, was an ardent Nazi whose glory in life lay in being an undercover agent for the German Gestapo. Among her diverse assignments, she reported to the authorities all she learned about the clandestine contacts between American doctors who exchanged dollars for the marks of Jews or other imperiled Austrians intent on fleeing the country.

Two years after the war, Howard received a phone call from New York. A man at the other end of the line reminded Howard of their nocturnal exchange of dollars for marks, described the location, time and his appearance. Convinced this was a legitimate call, Howard welcomed the man to the United States and sent a check at the address given. A few days later the same party called Howard to thank him, adding that not all the doctors he had contacted had fulfilled their obligation.

By late November 1938 when Howard and Helen left Vienna, the University of Vienna which had seethed with a virulent anti-Semitism long before the rise and triumph of the Nazis, was now completely politicized. Junior figures, professing ardor for the Nazi cause, were grabbing university and institute posts formerly held by senior professors who had been driven into exile or were already banished to concentration camps. In time, however, the grabbers were themselves grabbed by the iron hand of fate. Russell Fisher recalled that of the assistants and docents he knew in 1938-1939, one half were killed while serving in the armed forces and the other half were scattered to the winds.

Throughout their European sojourn, Howard seldom paused in his schedule merely to enjoy himself. As he neared the time for returning to the United States, Howard decided he owed it to Helen to ease up on his strict regimen of work, but it was difficult to enjoy himself at random and he continue to justify his stops medically in various cities after he and Helen left Vienna.

Their first stop was Zürich where he visited Professor Lorenz Reudi, head of the ENT department at the University of Zürich Medical School. Reudi not only extended the hospitality of his home to the Houses but he went out of his way to show Howard anything that might be of professional interest. Professor Felix Nager, another

Zürich-based authority, like Reudi received the Houses cordially and spent hours showing Howard sets of fascinating slides of various diseases and deformities of the ear from his specialization on the histopathology of the temporal bone. Nager would be the first ENT specialist to receive an honorary fellowship in the prestigious Royal College of Surgeons of England many years before Howard would be the second so honored.

From Zürich, the Houses traveled south to Milan, but the role of the inquiring student, along with its fruits, had reached the point of diminishing returns. Proceeding to Florence and then Rome, Howard settled down and was content to enjoy taking in the sights of the two cities, before boarding a train for Paris where Howard tried to see Dr. Sourdille and his fenestration work.

Throughout Europe, as had been his experience in America, whenever Howard presented himself in a medical office as a young doctor on a tour of post-residency training, he was consistently extended every professional courtesy, if not social hospitality as well. Sourdille, however, was the sole exception. In spite of Howard's successive attempts to see him, he like George Shambaugh before him, was rebuffed. Abandoning further futile attempts, Howard spent three days in Paris taking in the sights with Helen.

As the winter storms began to blow, the Houses took a December sailing on the Queen Mary for New York. Howard dealt with his sea sickness caused by the heavy winter seas by taking doses of Nembutal that put him to sleep for most of the ocean passage. Helen had no trouble on the voyage and sometimes found herself to be the only passenger in the huge dining room.

The Queen Mary was a day out of New York when Howard received a radiogram from Doctor Mosher in Boston—to whom he had written from time to time keeping him abreast of his progress in Europe—with an invitation to stop in Boston and address the ENT faculty and residents of the Harvard Medical School, describing what he had seen and learned through his extensive trip.

By return radiogram, Howard immediately accepted "with pleasure," but then for the rest of the journey was enmeshed in a quiet debate with himself.

17

Moral Test at Harvard

While Howard was still in Europe, the wall American otologists had raised between themselves and Lempert had begun to erode around the edges. Two of Lempert's major reports had been published in the *Archives* by its new editor, Dr. George Coates. The first appeared in May 1938 and was a sequel—separated by ten years—to his earlier article on the endaural approach to mastoidectomies. Having now attended 1,780 patients of all ages with every kind of pathology, the reported results of these cases were extraordinary: complete cures without complications in all but 37 operations performed *before* antibiotics were available.

Archives published Lempert's second article in July 1938 under the title, "Improvement of Hearing in the Cases of Otosclerosis: A New One-Stage Surgical Technique." The text of 55 pages presented the results Lempert had achieved with 23 patients who had undergone his new fenestration operation between September 1937 and April 1938. Among these were operations Howard had witnessed before leaving for Europe.

Not all in the initial sample were successful—as Lempert himself acknowledged—but the article would eventually be recognized for its historic importance for it ushered in a new day in ear surgery for deafness. Every detail that bore on the one-stage fenestration operation was covered, including luminous "how to do it" drawings and photographs, with the usual biographical data concerning the patients.

In concluding his article, Lempert struck a note which prefigured his future conflicts with even his most ardent disciples should they presume to introduce small variations on his regimen for a fenestration operation:

> To obtain the desired result, it is essential that every step in this technique be patiently and skillfully executed in its minutest detail. To bring this operative procedure to a successful conclusion, it must be performed in the exact order described. Each step in this technique is the foundation for the next step and unless each step is concluded successfully, the next step and therefore the rest of the operation is doomed to failure.

With the publication of this second article, senior otologists who had been indifferent to Lempert's other reports, were drawn by curiosity to call on him in New York. Some expressed friendly skepticism regarding the lasting benefits of the remarkable fenestration operations they had witnessed. Lempert agreed that a "wait and see" attitude was scientifically "correct," considering that many previous attempts to treat otosclerosis by surgical means had failed outright or led only to transient improvements in hearing.

Others, like Drs. John Lindsay and Samuel Salinger of Chicago, came away from a visit with Lempert in awe of his surgical skill, but concluded its techniques, they said, were not readily transmittable to otologists generally, because few of them had the required surgical talents. As Dr. Salinger put it, "Not more than a dozen or fifteen otologists in the country are capable of carrying out Dr. Lempert's technique."

At this point in Lempert's career, he was neither a member of his city, county or state American Medical Association, nor was he a member of any of the recognized national ENT societies. In essence he was not wanted, though in later years he would become a member or honorary member of all national and numerous international ENT societies—and would also be honored for his work by many foreign governments.

For the moment, Lempert was grateful to the otologists who expressed interest in his one-stage fenestration operation, even when they still reserved judgment about its durable worth and was delighted when an otologist who embodied everything he thought he needed to tilt the scales of judgment decisively in his favor showed up in his office in late 1938. Dr. Samuel Kopetzky had authored a major textbook on ear surgery as well as numerous scientific articles, and besides was an army general and a leader in all ENT professional organizations.

Like other senior otologists in the East, Kopetzky had astutely shunned Lempert from one year to the next. Now he was driven by irritation into contacting him, for several of his patients—whom he had failed to help in cases involving otosclerosis—had regained their hearing after undergoing Lempert's one-stage fenestration operation. When Lempert had released these patients he had asked them to return to Kopetzky to show him the evidence of Lempert's success (or more pointedly, to remind him of his own failure).

When Kopetzky called on Lempert he began imperiously, "I have never before taken the trouble to meet you and for obvious reasons,"—which was an allusion to Lempert's fee splitting in the 1920s. "Now, however, I would like for you to teach me how to do your fenestration operation. If you do that, we will prepare a paper together on the results of the operations for presentation next spring at the Atlantic

City meeting of the American Otological Society."

Meetings of the Society were open to all ENT doctors, but membership was by invitation only—and was confined to around 100 active members who were viewed as the professional elite among ENT surgeons. Kopetzky, unlike Lempert who belonged to nothing, was a past president of the society. Lempert was thrilled by the prospect that this very imposing figure would make the presentation in their joint names. Kopetzky could be the instrument of proof that the new fenestration operation could be mastered by any otologist with an intimate knowledge of the anatomy of the ear. Besides, Lempert's claim of success with the fenestration operation, standing alone, would have nothing like the scientific integrity of a claim that also bore the imprimatur of a highly respected authority such as Kopetzky.

Lempert set aside many hours from his heavy work load to rehearse with Kopetzky again and again, step by step, every stage and fine point of the operation. The training was done in the basement of the Lempert hospital on specimens preserved there with Kopetzky standing by Lempert's side to hear and see his detailed explanations while he operated on patients.

None of the new developments affecting Lempert had drifted across the Atlantic while Howard was in Europe, so that when he and Helen boarded the train for Boston, an internal debate raged inside him about what he would say at Harvard—based on the evidence of what he had seen with his own eyes during the four days he had spent with Lempert in early 1938.

Howard was apprehensive about the danger awaiting once he was shepherded by Mosher into the vast lair of power that was the Harvard Medical School. He knew Mosher both expected and wanted him to say something like:

I have spent a year and a half working in the United States and Europe with all the great figures in the field of otolaryngology; and now, based on what I have seen, there is no reason to leave Boston. The best place to be trained in otolaryngology is right here. This is where the highest level of professional competence elsewhere can be judged.

Of course, the lie at the heart of any such confessional concerned the subspecialty of otology. Nothing Howard had seen of ear surgery at Harvard or anywhere else in the United States or Europe—not even at the side of Gunnar Holmgren of the Karolinska Institute—was in a class with the revolutionary concepts and the dazzling surgical technique and skill of Dr. Julius Lempert—who was a first-rate genius among ear surgeons.

What made Howard hesitate telling Mosher and the other members of the Harvard faculty what he really believed was his loyalty to Mosher, yet he knew Mosher's perception of Lempert was distorted by the lens of anti-Semitism. Howard sensed that Mosher would never see, much less admit, that anyone might say a good word about Lempert and woe to anyone who ventured to judge Lempert simply by the dry criterion of merit.

Helen urged Howard to speak his true convictions without thought of the consequences. At the same time Howard's memory chamber echoed one of his father's refrains, "It's all right to fool the other fellow, but never fool yourself."

In Boston he and Helen were warmly received by Mosher and then taken to an impressive hall where 70 members of the Harvard medical faculty, their wives and residents, had assembled solely to hear Howard report on his travel experiences. Many in the audience had been present the year before when Howard had received the "Mosher prize" as the best student in the course on head and neck surgery, and he was now reintroduced to the audience by Mosher in flattering terms—which only increased Howard's internal strain as he began to speak.

Discussing his 18 months of post-residency experiences, Howard detailed what he had absorbed in the United States and Europe from the great figures he had met, acknowledging the immense debt he owed to Mosher and his faculty for all he had learned from them. Howard pointedly expressed his gratitude for Mosher's personal generosity, drawing out his remarks as though he was seeking a safe passage through a mine field. Still he was undecided about the conclusion he must draw. He could go either way. If he said nothing about Lempert, he could justify the silence on the ground that, after all, this was only one evening and that as Mosher's guest and debtor he should say only what pleased him—in another time and place, Howard could say what he really believed. Or, despite knowing how Mosher felt, Howard could speak the truth of his conviction and pay public homage to Lempert.

Perhaps he was driven by the same honesty that prompted him at the age of 21 to confess that he occasionally "smoked," or perhaps the hidden mainspring was his father's remark that he possessed a moral quality of central importance to any doctor—integrity. In any event, before sitting down Howard finished his remarks saying:

I have had the privilege of visiting all the great doctors in my chosen field, both in this country and abroad. I did this at the right time in my life, when I was free to move around. What I experienced in the last year and one-half has changed my whole outlook and my plans for the future. The greatest of all things I saw during this trek was the marvelous ear surgery of Dr. Julius Lempert of New York. I refer not only to his new approach to mastoidectomies, but to his one-stage fenestration operation to restore serviceable hearing to patients with otosclerosis. I examined his patients before their surgery when they were withdrawn and depressed because of their deafness and I examined them afterward. Their joy at being able to hear again transformed virtually everything about them.

The more he talked about Lempert's work, the more the hushed room crackled with the tensions of static electricity. Every doctor present knew that Mosher detested Lempert. Howard wound up his remarks by again thanking Mosher and others at the Harvard Medical School for the knowledge he had received from them and for the kindness they had shown. When he sat down, very few hand claps broke the sepulchral silence. The hostile reaction he had anticipated for speaking the truth of his convictions came in the form of a volley of enraged words.

"House! Stand up!!" Mosher commanded in a rasping voice.

Howard stood and listened to an infuriated Mosher, "You are a young man," he said, "and will be going back to Los Angeles to open your office. You will do well, but take a word of advice from me. Keep your eyes open and your mouth shut!"

With that Mosher stomped out of the room. The rest of the faculty followed. Few as much as paused to greet Howard and Helen. They would not cross their chief by acknowledging in any way the tribute to Lempert even though in subsequent months, some of these same doctors sought Howard out in professional meetings to learn more about his experiences and to compliment him on the talk he gave in Boston.

Conceivably, Mosher's violent reactions to Howard's remarks may have been fueled by evidence that certain senior otologists elsewhere in the country were either spending time with Lempert or were inclined to be open-minded about the ultimate worth of his work. Or he may have expected Howard to hew to the line of orthodox contempt for Lempert. Instead, he had been treated to a confession that Howard was already a Lempert enthusiast—as was true of two other rising stars who had trained with Lempert: George S. Shambaugh, Jr., who had been Mosher's resident, and Philip Meltzer. Possibly Mosher thought that Howard, who had been thoroughly preparing himself to be among the carriers of the future in otology, had already betrayed that future to Lempert.

Howard got little sleep that night, even though Helen kept assuring him "he had done the right thing." At least Howard's conscience was clear, even though he feared the price would be high. Mosher, an organizer, member and past president of the American Board of Otolaryngology, might not let him pass the board's certifying examination Howard still had to take or else block his future election to select professional bodies such as the Triologic or the American Otological Society.

Howard would be proven right in predicting some of the "fall out" of his remarks at the "welcome home" meeting at Harvard. In the decade ahead, whenever his path crossed Mosher's at professional meetings, Howard would make it a point to greet Dr. Mosher, who would walk past him in stony silence—even though whenever he saw Helen alone Mosher always spoke to her in cordial terms.

To keep Mosher's complex character in perspective, it is important to note that when Kopetzky was studying with Lempert, Kopetzky called Mosher to let him know that when the American Otological Society met in Atlantic City in the spring of 1939, he wanted to present a paper on the results of his fenestration operations.

Mosher, who was due to preside over the meeting in his capacity as the society's president, could not readily deny Kopetzky a place on the program given the latter's professional eminence, yet he knew—as Howard had learned through direct observation—that Kopetzky was not a good surgeon. Moreover, he thought it strange that Kopetzky was performing the fenestration operations in Lempert's hospital and not in the one he regularly used.

With this in mind, Mosher contacted three otologists—Gordon Hoople of Syracuse, Philip Meltzer of Boston and Robert Morehood of Brooklyn—informing them of his conversation with Kopetzky and asking that they arrange to be in Lempert's hospital to observe one of Kopetzky's fenestration operations.

This was done and all three were present on the day scheduled for the surgery. The patient was on the operating table and Kopetzky was scrubbing up for the surgery when there was an "emergency" telephone call. When Kopetzky returned, his face crumpled with a show of concern, he said, "Sorry, I have an emergency and must leave right away." He then turned to Lempert and asked, "Will you do the operation for me?"

The three onlookers subsequently contacted Mosher to report on Lempert's "beautiful" work, but Mosher rejoined, "I didn't want you to tell me about Lempert. I wanted you to tell me about Kopetzky's work."

They could tell him nothing. Arrangements were made for the three to come back when Kopetzky was scheduled to perform another fenestration operation, but the pattern was again repeated. Kopetzky was called away from the operating room at the last minute by another "emergency."

There would be no more outside eyewitnesses to his work, though he eventually got around to performing some fenestration operations on other occasions. The climax of the story remains to be told.

18

Reunions

By daybreak after the sleepless night in Boston, Howard's fear that he had "ruined his career" was displaced by a defiant mood. He told himself that no one could strip him of his knowledge or surgical skills—no more than the tyrants of the medical establishment could stop Julius Lempert's single-minded drive toward preeminence in his field. Having just completed the most productive year and a half of his life, Howard wished there was some way he could repay his teachers and also hoped that in time his own achievements would make Mosher regret the way he had treated him simply because he had praised Lempert's innovative work in surgery.

Happy to be heading home at last, Howard and Helen once again crossed the continent and on reaching Los Angeles headed for the home of Helen's parents where they were to stay, pending a decision about where Howard would start a practice.

The next few days were spent in reunions with family members, friends and Howard's former mentors at the USC Medical School. Inwardly Howard hoped he might be asked by Dr. Brown to become an associate in his office practice, but no such invitation was extended. When Howard took his boards, he passed them despite his prior fear that he would flounder on the rock of Mosher's enmity.

Being reunited with their families constituted a great pleasure. Milus was now 61 years old and Howard was reminded anew of how much he owed to him—most recently for suggesting and backing this invaluable plan to study with all the "great" ear, nose and throat specialists in the United States and Europe. This venture had endowed Howard at age 31 with a fund of professional knowledge whose scope and depth had few equals among ENT surgeons of his own generation. Could he, in his own career, possibly do as well as his father had done and continued to do?

The tributary streams which contributed to his father's income were at their full flow. Milus now carved and baked artificial teeth based on their size, shape, color and relation to facial form and size. Dentists in western states formed what were known as the M.M. House Study Groups and 13 such groups came to Whittier each month with their patients in tow to make dentures under Milus' guidance while using the articulator and grinder he had designed and the false teeth he had perfected.

Each summer Milus reserved two months for teaching the professors of prosthetics from various dental schools in the United States and Canada, and fully 80 percent of professors of prosthetics then on the faculties of American dental schools had studied with Milus—in the grove where he had displaced the old chicken house with a sturdy, concrete combination classroom-laboratory-library-projection room and clinic for patient care.

The more interesting patients or visiting dentists were often invited to stay for supper—which meant extra work for Alta, but she nonetheless encouraged the invitations. When guests were present Milus seemed at his most relaxed and his table talk flowed freely, to the delight of his listening sons.

Howard found the 18-month separation had produced some changes in his three younger siblings. Of course the three growing boys were still bound to a routine of assigned ranch chores—which also included sorting and washing extracted teeth sent to Milus by dentists for his classification and study. (Howard often said he dreamed of teeth coming out of his ears.)

Warren was now a "pre-vet" major at Michigan State University, but when he was home, he was expected to do his full share of work on the ranch. An extrovert by temperament and compassionate in his touch, Warren would always be a source of special delight for Howard and for his wide circle of friends.

Viewed from afar, Bill, 16 and a sophomore in high school, had only one visible achievement—surviving the long string of concussions and broken bones that were the rewards of his ill-fated experiments, or of his stubborn indifference to sober words of caution. In his schoolwork Bill thought of himself as a poor student. It would take an exceptionally prescient teacher to guess that this raw-boned youth was quietly seeking, sifting and seeing things that bore on problems he defined for himself rather than concentrate on commonplace class-room problems.

The impression Bill gave of being "a dull boy" underlay the advice he received from his high school counselor that he should not attempt going to college because he wasn't "college material" and it would be a waste of his time and his father's money. Rather Bill should scale his ambitions down to the level of his talents, and specifically, the counselor told this unregimented youth he should enlist in the navy. Some advice!

Jim's efforts to equalize the distance between himself and his older brothers tended to founder on hidden reefs and shoals. His deeper wound, aside from his disfiguring acne, was the undetected dyslexia which made him appear incapable of learning anything. His high school counselor also said, without equivocation, that Jim should not even try to get a college education.

After the round of reunions with family and friends, Howard began to cast about for "connections," starting with his teachers at USC Medical School and County Hospital who welcomed him onto the faculty at USC. Howard also found temporary work at the Georgia Street Receiving Hospital in Los Angeles, which is located in big-city life at the intersection of the emergency needs of the police and fire departments and a segment of humanity which seems to live under the dominion of virtually every kind of disaster. His shift at the hospital was between five and eight every evening, plus all-night work twice a week. The pay was good and the schedule suited him well for it gave him free hours during the day to explore places where he might want to start an ENT practice.

Howard's return to the Georgia Street Receiving Hospital exposed him again to the troubling questions that had not been answered during his days as a medical student, intern and resident: How was one to be certain a death could have been avoided, but for the failure to operate when the situation demanded it? Conversely, was the cause of death due to untimely surgical intervention? How could one determine whether an unsuccessful surgery performed in a context where the absence of an agreed-upon scientific standard of conduct made such action inappropriate?

More clearly than ever, Howard perceived the raw truth about surgeons and surgery: The technical and judgmental problems related to the assessment of errors and their control were at the bottom of moral challenges to the individual surgeon. Surgeons that held themselves to strict accountability for the consequences of their acts—of omission or commission—were challenged in such a hospital for here they could test how hard they would strive to avoid any errors in treating the case of a derelict off the street as compared to the case of a prominent figure in the public eye.

In canvassing places to start a practice, Howard always kept their future children in mind—an indication that the strains of their first year of marriage had been eased during the months he and Helen spent together in Europe. Favoring a place that would offer his children the benefits of the small town milieu he had known back in Indiana, or that environment his father had provided in Whittier for Warren, Bill and Jim, Howard began to consider La Jolla and Santa Barbara.

There was only one ENT doctor in La Jolla who served both the town and the patients at the Scripps Clinic and he wanted to retire. The director of the Scripps Clinic assured Howard and Helen when they went to visit, that if Howard took the place of the retiring doctor, the clinic would send him all their ENT patients—which guaranteed them a "good living" the moment his office was set up. As they left La Jolla, Howard and Helen stopped on the crest of a hill as the sun was starting to set over the lovely, little town nestled in its beautiful Pacific Ocean cove. The natural beauty of the scene was more stirring than the pomp of any human-made pantheon they had visited in Europe. Here, they agreed, was a "perfect place to start a family."

Still they went as planned to explore the possibilities in Santa Barbara where they found living and professional prospects very promising.

Where then should it be? La Jolla? Santa Barbara? Howard turned for advice to Dr. Brown, who advised against either. "Your proper place," he told him, "is in a big city and with your special qualifications you will quickly stand out in the crowd."

Howard was not convinced. Certainly his father had built a remarkable dental practice and had brought the world to him in a rural setting far off the beaten path. Why couldn't he do the same and make himself known beyond the boundaries of a small town?

In their indecision, he and Helen returned to La Jolla and stood on the crest of the same hill where they previously had been overwhelmed by the physical beauty of the scene before them. As they stood contemplating their future, Helen suddenly cut through the mists of illusions, "Howard," she said, pointing to La Jolla whose length she covered by a wave of her finger, "you will never be happy here. You really want to be where the action is. You want to be near a medical school where you can teach and be involved in research on something you enjoy. Los Angeles is the place for you."

Howard nodded his head in silent agreement and they drove back to the megalopolis of Los Angeles.

19

The Faces of Ambiguity

In 1939 the Moore-White Clinic was the most prestigious private medical clinic in the Los Angeles area. Its style made it the Los Angeles equivalent of the medical establishments on London's Harley Street which minister to Britain's aristocracy of birth, beauty and wealth.

Dr. Clarence Moore, who had been among Howard's volunteer professors of surgery, was one of the five partners of the Moore-White Clinic, along with Drs. White and Van Fleet, both internists, Hill, a pathologist, and Tollefson, gynecology and obstetrics. Each partner was regarded as being the leader in town within the different specialties and the ten other doctors, who comprised the rest of the staff, were viewed as "comers" in their own specialties.

Helen's words about Los Angeles still rang in Howard's ears when the pair returned from La Jolla to her parents' home where they found a message waiting from Dr. Moore. Howard quickly returned the call and Moore explained that through Dr. McKenzie Brown he had learned of Howard's recent tour and he would welcome a chance to talk to Howard before he made up his mind about where to settle.

When the two met, Moore explained that since their clinic covered all branches of medicine and surgery except eye, ear, nose and throat work, the partners had decided to establish an ENT department. Would Howard be interested? If so, his starting salary would be $14,000 the first year, $17,000 the second and $20,000 the third—very attractive salaries in 1939. Howard would also have the right to select and train his own nurses and have them by his side in the operating room.

Howard agreed to think over the terms of the proposal and immediately went to Whittier to discuss it with his father—who proceeded to recommend a counterproposal Howard should tender: Accept the first $14,000 offered to organize the ENT department at the clinic, but forgo any salary increases after that. Since Howard should have a goal that would encourage him to be more productive and be rewarded accordingly, propose that he receive a percentage of the clinic's income. If the overhead of the clinic was 50 percent of all income, then at the end of the first year, Howard would get 25 percent of what he brought in excess of overhead. On the same basis, his percentage should be increased each year. At the end of four years, he should get all the income he earned for the clinic beyond the overhead except for 5 percent. That would go to the partners as payment for their good will.

Milus believed the deal would be fair to all, yet it was with fear and trembling that Howard returned to the Moore-White Clinic for a meeting where all partners were present. He laid out his counter-proposal and the reason why he only wanted a fixed salary for the first start-up year. His terms, the partners said, were unacceptable. Everyone at the clinic, except for the partners, was paid on the basis of a set salary schedule. Furthermore, since most of the patients he would treat would be referred to him by the clinic staff, it would be unfair for Howard to stake out a special claim on income for treating patients who "belonged" to the clinic as a whole.

There was no meeting of the minds and Howard left the meeting wondering what he would do next. The following day Dr. Moore telephoned to say he and his partners had decided the terms would be acceptable after all. Howard was delighted, but there was one small hitch—he had committed himself to the Georgia Street Receiving Hospital for several hours at the end of the day and to an all-night schedule twice a week. He didn't want to quit the hospital until a replacement could be found.

Dr. Moore agreed that Howard continue at the hospital provided it did not interfere with his work at the Moore-White Clinic, so Howard signed on to the prestigious clinic and he and Helen moved out of her parents' home into a rented duplex on the edge of Beverly Hills—whose other side was rented by another young couple, friends from Helen's school days. Their first two sons would be brought back to this apartment after their births—Kenneth, born in 1942, and John the following year.

In his first professional decision after the contract with the clinic was signed, Howard called on Margaret Pierce, chief nurse on the ENT ward at the Los Angeles County Hospital. As an intern and resident, he had noticed that she not only wore a fresh uniform every day but to avoid getting any wrinkles in it, she never sat down—but always remained on her feet. This immaculate, starched whiteness might have appeared to be a virtue carried to an obsessive excess, but Howard realized her appearance mirrored the fact that to Margaret Pierce, nursing was the equivalent of a religious vocation.

The blend of her vigilance and kindness toward the nurses who worked under her supervision in the ENT ward went far toward reducing the kind of errors that are the despair of doctors anywhere—scheduled medication improperly provided, intravenous solutions that were not replaced on time or were run too quickly or too slowly, tests that were ordered but not carried out, blood samples that were drawn only to be contaminated and worrisome changes in a patient's condition that were not promptly reported. The patients loved her.

Howard had come to ask Margaret Pierce if she could recommend a nurse who could work with him at the clinic and be trained in his ways. "Yes," she said, "I know one. Me."

And so Margaret Pierce became Howard's first office and surgical nurse, working with him for many years until she retired from nursing to begin a happy marriage with the mayor of Santa Barbara.

When Howard's practice expanded dramatically, he engaged another gem, Billie Doyle, as the nurse-receptionist. Soon he added Nan Bundy to his office nursing staff. When the continued expansion of his practice required still another surgical nurse, Howard was again fortunate, for Margaret Pierce's closest friend, Lucille Carnes, then chief surgical nurse on the ENT service at County Hospital, also agreed to join the team. So with the addition of this top-flight ENT surgical nurse, (who retired 32 years later to live near her son in Texas) Howard came to be flanked in his practice by the best of ENT office and surgical nurses. The pattern they set was followed by many others as his staff continued to enlarge.

The skill of the surgical nurses and his refinements of surgical procedures enabled Howard to reduce the time it commonly took to complete a particular operation. This team efficiency not only reduced operating time, thereby decreasing the high risk of infections, but it also enabled them to schedule an exceptional number of operations for a single day. The moment one case was finished, his nurses would have another ready for Howard in an adjoining room.

The partners' view that Howard should not expect many referrals from outside doctors was based on solid experience, for most doctors feared that patients sent to a clinic for special treatment might return to the same clinic with other ailments. Howard, however, decided to change that and set out to get many patients from outside sources and thus be more "productive," as Milus had phrased it.

Many things worked in Howard's favor. He had attended college, medical school and completed his internship and residency in Los Angeles—so was already well-known to many practitioners in the area, including Lawrence Chaffin, chief surgeon for the Santa Fe Railroad, who asked Howard to accept an appointment to the ENT service for the Santa Fe. Soon after he was asked to be an ENT consultant to the Barlow Sanitarium, a private institution devoted to tuberculosis, to the Union Pacific Railroad and to the County Sheriff's office—a position he got through a patient and good friend, Sheriff Peter Pitchess.

The personal initiative Howard took to widen his horizons recalled the advice he had received from "Hot Point" Percy— he immediately joined County and California medical societies, the American Medical Association, the Pacific Coast Society of Ophthalmology and Otolaryngology and the larger American Academy of Ophthalmology and Otolaryngology—both of which in later years he would serve as president and still later as guest of honor. In addition to his appointment at the County Hospital, he was rapidly appointed to seven other hospitals—California, Eye and Ear, St. Vincent Medical Center, Queen of Angels, Hollywood Presbyterian, Good Samaritan, Children's and Santa Fe.

He regularly attended the staff meetings at all seven, had breakfast with doctors in one hospital and lunch at another, repeating the pattern throughout the week including Saturday, when the Moore-White Clinic was open until one p.m. If he had two surgical cases the same morning, he would schedule the first in one hospital and the second in another, so his name would appear on the surgery roster in each hospital—because to Howard the surgery roster, not fine clothes nor fine cars, was his emblem of success.

It was one thing for Howard to become a familiar figure at various hospitals and medical associations, but another to respond to his patients' needs so they would refer more patients to him. Surgical skills, psychological antennae, choice of nurses and compassion, worked in his favor. Then from the start of his career he was busy performing the submucous resection of the inferior turbinate, the "stuffy nose" operation he had perfected as a resident. He was also the first ENT doctor in Los Angeles to perform cosmetic nasal surgery.

One hospital that brought Howard onto the staff told Howard he could not bring his own anesthesiologist, Dr. William Meals, and surgical nurse when he operated; whereupon he wrote to the director in charge saying he would resign on the principle that he would not compromise the welfare of his patients, and then sent a copy of the letter to the chair of the board. When the chair called to ask what he meant by "compromising the care of his patients" at the hospital, Howard told him he could not adequately explain over the phone, but would be pleased to appear before a meeting of the board.

When the board met Howard appeared and asked the assembled group to assume they were hard of hearing and were to have the delicate fenestration operation. Howard explained, "I could take you to another hospital which would allow me to use my own nurses and anesthesiologist, or I could bring you to this hospital where I would be working with a nurse unfamiliar with the fenestration operation. Since the instruments are extremely delicate, some of them— because they were being handled by an inexperienced nurse—might be bent when I began to work on your ear, and I would have to stop and re-bend them into a proper position. I would also have to look up from the operating microscope to pick up my instruments on the tray, because the nurse would not be familiar with them. In other words, I would have to take my eyes off the microscope at every stage of the operation."

As if that was not enough, Howard continued, "Since the anesthesiologist would be administering the sedative from the head of the table instead of through the vein at the foot of the table and would also be unfamiliar with the kind of special anesthetic and procedures used in the operation, I and the surgical nurse operating at the head of the table would constantly have to walk around the anesthesiologist. For all these reasons, the operation would take twice as long as usual and your chance of infection and further hearing loss would be doubled." Howard finished, "I hope you now understand why I stressed that my primary interest was in the welfare of my patients."

The chair of the board turned to the director in charge of the hospital and asked if this was an accurate analysis. The director concurred and then Howard was asked how he would handle the training of their nurses. He agreed to have a nurse scrub in on the case and observe the procedure and soon arrangements were made in accordance with his wishes.

At the height of Howard's career, the roster of patients whom Howard treated for hearing problems included a Who's Who in virtually all realms of endeavors. Since they came to his office it was easy to treat them as one more of the anonymous crowd who surfaced as his patients.

There was, however, a special excitement to Howard's first house call as a member of the Moore-White Clinic because never before had he been exposed directly to the inner citadel of the truly Rich and the Famous. One night Dr. Clarence Moore telephoned him at home. It was eleven p.m. "Howard," he said, "I'm sorry if I have awakened you, but I've just received word from Bill Hearst that Marion

Davies has a bad earache. You know the Hearst place on the Pacific Coast Highway in Santa Monica. The guard at the gate expects you. One more thing. Remember that Mr. Hearst is a teetotaler and Marion is a "tippler."

Howard did not know what the term meant, but thought Moore was saying Marion might tip him. When he told Helen what the phone call was about, she was agog with excitement. "If I am asleep when you get back," she said, "wake me up and tell me all about it."

Howard arrived at the Hearst mansion sometime after midnight and told the guard he was Dr. House. But what to call the patient? Mrs. Hearst? Marion Davies? Marion? He settled on, "I am to see the lady with the earache."

He was escorted to the house where a butler opened the front door and ushered Howard through an elaborate hallway to a gold inlaid elevator which took them up to the third floor where Howard was turned over to the third-floor maid who led Howard down the hall in the direction of a vast bedroom ornate with laces, ruffles and satin. There he was introduced to "the lady's private maid."

The center of the room contained an immense oval bed and in the middle of this was the little blonde head of Marion Davies. As Howard moved toward the bed with what he hoped was the certified dignity of professional authority, several Pomeranian dogs began yapping menacingly, jumping at Howard and generally causing a tremendous commotion. Resolutely Howard continued toward the bed, dragging the frenzied dogs along with him. At the bedside, he simply said to the patient, "I'm Dr. House and I'm so sorry to hear that you have an earache."

Marion Davies acknowledged his presence with the wan smile of Camille dying and a small wave of her hand where one finger followed the other as in a child's hesitant piano exercise. By this time the ignored dogs had quieted down and Howard put his instruments on the bedside table, asking the maid where he could wash his hands.

"The lady's private maid" led him to a gold brocaded bathroom with gold fixtures where Howard looked things over while scrubbing his hands longer than he ever scrubbed for surgery. Returning to the bedroom, the dogs once again started to yap and jump all over him.

"Tell me," he said, trying to maintain some professional dignity, "how long have you had your earache?"

"I dunno," she answered blankly.

"Which ear bothers you!" he asked.

Again the vapid answer, "I dunno."

"If you will come over to the edge of the bed," Howard said "I will examine your ears."

With a beckoning finger and an impish grin, she said, "Oh no! You come over to me."

She seemed to be ten feet away in the middle of this enormous bed. With otoscope in hand, Howard began to crawl on hands and knees towards her, which again set off the dogs again while he worked his way toward her right ear, praying it was the one that gave her trouble.

The right ear was normal! He examined it for some time while deciding what to do next. Should he back off the bed and come in from the other side, or should he turn her head over and literally lay across her body to examine her left ear? He decided on the latter course. He used his elbows to lessen his weight on her tiny body, hoping this would not set off the dogs again. The left ear was also perfectly normal.

Out of the corner of his eye he could see a large man. He studied the ear for some time while he considered his plan of action. This had to be William Randolph Hearst. What to do? Crawl over Marion's body or back off bottom first in the direction of Mr. Hearst? He decided to back off the way he came.

Hearst greeted him affably. "Oh Dr. House," he said, "I'm sorry to get you out at such a late hour. I appreciate your coming here to see about Marion's earache. Is it serious?"

Knowing he could make a mortal enemy out of Marion if he reported there was nothing wrong with her ears, Howard said in a voice heavy with solemnity, "I examined both ears, and both are a little inflamed."

Not wanting to provide Marion with a pretext for saying the next morning that he had treated the wrong ear, he continued, "Have the maid put two drops of this medication into each ear." He handed the maid a small vial of baby oil, adding, "I will give her a capsule to ease the pain and put her to sleep. However, an earache like hers often causes a headache, nausea and slight dizziness. If she awakens with a headache tomorrow, put some witch hazel packs on her eyes and forehead. By noon the headache should disappear. Please call me tomorrow and tell me how she is."

The next afternoon Dr. Moore called Howard to his office. "Howard," he said, "in 40 years of active practice, this is the first time I learned that an earache causes headaches that can be cured by witch hazel pack." He added that Mr. Hearst called to report, "After Dr. House's treatment, Marion did go to sleep and in the morning did have nausea and a headache that Dr. House mentioned might be present. The witch hazel packs cured the headache and now she feels fine. You have a very sharp young man heading your new department. Tell him thanks for what he did for Marion."

Howard thanked Dr. Moore for his diagnosis that Marion was a "tippler."

Another episode early in Howard's association with the Moore-White Clinic also involved a deliberately fictitious diagnosis which also began with a midnight phone call from Mrs. Will Rogers to Dr. Clarence Moore.

Her call concerned her 16-year-old daughter Mary who had just returned home from one of her first dates. She was dizzy, unsteady and nauseated. The mother did not know what was wrong, nor could her daughter shed any light on what might have brought on her alarming condition. Dr. Moore contacted Howard and asked if he would drive to the Rogers' home and see the girl.

Will Rogers, who had vanished along with Wiley Post on their planned flight around the world, had been a long-time patient of the clinic, as were many other Hollywood celebrities. Will had claimed that every time a new doctor was summoned for a house call, he could tell the size of the medical bill he was going to get depending on the sound of the doctor's car coming up the hill to Rogers' home. If the car purred its way up the hill without shifting gears, he knew he was in for a good-sized bill. If the car shifted gears once, a moderate bill, if twice, he was always greatly relieved.

Howard, in his Buick, made it up the hill by shifting gears once. Mrs. Rogers greeted Howard and took him into Mary's bedroom. Just at that moment the young girl sprang from her bed and raced unsteadily for the bathroom for a seizure of vomiting. Instantly Howard knew, by sight and smell, what the trouble was, but Mrs. Rogers—a strict teetotaler—was too innocent to suspect that her daughter had had too much to drink.

Howard, for his part, would not betray the girl and after helping Mary back to her bed, spent enough time on a systematic examination to warrant a verdict: "Your daughter," he said to Mrs. Rogers, "has a case of 24-hour flu. But you have nothing to worry about. Soon her stomach will settle and she will sleep with the medication I am prescribing. In the morning she may have a headache, but some witch hazel packs on her forehead and two aspirin tablets will help ease her discomfort."

The next day Mrs. Rogers called to say that Mary was feeling much better, expressing her gratitude for the good care of her daughter's illness.

An epilogue to this story occurred years later when Mary, by now married and the mother of a little boy, walked into Howard's office. Her son needed a tonsillectomy, but the mother had something further on her mind. "Dr. House," she said, "I never had a chance to thank you for your diagnosis of my own case ten years ago. It would have broken my mother's heart if you had told her the truth. You spared us both great pain with your flu diagnosis."

On another night Howard received a call from Charlie Chaplin who said that Paulette Goddard was screaming with severe eye pain. Chaplin was pacing the porch when Howard arrived and immediately rushed him into Paulette's bedroom.

Paulette's eyes were swollen and bright red with inflammation. She had been exposed to Kleig lights all day at the studio and had received severe ultraviolet burns. Howard applied an anesthetic ointment to both eyes and covered them with eye pads. The pain stopped immediately.

"A miracle, a miracle!" shouted Chaplin. Howard then showed him how to use the ointment if the pain returned. Paulette was told to stay away from the studio for at least two days.

Chaplin invited Howard to have a liqueur with him and Howard took the opportunity to toast him for the joy he had brought to so many people throughout the world. Chaplin then noted it was after midnight and told Howard he should be the first to toast him for another reason—his birthday. From a stack of telegrams on his desk, he took one of which he was most proud and showed it to Howard. It was a greeting from Joseph Stalin.

The year 1939 brought other portentous moments to Howard, mainly because of the moral they pointed up. In the spring he attended the American Otological Society meeting in Atlantic City where Dr. Samuel Kopetzky was scheduled to present a paper at the opening session on a new otosclerosis operation.

Howard entered the lecture hall where he saw an isolated man sitting alone, marooned within a ring of empty seats. Walking over to Julius Lempert, Howard asked if the empty seats were being "saved."

He was assured they were not reserved and so sat down and proceeded to bring Lempert up-to-date on his own career moves before the session was gaveled to order by Dr. Harris P. Mosher who was presiding.

Lempert was interested in hearing about Howard's visit with Holmgren and his analysis that Lempert's ear surgery had no equal anywhere. For his part, Lempert briefed Howard on the importance of this particular meeting and that Dr. Kopetzky, who had come to him for training in the fenestration operation, would be giving full credit to Lempert in this paper.

Lempert was convinced the hour had arrived when his work would be legitimized by a leading ear authority and in the presence of the elite among otologists.

However, as Kopetzky intoned his paper both men sat stunned. Not once was Lempert's name mentioned. Rather the text gave the impression that Kopetzky, alone and in a springtime torrential gush of brilliance, had brought the one-stage fenestration surgery to its current state of development.

At first dumbfounded, Julius Lempert was rocked to the core. He had eagerly anticipated the moment when he would finally be granted a mark of respect in the company of fellow professionals. "Howard," he said as tears welled up in his eyes, "Why should anyone want to do this to me?

Whom have I harmed? I am going back to New York immediately."

Beyond consolation, Lempert rose from his seat and walked out of the hall, with Howard following lamely, not knowing what he could say. Silently he walked Lempert to the train station and saw him off.

Kopetzky's scandalous behavior was like a storm that clears a foul sky, for it set in motion a series of events that eventually led to Lempert's sweeping vindication. The process got underway the moment Kopetzky finished his presentation.

Howard later learned that as soon Kopetzky sat down, Dr. Mosher himself had jumped to his feet, pounding his gavel, he rasped out a command, "There will be no discussion of Dr. Kopetzky's paper. I am calling an emergency meeting of the council promptly at noon in my suite."

To Mosher, Kopetzky's affront to professional ethics transcended the undertow of his own fierce antipathy to Lempert personally and of his known strong skepticism about the worth of the fenestration operation. At the emergency meeting, Kopetzky was assailed by questions fired at him by council members.

In view of Lempert's previous 55-page article in the *Archives* on fenestration surgery, why did he think he could ignore Lempert altogether? Wasn't it true that his own paper was based on Lempert's work? Wasn't it true that he had mixed the fenestration operations he had done with those Lempert had performed? Wasn't he aware that some council members had visited Dr. Lempert to see his work with patients? Wasn't he aware that many otologists had come to recognize Lempert's genius as a surgeon? What made Kopetzky think he could falsify the truth by omitting any reference to Lempert's role in the cases that were reported?

Kopetzky was reduced to the weak begging of a hopeless case. He broke down and admitted it was "all Lempert's work," and that he "should not have presented the paper as though the work it covered were all his own." He said he was getting on in years and this was a final chance for "glory." Lempert would have other opportunities that would secure a high place for him in the history of otology, etc.,etc.

The more he talked, the less sense Kopetzky made. The council voted to expel Kopetzky from membership in the American Otological Society—the first member ever to be formally expelled. The action was all the more striking when one took into account that Kopetzky was a past president of the society and a retired general in the U.S. Army.

Howard left that meeting with two strong convictions: One was that Kopetzky was a disgrace to the medical profession despite his authorship of a textbook on the ear; the other was that sometime in the near future he needed to take a leave of absence from the clinic to go to New York for the six-week course Lempert offered on fenestration surgery.

Rather than assume responsibility for his tribulation, Kopetzky bitterly blamed Lempert and in his disordered way, waited for a time to ambush Lempert in revenge for what he had suffered.

Lempert had always cautioned his patients of the risks of his one-step fenestration surgery, based on his own statistics which showed that in two percent of his patients their hearing was worse after the operation, while about one percent suffered a totally deaf ear. Since hearing was substantially improved in 80 percent or better of the cases, this two percent negative outcome was a risk virtually all patients were prepared to take.

One of Lempert's patients who emerged from the operation with a dead ear subsequently met Kopetzky—who

173

saw in him an instrument of retaliation. Kopetzky told this patient he was prepared to testify in court that "Lempert should not have performed the operation at all." The patient sued and Kopetzky appeared as such a convincing "expert witness" the jury awarded the plaintiff $25,000 in damages.

Because of his past history of fee splitting combined with having no membership in recognized medical societies, Lempert had no malpractice insurance. Hearing the verdict, he walked up to the presiding judge and asked, "How and where do I pay?" and proceeded on the spot to write a check for $25,000.

Howard, too, had his own medical difficulties. Though he got off to a fast start, it would be false to suggest he always knew exactly what to do and that everything he did worked out well. One day he received an emergency telephone call from Dr. Chaffin who reported that a vice president of the Santa Fe Railroad was in the hospital with a profuse nosebleed that went with the patient's history of high blood pressure.

Taking with him the equipment he would need, Howard sped to the hospital. In those days the accepted procedure for controlling such a hemorrhage was a tight gauze pack that added to the misery of the patient. The procedure worked, staving the blood flow. As usual, after two days Howard gently removed the pack, only to have the severe bleeding resume. His only alternative was to repeat the miserable procedure, which again stopped the bleeding. But this cycle repeated itself when another two days passed and he again removed the pack. For the third time he repeated the procedure to quell the fresh flood of blood.

If this failed, Howard knew he would have to operate and tie the artery that carries blood to that area. But before undertaking so radical a step, he called to consult with Dr. Simon Jesberg, one of his mentors during the days of his residency at the County Hospital. When he explained the difficulty he was experiencing in controlling the bleeding, Jesberg at once came to the hospital.

Howard, at the bedside of the vice president, expansively introduced the notable visitor, saying, "This is Dr. Jesberg. He is an expert on your kind of problem."

Jesberg proceeded to draw from his medical bag a jar containing salt pork strips. Howard, wondering what on earth was his teacher up to, fought hard not to betray his own embarrassment. He had never heard of salt pork being used to control a nasal hemorrhage, but Jesberg assailed the problem before him with calm confidence. Removing the gauze pack from the vice president's nose, which immediately caused the hemorrhage to reoccur, Jesberg began to stuff salt pork strips into the patient's nose.

The bleeding stopped. Howard was astounded.

The patient admitted the salt pork strips in his nose were far more comfortable than the surgical pack. Howard was still incredulous and later challenged Jesberg with a question. How long will you leave those strips in the patient's nose?"

Jesberg replied, "I'll be by tomorrow to remove them."

Howard made sure he was on the scene when Jesberg removed the salt pork strips. A miracle! No more bleeding! The patient was very grateful.

Following Jesberg into the hall, Howard asked, "What happened—how did the salt pork work?"

"I don't know," Jesberg answered, a slight smile on his face. "It's an old treatment I heard of years ago, but I try to make it look as scientific as possible."

Howard was as baffled by the fortunate outcome as he was baffled by the infection-free work of the ophthalmologist in Zambathay who worked in a sea of filth and by a Swedish surgeon he observed remove a pituitary gland through the nose in order to relieve the pain of a patient with metastatic cancer.

Another experience, however, staggered all parties touched by it—and recovering confidence after the shattering blow did not come easily. Usually surgeons discuss incidents as this one among themselves in low, confidential voices. It began with a telephone call Howard received one evening from a fellow doctor who explained that a half hour earlier when he put his three-year-old son to bed, he noted the child showed symptoms of having a little cold. Now he was having trouble breathing and was getting feverish. Howard directed him to bring the child to the hospital immediately where he would meet them.

Upon his arrival, the child was having serious trouble breathing and his temperature had already skyrocketed to 104°. His throat was swollen like a balloon—something Howard had never seen before—and the swelling was in the epiglottis at the base of the tongue which by now had almost closed off the trachea.

To reduce the swelling, Howard immediately put the boy on steam inhalations and antibiotics and then stayed at the child's bedside until he was breathing more easily and seemed much improved. Howard felt he could go home and the boy's father walked out with him to get a cup of coffee. When he returned, his son was dead.

Subsequently it was established that what had caused the epiglottis to swell was a particular strain of influenza, "Type B," which had never been recognized before. Since then, many cases have been reported, and it is now known the results are often fatal unless a tracheotomy is done immediately.

Even though all that could have been done—based on existing knowledge—was done, still everyone was devastated. Howard was aware that the very nature of his work made him accountable not only to other physicians but to a court where he was the judge and jury. For a long time he was tormented: Should he have known what he didn't know? Could he have known more than he did? Were there any lessons to be drawn from the failure itself?

Balancing out these harsh blows were instances when he was acutely aware that he was a "lucky" person—though he never boasted about it. One such time involved a case that marked the first time Howard "hit the press."

A child in Las Vegas was choking on a peanut that had lodged not in the lung but in the trachea. Howard received a frantic call from a doctor in Las Vegas describing the condition of the child who was intermittently blue from the lack of oxygen. Howard advised his fellow physician to give the child oxygen and then hold him upside down by his feet shaking him to try to get some air in past the peanut.

At the same time, emergency steps were taken to rush the child from Las Vegas to the Children's Hospital in Los Angeles. A TWA plane, about to depart from Las Vegas for Los Angeles, was alerted. Three people were bumped off to make room for the doctor, the child and his father.

Howard dashed to the hospital where he and others were kept informed by radio messages from the pilot. One moment he would radio that the child had stopped breathing. The next moment the message would come through: "No! No! The child is breathing again." So it went in a nerve-wracking round of despair and hope. By the time the plane landed, all the passengers were emotionally wrapped up in the fate of the gasping child who was being held intermittently upside down in the aisle and jiggled by his legs so some air could pass into the lungs.

The press meanwhile picked up the desperate radio calls from the plane and numerous reporters and photographers were at the hospital by the time the ambulance arrived with the desperate trio. They watched as the father and the Las Vegas doctor rushed into the elevator being held at the ground level carrying the half-dead, blue-faced child whom they held upside down by his feet.

The elevator doors closed on the grim drama, whisking the child out of sight. Some reporters waited below. Others stood in the hall outside the operating room where the blue, cyanotic and semi-conscious child had been rushed.

Howard instantly passed a bronchoscope down the child's throat into the trachea. When he peered into it he could see nothing but blackness. Quickly he pulled the scope out to ascertain whether the light bulb was working and to his immense relief discovered why he could see nothing. The bronchoscope had irritated the semi-conscious child who had coughed, blowing the peanut into the opening of the scope. The peanut had blocked the light. When he removed the scope the peanut came out with it.

There it was—an innocent looking strangler! A moment before, Howard had a half-dead child in the operating room. Now here was an alert child with normal breathing, good color and a husky cry. The press pounced on the dramatic turnabout and made the most of it in front page stories. The child's doctor, the TWA pilot and the airline itself were hailed for their part in the rescue mission, but Howard was the celebrity of the hour.

Should he have been acclaimed for what he did? When he reconstructed the event, Howard knew he had made a dreadful mistake. He admits, "Despite the acclaim of the press, my mistake was put squarely to me by my friend Simon Jesberg, who said, 'Howard, you had only a few seconds in which to work. You should immediately have done a tracheotomy first and then put in the bronchoscope. You were lucky this time, but don't press your luck in the future!' "

Children's Hospital and Howard subsequently tried to get the newspapers to publicize the problems peanuts create for children. Bowls of peanuts are often within reach of small

Milus, the young dentist, at the time of his first marriage.

Howard and his mother.

Howard sailing to Europe,
almost 5.

Howard, almost 7, and his
first bicycle.

Howard, 2nd from left, with young friends
(the two brothers who drowned are on right).

Howard's first pair of long pants as he starts high school.

Howard takes Warren for a ride.

Bill, Jim and Warren.

Howard, Floyd, Mary, Burnice, Dorothy and Grandmother Payne
pose at Yosemite's Wawona Giant Sequoia on their grand tour.

Burnice, Mary and Howard on the Pacific Coast car trip.

Floyd tries flying one of the first planes.

Milus in California after regaining his health.

The House clan gathers, l. to r., Granddad House, Alta, Jim, Grandmother House, Milus, Bill, Warren, Helen with Uncle Ben (the minister who married all the House boys) and Aunt Mabel.

Helen in college days.

Howard, the aspiring medical student, on his 21st birthday.

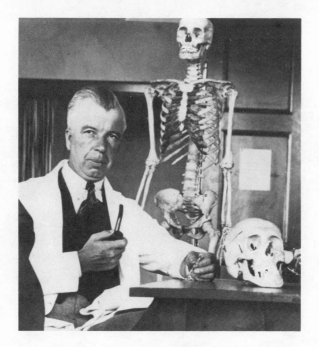

Dean Paul McKibben who let Howard into medical school.

J. Mackenzie Brown, a great teacher and adviser.

Howard, with his father, proudly holds his M.D. diploma.

Harris P. Mosher

Howard taking Mosher's course.

Helen and Howard in Paris, 1938.

Professor Gunnar Holmgren.

Milus and his four boys—Jim, Bill, Warren and Howard.

Howard and Helen's rented home near the hospital during his E.N.T. residency.

Alta, Warren, Howard, Milus, Helen and Bill surround
the new addition to the family, baby Kenneth.

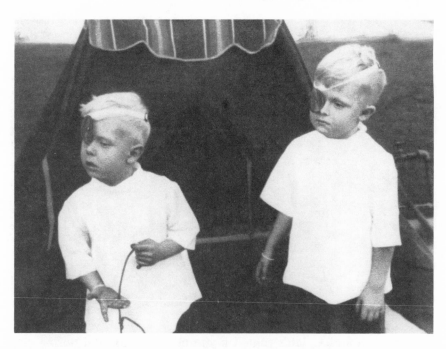

John and Kenneth waiting for their first patients.

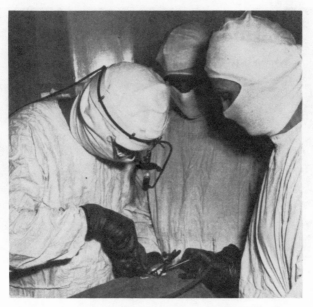

Howard doing a fenestration on a *Saturday Evening Post* writer
who published an article about the experience in 1946.

Julius Lempert receiving the
Deafness Research Foundation Award.

Howard in front of the Los Angeles Foundation of Otology which was founded in 1946.

George Eccles, principal motivator behind the Los Angeles Foundation of Otology.

Young naval cadet Bill in dental school.

Bill and June with Howard and Helen.

Howard, Helen, Carolyn, Ken and John in 1959.

Carolyn made the Olympic Swim Team in 1960 and held two world records.

John was captain of the USC swim team which went to four national championship playoffs.

George Kelemen.

Dean Lierle, professor of E.N.T. at Iowa Medical School.

Aram Glorig who wrote the "Bible" on hearing loss due to noise in industry.

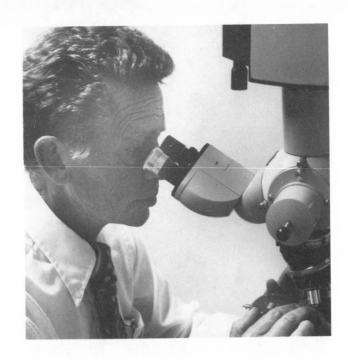

Fred Linthicum, member of the original O.M.G.

Dr. Sam Rosen who reactivated the stapes mobilization
surgery.

Howard with George Shambaugh and Victor Goodhill.

Harrell J. Harrell who made the first substantial
endowment to the institute.

The Ear Research Institute on 3rd and Lake.

Bill, Howard and Ed Ethell watch the new name go up
on the building leased from St. Vincent Hospital.

James Sheehy, member of the original O.M.G. formed in 1959.

John Shea, fellow at H.E.I. and O.M.G. who
reactivated the stapedectomy surgery.

Bill in his laboratory.

Jack Urban and Bill working on the cochlear implant.

Bill Hitselberger who helped develop the ear tumor surgery.

Tracy Husted, first child with cochlear implant in 1981 (now a
student in a regular junior high school) is observed by
Dr. Bill as she hears for the first time.

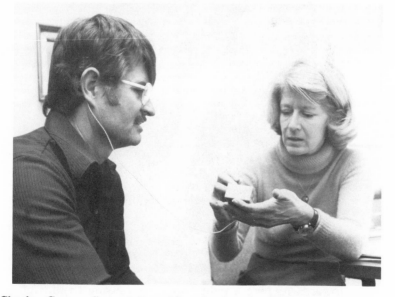

Charles Graser, first adult cochlear implant in 1970 (now working as
a librarian) with Norma Norton, M.A., director of rehabilitation.

Howard and Helen, his wonderful, loving wife of 40 years.

Howard, keeping a tight grip, after bowing to the
Queen and Prince of Sweden.

Bill and June with state-of-the-art testing equipment.

John, with his halo, making a miraculous and
complete recovery.

Joe Van Der Meulen, Alden Miller, Dean Allen Mathies
and Howard commemorate the institute's affiliation
with the USC School of Medicine

The Howard House family gathers to celebrate
Howard's 75th birthday.

Ruth Barnes, Howard's executive secretary for four decades.

Mrs. Athalie Irvine Clarke, trustee of the institute and
founder of the first auxiliary, "The Associates."

Howard guest acts his part on the popular TV series, "One Day at a Time," with Valerie Bertinelli, Pat Harrington, Nanette Fabray and Bonnie Franklin. Copyright © 1982 Embassy TV.

Nanette Fabray, good friend and editor, helping with the biography project.

A model of the soon-to-be-finished 120,000 sq. ft. building.

Steel going up on the new House Ear Institute building.

John, Howard and Bill inspect construction progress
of their dream come true.

children, especially when cocktail parties are held in a home. A child who grabs a handful of peanuts may be caught, spanked and begin to cry which causes the peanut to be aspirated into the lungs. Parents are often unaware of anything wrong until later at night when they notice that the child wheezes as he sleeps. If not diagnosed by history and special X-rays, the peanut in time causes a lung abscess which might require the removal of a lobe of the lung.

Unfortunately their attempts to publicize these problems got nowhere. The peanut industry apparently had a strong voice where the press was concerned.

20

Disengagement

Howard's link to the clinic might have been changed in 1942 if he had been tapped for war-time duty with the armed forces. He volunteered, but when his color blindness showed up on his physical examination, he was judged to be medically unfit for military duty as an officer, deferred from the draft, declared essential and told to continue his practice and his teaching at the USC Medical School.

At this point roughly one-half of Howard's practice entailed "eye work" with the remainder divided among ear, nose and throat cases. His heart was set, however, on performing Lempert's kind of surgery for he was convinced that fenestration held the key to the relief of hearing loss due to otosclerosis for some patients.

Lempert himself was no longer scorned by the high priests of the medical establishment. The cumulative evidence he offered—backed by tests made by the newly perfected audiometers—convinced most skeptics that he had permanently improved the hearing in 80 percent of properly selected patients suffering from otosclerosis.

Until 1942, however, knowledge of Lempert's work was largely confined to medical circles—and to word-of-mouth reports by patients Lempert had helped. That year, however, the *Reader's Digest* published an article by an author who described his own strikingly successful fenestration operation. Soon an avalanche of patients converged, not only on Lempert, but also on George Shambaugh, Jr. in Chicago, who was mentioned in the article as someone Lempert had trained.

Howard, now 36, felt the time was ripe to arrange a leave of absence from the clinic so as to take Lempert's six-week course in fenestration surgery. He also reasoned that the clinic might pay the tuition of $1,500 because on his return he would be, with the exception of the older Dr. Sylvan Goldberg, the only surgeon in the West trained by Lempert. The inevitable result would be a mass of new patients, leading in turn to an increase in the income of the clinic as a whole.

When Howard made his proposal to the five partners of the clinic, he was rejected out of hand on the basis that the leave would entail an immediate loss of income to the clinic, besides the clinic never paid for the courses staff members took to upgrade their skills. Deciding not to press matters further, Howard kept his thoughts to himself and waited for the first chance when he could study with Lempert.

Meanwhile on the home front, Howard had become a father when Helen bore a son, whom they named Kenneth. Just as she was giving birth in the California Hospital, Howard, on the floor above, was performing a tonsillectomy on a child. The coincidence confused the child's parents who heard the announcement over the hospital public address system, "Mrs. Howard House has just delivered a fine baby boy and Dr. House is now a father."

When Howard emerged from the operating room the waiting parents said, "Doctor, we thought you were operating on our son. We had no idea you were involved in the delivery of your son."

Howard assured them he had performed the tonsillectomy on schedule and with no complications.

John, the second son in the House family, was born 14 months later, some ten days before the estimated time of arrival. It was a very warm California night during the ninth month of Helen's pregnancy. She and Howard finished dinner at home and though Helen was feeling fine, Howard was troubled by a backache. He thought it safe to leave Helen while he went to a health club a block away for a rub-down. A half hour later, Helen telephoned him at the club to say she was going into labor.

Howard ran home—and into another problem. Who would look after the infant Ken? The next door neighbors were away. Howard called Mrs. Anita Burdick, who had been helping Helen and had become like a second mother to Ken. When they explained the situation and asked if she and her husband, a Los Angeles policeman, could come at once to look after the sleeping baby, Mrs. Burdick agreed.

They were momentarily expected, but Howard felt that they shouldn't delay. In the last flurry of activity, they deposited the sleeping baby in a playpen in the backyard, since they would not leave him alone inside fearing a possible fire could occur.

Howard raced Helen to the hospital where she was immediately wheeled into the delivery room. Suddenly there was a frantic telephone call from Mrs. Burdick. On entering the house, she and her husband found Ken's crib empty, with the baby nowhere in sight. Howard apologized for the breakdown in communication. At his belated suggestion, she stepped outside into the backyard and found Ken snug asleep in his pen.

The war years also saw important developments in the life of Howard's half-brothers and father. Warren graduated from Michigan State with a degree in veterinary medicine and entered the veterinary services of the U. S. Armed Forces. When Bill graduated from high school, he fortunately ignored his counselor's opinion that he was not "college material" and entered Whittier College where he was accepted as a pre-dental student. With the Japanese attack on Pearl Harbor and the U.S. entering the war against the Axis powers, many young men at Whittier volunteered for service in the navy.

Within a month, however, word reached campus saying the navy could not as yet handle all the volunteers, so the young men were advised to "keep on going to school" until they were called up. Bill accelerated his program, completing the equivalent of four quarters of pre-dental work in three, so he soon had enough credits to qualify for entry into a dental school. His applications were accepted at both the University of California and the University of Southern California.

Something else, however, was on Bill's mind. The U.S. Navy maintained a recruiting post in Los Angeles for prospective naval flying officers. If accepted, college students were assigned to what was known as the college-based V-12 program. Bill, then a gangling, skinny youth, went to the recruiting station, applied for the V-12 program, took the physical examination and was flatly rejected. He did not fit the Navy's theory that flyers should conform to the mold of a specific body type—muscular, broad shoulders and heavy neck.

Bill was crestfallen but Milus advised him in his own inimitable way, "to go to hell!"—his general counsel for all blockheads. "You go right up to San Francisco, start in at the University of California Dental School and see what happens." So he did.

In the fall of 1943 Washington ruled that all male medical and dental students had to be in uniform and part of the V-12 program. When Bill drew unwelcome attention to himself by wearing civilian clothes, he was summoned and asked why he wasn't in the V-12 program.

"I applied for it in Los Angeles," Bill replied, "examined and told I was not qualified."

"Well, you are qualified right now," he was told and immediately issued a uniform and ushered into the V-12 program. It was one of many head-on clashes Bill was destined to have with a range of authorities.

Jim, like Bill, also ignored his high school counselor's advice about not attempting college because he wasn't college material and entered Whittier College. Because of his unsuspected dyslexia, he did poorly in his studies and welcomed the moment when he was inducted into the navy where he spent three years, first as an orderly in a San Diego naval hospital and then as a dental assistant aboard a naval ship in the South Pacific.

By 1943 Milus was able to supply porcelain reproductions of natural teeth in 183 different molds, sizes, shape and color in relation to face forms and skin tone. He was now ready to make this available to commercial dental houses. Howard traveled east with his father for a meeting in New York City with John Shepard, a close friend of Milus who was president of the Dental Supply Company.

Shepard, surrounded by other executives and several attorneys, announced to Milus that their company wanted to purchase the rights to manufacture and distribute the products Milus had developed and then handed Milus a contract several pages long detailing the terms. Milus thanked the group and arranged to meet with them the next morning once he had looked over the document.

Back in their hotel room, Milus studied the contract and asked Howard if he could suggest any needed changes. The terms were excellent in Howard's view and he was amazed by the sum of money at stake and was certain his father would sign up.

As the group convened the next morning, John Shepard opened stating that after a night's reflection, he concluded the contract did not sufficiently compensate Milus for his contributions to dentistry. Therefore he proposed doubling the money originally offered and hoped this would prove satisfactory to Milus.

Howard was aghast to hear his father respond saying it was unsatisfactory, but not for monetary reasons. Milus explained he would not sign the contract as written because it contained the word "exclusive." A company to which he granted the rights to his molds might use that monopoly to protect its investments in its old style molds—by *not* tooling up for the production of the new molds it acquired. If, however, that word were removed from the contract, he would accept the original financial terms and would forgo the proposed doubling of the sums involved, adding that he was leaving that afternoon for Philadelphia where he would be offering the S.S. White Dental Manufacturing Company the same contract he was prepared to offer Shepard's firm, with no "exclusive" rights granted.

Shepard signed a contract on Milus' terms, as did the S.S. White Dental Manufacturing Company. Milus retained the privilege of manufacturing teeth in the state of California because he was making his own teeth anyway and teaching other dentists how to do so in his Whittier laboratory. During his lifetime he was to receive a half-cent royalty for every artificial tooth sold manufactured on the basis of his molds—but there would be no royalty payments to his estate after his demise.

By this time Howard had been with the Moore-White Clinic for four years and had more patients referred by outside doctors than any other doctor in the clinic plus the second largest number of referrals from other patients. This was the year in which he would receive all he earned beyond the actual overhead, except for the five percent that was to go to the five partners.

That was the background for an invitation he received to come to Dr. Moore's home for a business dinner where the other four partners of the clinic were also to be present. Dr. Moore remarked at the outset that all the partners were in agreement that Howard had done a "helluva job." He was producing more income for the clinic than anyone except Moore and Tollefson, but his success, however, had created a problem. Many doctors on the staff with far more seniority were receiving salaries well below Howard's income.

"We feel," Moore concluded, "that this disparity can adversely affect morale. For that reason we have decided we cannot continue to pay you on a percentage basis."

Howard was shocked, for he could not believe Moore and the other partners could look upon their contract with him as revocable at their own discretion. Trying to collect his thoughts, Howard managed to say he had no choice but to leave the clinic, though he would agree to give the partners a chance to find a replacement if they so desired.

To soften the response, Howard added that he had been thinking of leaving the clinic anyway, because he realized that ultimately in order to limit his practice to the ear, he must have many references from many doctors instead of mainly from the few doctors within the clinic. As things stood, most doctors in the Los Angeles area avoided sending him cases for fear they might lose their patients to other doctors within the clinic and Howard cited instances where local ENT doctors had referred patients with otosclerosis to Lempert in New York or to Shambaugh in Chicago for surgery, who in turn, would refer them back to Howard for their post-operative care.

Don Tollefson, the youngest of the partners, made a shift in the tone of the conversation, observing that Howard had made a generous offer to stay with the clinic while the search was on for someone to take his place. More importantly, he disagreed with the senior partners who wanted Howard to stay and to develop his ear work at the Moore-White Clinic while dropping eye, nose and throat work.   Turning to Howard, he said, "I agree, Howard, you will do better on your own concentrating on otology instead of handling everything that comes along in the ENT field."

Another partner observed that if Howard left the clinic to concentrate on the ear, it would mean an immediate drop in his income. Howard concurred, but said he assumed that he could look forward to a sharp upturn in his income once he had been trained in Lempert's fenestration surgery.

The meeting, ending on an inconclusive note, was followed by another three days later, when again dinner was held in Dr. Moore's home with all the partners and Howard on hand. Again Dr. Moore opened with a surprise. Speaking for the rest he said, "Howard, we have decided that if you stay with the clinic, we will give you a full partnership. That will get rid of the percentage problem."

Howard voiced his thanks for the offer, but noted that if he were made a partner over the heads of other doctors who were his seniors on the staff, the effect would further exacerbate the "morale problem" that created the initial difficulties. Besides, the financial factor was not the real reason why he thought the time had come for him to leave the clinic. He had taken his stand on the issue of percentages only because he believed that promises should be kept. The conviction was growing that the time had come for him to limit his practice to the ear, as Lempert and Shambaugh had done.

Again, trying to soften the blow, Howard expressed how much he had enjoyed his relationship with the partners, valuing what they had taught him, as well as the doors they had opened for him. "Before I joined the clinic," he remarked, "I was learning the science of medicine. At the clinic, I learned the art of medicine, as well as the procedures for the efficient management of a large medical setup."

So that was it. In the fall of 1943, though his replacement in the clinic had not yet been found, Howard took a leave of absence for what was originally to be six weeks of training with Lempert. Prior to his departure for New York, he told ten of his patients who were good candidates for the fenestration operation that he would soon be trained in its procedures. If they wished to undergo the operation at his hands when he got back, he would charge them nothing. If they were uneasy regarding his competence, he strongly urged them to turn to Lempert, Shambaugh or, locally, to Sylvan Goldberg.

All ten said they would wait for Howard until he was "ready."

21

New Beginnings

During the six-week course, Lempert, the expert, was impressed by Howard's surgical skill, and particularly by the swift way Howard could complete an operation on the ear of a cadaver without tearing the delicate skin flap used to cover the fenestra (window).

The end of the course came at a time when Lempert was planning an exhibit on fenestration surgery for a meeting of the American Medical Association. With that in mind, Lempert made a proposal to Howard. If he were provided with specimens of six half-heads, would Howard do the fenestration operation on them in ways where each would represent a given stage in the surgical procedure? The heads would be mounted in cases with electric lights, a magnifying glass and properly labeled descriptions. An observer who moved from specimen to specimen could then see and read the sequence of the procedure from start to finish.

Howard construed Lempert's request to be a compliment and placed two calls—one to Helen and the other to the Moore-White Clinic—to advise them that he would not be returning for another week. He then happily tackled his assigned project, working from early morning until dinnertime when he would join Julius and his wife, Flo, at the 21 Club where they customarily dined. This time together further reinforced the bonds that were drawing the older and the younger men even closer.

The work itself progressed in fine style and so expeditiously that Howard asked Lempert if he could make a second set of specimens for his own teaching purpose—not only of the fenestration operation, but of the simple, modified and radical mastoidectomy technique he himself had perfected. In this way, Lempert could include the mastoidectomy examples as well in his exhibit. Lempert welcomed the suggestion.

By the end of the week, Howard had produced two sets of twelve mounted and shellacked specimens. To protect the mounting against damage in transit, specially designed cardboard containers were acquired, one for each head.

During Howard's affectionate farewell with Lempert he was surprised when Lempert asked if he would join him in practice and offered him what Howard thought was an "outrageous" salary. Flattered, Howard promised to give the matter serious consideration. Then Lempert's chauffeur helped Howard carefully place his twelve boxes into Lempert's limousine and later on the train for the homeward-bound trip.

To be sure that the heads were safely kept, Howard checked his personal luggage into the baggage car so the twelve boxes would fit into his roomette. The journey was without incident between New York and Chicago, but on the second leg from Chicago to Pasadena—where Helen would be meeting him—the air within the closed roomette grew dank with the smell of malodorous formaldehyde.

Howard was unfazed by this familiar smell, but the Pullman porter who attended the car could not avoid the sense of a "spectral presence." Trying hard not to pry, the porter continued to act as though nothing was out of the ordinary. Finally as the train was slowing down for the Pasadena stop, the porter gingerly asked Howard what was in those boxes.

Nonchalantly Howard said, "Half-heads—twelve in all."

"What kind of heads?"

"Human heads," Howard replied, explaining that he had been dissecting them on a medical project.

This was too much for the porter, who recoiled in horror from Howard's request to help carry the twelve boxes off the train, and so Howard removed the boxes unaided.

Helen was waiting for him as he lumbered off the train, burdened with his strange load. On the way home he discussed with her Lempert's offer which he had mulled over on the train ride home from New York. Howard was inclined not to accept it and Helen agreed, so he called Lempert in New York to explain that he and Helen believed it best to remain in Los Angeles because it provided a more congenial environment in which to live and rear their children.

Lempert, although disappointed, respected these reasons and wished Howard well in his new practice in Los Angeles.

Other matters intervened before Howard undertook his first actual case of fenestration surgery. Office space was hard to find, but he learned from Dr. Brown that a large office at 1136 West Sixth Street, close to St. Vincent Medical Center and Good Samaritan Hospital, was available. Howard thought that its 3,600 square feet far exceeded his need.

"Take the office now," Dr. Brown advised. "Some day you will need all this space and a good deal more."

Howard remained skeptical because Brown's own office in the same building was only some 1,000 square feet. Time would prove that if Brown erred in his judgment, it would be on the side of understatement.

Howard signed a five-year lease which he would renew with more space three times before the time came and he bought land and built his own 22,000 square foot building at 2122 West Third Street. He continued working at the clinic, because they still did not have a replacement, but also oversaw the purchase of necessary furnishings and equipment for his new office.

Helen, on her part, began to look for a new home in a location no more than 20 minutes from the new office, convinced that Howard should not have to drive against the sun, cross railroad tracks or drive on a freeway. She also wanted the children to have ample roaming grounds and be close to schools while the site must be conducive to privacy, have a "nice view," and be near a shopping center.

The home Helen eventually found was on Waverly Drive in Los Angeles, twelve minutes from Howard's office. They sold their duplex and bought their new home, paying for it in cash, which on top of the expenditures for the new office, left them "nearly broke." Years later Howard computed how much time he had saved by living in the Waverly Drive home for 40 years, contrasted with most of his medical associates who averaged 45 minutes in travel time, one-way, between their respective homes and office, and calculated that thanks to Helen's foresight, he had saved roughly two and a half years just in travel time between his home and office.

Finally in April 1944 his replacement at the Moore-White Clinic was found, so with the help of his three personal staff nurses—Margaret Pierce, Billie Doyle and Nancy Bundy—he moved out of his facilities in the clinic one Friday night to open his new office on Monday morning.

During this transition period he had shrunk from telling Mrs. Bundy that he doubted if his practice would be large enough to support three nurses so there would be no place for her in the new office. She reported for duty in her usual conscientious way, on Monday and he again delayed. It turned out to be a fortunate error, for not only her services but those of additional nurses would be needed as Howard's practice boomed.

The time had at last come when Howard was ready to perform fenestration surgery. His first patient was not one of the original ten who were waiting in the wings, but rather someone recommended to him through a secretary at the Los Angeles County Medical Association.

"Dr. House," the secretary said, "we have a deaf young man in our office from Brazil who can't speak a word of English, but who has with him a close friend acting as his interpreter. Somehow his family in Brazil has heard of a new operation you are starting to perform that can restore hearing. Is there anything to the report?"

Howard replied that he had been trained to do the fenestration operation and would be glad to see the Brazilian youth. Within minutes the young man and his friend arrived from the nearby quarters of the Medical Association. Tests showed the patient was suffering from otosclerosis and was an ideal candidate for fenestration surgery. When this fact, along with the risks and rate of failure, were explained to the youth, he said he understood what he faced and was prepared for whatever might happen.

The operation was set for the California Hospital on the afternoon of the following Saturday—when other surgeons would not likely be around to distract Howard's attention by poking their heads into the operating room to see what he was doing. On Saturday morning Howard sent Margaret Pierce to the hospital with instructions to scrub the operating room from top to bottom—walls, floors, lights, table legs, racks, doors—the works.

That afternoon, when Howard walked into the operating room ready to go, both he and his surgical nurse were confident that the long drills with cadavers would enable them to complete, without a hitch, their first fenestration operation.

The anesthesiologist, Dr. William Meals, was not as confident. This was his first experience with fenestration surgery and he was doubting Howard's recommended dosage of anesthetics to use. Howard explained that, according to the Lempert rule, one half grain of morphine and six grains of seconal, were to be given one hour before surgery.

Meals was convinced there must be some mistake for such a dosage would "knock a patient sky high." To check on the accuracy of Howard's instructions, he called Lempert's anesthesiologist in New York, saying he did not believe anyone could safely take that much medication. The anesthesiologist confirmed this was what Lempert regularly used.

"Well," Meals shrugged to Howard after the long-distance telephone conversation, "if that's the way they do it in New York, that's the way we will do it in Los Angeles."

Clearly, however, he was in no way reassured. In contrast to Lempert's method, Meals was to be at the foot of the table to be out of Howard's and the nurse's way. Presently the Brazilian youth was wheeled into the operating room, still very much alert. Meals administered pentothal into the ankle, pausing each second as if to invite Howard to "overrule New York." There was no such reprieve. Lempert's advice had stretched across the continent to govern what was done in the operating room of the California Hospital.

The operation itself went as smoothly as if it had been performed by Howard and his surgical nurse 1,000 times before. Howard anticipated the procedure would take up to three hours, but the preceding weeks of drills and more drills enabled him to complete the complex surgery in an hour and forty-five minutes. Howard was pleased by the procedures, but he had been infected by Meal's concern over the effects of the premedication that had been used.

In those days hospitals were without recovery rooms or intensive care units, but a private nurse stood by for this patient. Howard and Meals were each due to go to formal dinner parties that evening, though in different places and both left the hospital before the patient regained consciousness. The anxiety remained on Howard's mind after he returned home, got into a tuxedo and escorted Helen to the dinner party. During the evening Howard frequently called the hospital for reports about the patient and as soon as he could politely leave, he dropped Helen off at home and continued on to the hospital where he checked the condition of the Brazilian youth.

To his immense relief, Howard found that the lad could be aroused, though he was still very drowsy. All seemed well, and Howard walked down the hall to the elevator, whose doors slipped open to reveal on the figure of Dr. William Meals, also still dressed in a tuxedo. He too had left a dinner party early, drawn to the hospital by his unease over the condition of the youth. The two doctors paused long enough to congratulate each other over the way things seemed to be turning out and then parted for their respective homes.

Hours later Howard was awakened at four in the morning by an emergency call from the hospital. Something terrible was happening to the Brazilian youth who appeared crazed, shouting, running and staggering up and down the hall. He was beyond control.

Quickly Howard dressed and sped to the hospital hoping a police officer would stop him and clear the way with a siren, but none materialized. When Howard reached the hospital hallway and crossed the youth's line of vision, the latter lunged toward him, threw his arms around his neck and kissed him repeatedly. The youth's interpreter, who had also received an emergency summons to the hospital, showed up on the scene and they pieced together the story.

When the patient had awakened in the middle of the night and found he could hear human voices in the hall, his sheer ecstasy had triggered this lunatic conduct. With the help of the interpreter, Howard coaxed him back to bed and assured him that all the sounds in the outer world would still be there in the morning when he awoke from his sleep.

The post-operative effects included some dizziness, but after a five-day stay Howard released the patient from the hospital. The youth was eager to undergo an operation for his second ear, but this could not be done at once for a minimum interval of at least six months was needed before the second ear could be operated on. The youth accepted Howard's explanation and went off with his friend to celebrate his regained hearing.

The epilogue to the case was as ludicrous as it was full of wild menace. Howard told it this way:

A week after the young Brazilian had been released from the hospital, the interpreter called me to say that he must see me right away. The tenor of his voice suggested some sort of emergency so I told him to get to my office as quickly as he could. He was in a lather of excitement when he arrived and the nurse-receptionist waved him past the waiting patients into my office.

"Dr. House," he began, "you know how much I appreciate what you did to restore the hearing of my friend. That is why I feel terrible because of what I must tell you. I am going to kill him!"

"You're going to do what?" I asked incredulously. "What do you mean?"

"We were out with two girls last night and my friend insulted me in their presence. When he refused to apologize, I challenged him to a duel and he accepted the challenge. Once we are back in Brazil, we will have a duel and I will kill him."

"I can't believe what I am hearing," I said. "I don't know

much about duels, but isn't it true that you must take ten paces in opposite directions and then whirl around and shoot?"

"Yes and I am a very good shot."

"It's a gentlemen's challenge, isn't it? A matter of honor and done with honor?"

"Yes. Absolutely. He will have the choice of guns."

"In view of the code of honor that governs a duel, you wouldn't want to take unfair advantage of him, would you?"

"No, of course not."

"But you may be doing just that. After an operation such as your friend has undergone, he can be made unsteady by any sudden motion. You've seen that yourself. If he gets to the end of the ten steps and makes a sudden whirl, he'll have trouble aiming that gun. Who knows what he might hit? Are you still speaking to your friend?"

"Yes, we share the same quarters in the hotel."

"When you see your friend, ask him to turn around suddenly, without any relationship to the duel. You will find that he is unsteady."

"How long will it take before he is no longer dizzy?"

"It may take six months or more. You can honorably go ahead with your duel after that, but bear something else in mind. As you know, fenestration surgery is a relatively new operation. After you get back to Brazil, I want you to talk to his parents and tell them their son could make a contribution to hard-of-hearing people in the world, in the way I want to outline for you. Before the duel and on the assumption that you will kill him, they should arrange for me to get the temporal bone I operated on. I can look at it under the microscope and determine why his operation was so extremely successful. In that way, even when he is dead, he will help mark a new chapter in medical research history."

"That's a wonderful idea," the young man said. "Of course, I may not kill him, but if he dies as a result of our duel, I will surely do everything in my power to see that you get his temporal bone."

"Be sure it's the right one—the ear I operated on. And try not to hit it!"

The exchange took over an hour, to the disruption of the scheduled appointments with the patients waiting in the office. Some two months later, Howard received a lovely present and cover letter from the parents of the youth. Still later, the youth returned to Los Angeles for surgery on his other ear with the same interpreter.

When the pair walked into Howard's office, it was clear that they were great friends. "What happened to your duel?" Howard asked. "Did you miss each other?"

"Oh no," the interpreter replied, "he apologized to me."

Howard had to await some other "arrangement" before he got the temporal bone he wanted to study.

In line with his decision to concentrate on ear work, Howard gradually sloughed off the other things he had done at the Moore-White Clinic—first dropping eye work, then throat and neck work. When his close friend Alden Miller returned from military service, Howard stopped doing bronchoscopies and esophagoscopies—a Miller specialty—and referred all such cases to him. The last thing he gave up was plastic surgery of the nose, which he had thoroughly enjoyed.

Each time he dropped a segment of his previous practice he was certain his income would fall, but the opposite happened due to the rapid growth of his practice with patients having ear problems. At the time Lempert in New York and George Shambaugh in Chicago were the only other surgeons in the United States doing ear work exclusively.

Howard's success with fenestration surgery alone brought him so many patients he was booked six months in advance for appointments and a year in advance for surgery. His staff continued to enlarge. Lucille Carnes, the matchless surgical nurse, was to be with him for 36 years. Another incomparable assistant was Ruth Barnes, R.N. who left the Moore-White Clinic to become his secretary—a post she still holds along with a nurse, Lillian Healy, after 38 years. Besides these three, Howard engaged Dr. Edward Johnson when the latter obtained his Ph.D. in audiology at the University of Southern California. He was the first Ph.D. audiologist employed in a private office and he remained with Howard until his retirement 32 years later.

Howard was doing 14 fenestration operations a week including Saturdays, teaching at the USC Medical School and trying to spend every spare moment with his two small boys. Helen and Howard's home overlooked the city of Los Angeles, a broad valley and the ridge of a distant mountain range.

It was not equivalent to the family ranch in Whittier or to the farms Howard had known back in Indiana, but there was ample space around the house where the children could play and keep their collection of animals, for Howard tried to duplicate for his own children what his father had provided for his half-brothers. The Waverly establishment came to include a lamb, rabbits, ducks, chickens and a large police dog. The boys gathered eggs and sold them to the neighbors and their home became known as the House Zoo where children from a nearby grade school would come with their teachers to see the menagerie each year.

22

Twin Births—Sorrow and Triumph

There is no road whose route runs only through triumphal arches. In Howard's case, the pleasures of his work intersected with a grim event in his family life which began in 1945 when they found out Helen was again pregnant. Nothing unusual happened until the sixth month when she was examined by Dr. Tollefson at the Moore-White Clinic on V-J Day when the country was celebrating the end of the war against Japan.

Their participation in the festivities was short-lived, however, for Tollefson announced Helen was carrying twins. Though this was happy news, both he and Howard were concerned over Helen's tendency toward rapid or premature labor when Kenneth and John were born. So she was taken home—past the frolickers and all the excitement attending V-J day—and put to bed for a regimen of bed rest with a minimum of motion, while the ever-reliable Mrs. Burdick was summoned to attend to the needs of the family.

Three weeks later, Helen called Howard to say it appeared she was on the verge of labor pains. Immediately Howard went and picked Helen up, taking her on a slow and careful trip to the California Hospital where Tollefson did everything possible to stop the onset of labor. His best efforts only delayed matters by a week when Helen went into labor two months prematurely and bore identical twin girls.

That she had given birth to identical twin girls was all the overjoyed Helen was told. The babies, named Marolyn and Carolyn by Helen, were immediately placed in an incubator and given pure oxygen. It was not known at the time—the truth would be discovered the next year—that too much pure oxygen could damage the retina on the eye of premature infants.

The immediate cause for concern were X-rays showing that Carolyn had enough lung expansion to give her a chance for survival, whereas Marolyn's lungs contained fluid and were not expanding. A bronchoscopy to remove the fluid was the only procedure that might be taken, but Howard's experiences with premature babies suggested that Marolyn's chance for survival was not more than one in ten, for if the tiny three-millimeter bronchoscope designed by Dr. Jesberg was inserted into her lungs to remove fluids, the procedure in premature babies risked instant death through shock.

Due to the war, Dr. Harold Owens and Dr. Jesberg were the only surgeons in the Los Angeles area other than Howard who were capable of performing such a bronchoscopy. Both were out of the city and Dr. Alden Miller, another specialist, was still in the navy. Howard could not bring himself to apply the procedure to Marolyn— leaving him in an impossible dilemma: damned if in a desperate attempt to try and save his baby he would cause her immediate death and damned if she died because he did nothing at all.

With a heavy, penitent heart, his decision was to do nothing and the newborn infant died within a few hours. It was left to Howard to break the sad news to Helen. Today, due to advances in medical knowledge and resources, both infants might well have survived without complications the severe tests of a premature birth.

Carolyn was kept in the California Hospital for three months after Helen returned home. During the course of Howard's frequent visits to the hospital to check on her progress, he noticed that her eyes were not quite tracking and that one eye was slightly off to the side. Based on his own work in ophthalmology, Howard knew that the vision in an eye with nothing to focus on tends to deteriorate. He was not sure what Carolyn saw with the good eye, and he and Helen began to think of how to care for a blind child and have visions of a white cane and a seeing eye dog. Fortunately it never came to that, but the family did rally around to help Carolyn overcome her sight impairment difficulties begun with this unfortunate ordeal.

In the midst of this sorrow, Howard found himself facing a totally unexpected triumph in his own practice. Patients sometimes appear on the scene like seeds which travel on the wind and then take root on soil far removed from their point of origin. They can come to a doctor's office seemingly out of nowhere and either be a vehicle for a major advance in medical knowledge or can help set in place the means for what eventually evolves into a major medical institution.

The latter role fell to George S. Eccles, starting in late 1944. Eccles, a banker and a member of a leading Utah family, was a dominant figure in virtually all aspects of economic life in the inter-mountain West—once he emerged from the shadow of his celebrated older brother, Marriner S. Eccles, the innovative chair of the Federal Reserve Board.

As a young man of outsized mental and physical vigor, George Eccles had been afflicted by deteriorating hearing due to otosclerosis and was finally forced to wear a hearing aid whose bulky apparatus, common to the day, required oversized pockets sewn into jackets and pants as a pouch for the gear. To be without the aid meant silence that taunted a young man eager to grasp every whispered nuance at a meeting or during a personal encounter.

Whenever George or his wife Dolores learned of a doctor who reportedly could improve the hearing of deafened people, Eccles would seek him out. Thus in 1944 he found Julius Lempert in New York who assured him he was a suitable candidate for a fenestration operation.

Even though Eccles welcomed this finding, he was jarred by Lempert's manner—and was not alone in this respect. Others had been repelled by Lempert's imperious ways and off-put when he brusquely questioned them about their income, setting astronomical fees if they were well-to-do. (Another Lempert cast-off was another leader of American business—Leonard Firestone—who was destined to become one of Howard's patients and be a source of invaluable support in the development of what is now the House Ear Institute.)

Eccles was relieved by Lempert's suggestion that should he want the surgery done close to his home, he could see Dr. Howard House in Los Angeles. "Dr. Lempert," so Eccles recalled, "described Howard House as an experienced and exceptionally skilled surgeon—one of the best whom he had personally trained in fenestration surgery. With banker-like caution upon my return to Salt Lake City, I checked Dr. Lempert's judgment with my local doctors. They confirmed what I had been told."

He made an appointment with Howard in Los Angeles and had fenestration surgery on one ear. "The result," Eccles said, "made me a man reborn, though not without the usual initial difficulties. It took some time before I was comfortable hearing so much and also before an operation on the other ear enabled me to regain directional hearing so I could tell at a meeting where a voice was coming from."

Eccles, a gregarious man, brought the details of his regained hearing to the attention of Mr. Jean Witter of the nationally known stockbroker firm. Witter's daughter, Nancy, then 19, was afflicted with otosclerosis. In the spring of 1945 she and her mother came from San Francisco to Los Angeles where Eccles had already cleared the way for a prompt examination by Howard. The young woman turned out to be a very suitable candidate for fenestration.

Howard always had his fee quoted by a nurse before surgery so there could be no misunderstandings later. When Mrs. Lucille Carnes began to discuss the financial arrangements with Mrs. Witter regarding the standard fee of $500, Mrs. Witter interrupted to say she didn't care about the doctor's fee, she simply wanted Nancy's hearing back. Also, she informed Mrs. Carnes, she wanted a room for herself next to her daughter's, with special-duty nurses around the clock.

Mrs. Carnes excused herself and went to Howard's private office to discuss the matter with him, suggesting that in view of the extra time and special care the case entailed, the fee should be set at $1,500. Howard, who knew his father never inflated his own fees when treating wealthy patients, vetoed the suggested figure. The Witters would be charged the standard $500 plus $100 for extra time.

The surgery was successful and Nancy regained her hearing. Soon after the young woman and her mother returned to San Francisco, Howard received a very short note from Gene Witter expressing his appreciation for the restoration of his daughter's hearing. He went on to say he felt the fee was entirely out of line and was enclosing a check for the $1,000 to take care of the bill, adding that his attorney would be visiting Howard in the near future to discuss the matter.

Howard showed the letter to Mrs. Carnes who admitted that she had sent Witter a bill, not for $600 but for $1,000. She was overcome with remorse for having done "such a terrible thing" and apologized for causing any problems Howard might face with the attorney.

Shortly thereafter Witter's attorney arrived at Howard's office one afternoon without bothering to make a prior appointment saying he wanted to speak to the doctor face-to-face. Reiterating that Jean Witter was thrilled to have the hearing of his daughter restored, the lawyer explained that Mr. Witter was troubled by the fee.

"Fortunately," so Howard recalled, "he continued talking before I had a chance to take the $1,000 check out of my desk drawer and return it to him with my apologies."

The attorney went on to say that Witter wanted him to submit a bill commensurate with the true value of his services, suggesting a bill for at least $10,000.

Howard was dazed by the suggestion, but again declined to make any change. The attorney then asked if Howard had any children and when he found out there were three, he suggested that perhaps Mr. Witter could establish a trust fund to help in the education of the children.

By now Howard's head was spinning. "That would be very kind of Mr. Witter," he managed to say, "but I feel the education of my children is my responsibility."

The attorney then asked if Howard belonged to a medical school faculty.

When Howard mentioned his affiliation with the USC medical school, the attorney intimated that Mr. Witter would no doubt be favorably disposed to an arrangement where he could help finance research by means of a gift to the medical school earmarked for Howard's use. Howard promptly phoned Dean Raulston, then passed the receiver to the attorney.

After some ten minutes of talking with the Dean, the attorney thanked him and hung up. Then turning to Howard he said that any arrangements involving the university would not do, because donated funds would first go to the university, from there to the dean of the medical school and then to the chair of the department of ear, nose and throat—who, no doubt, would pass the funds on to Howard.

There were simply too many bureaucratic steps in the way and the attorney pressed Howard: Had he ever heard of a foundation? When the attorney realized how naive Howard was about nonprofit foundations, he declared he would prepare in draft form the papers necessary to establish a nonprofit foundation to receive funds for ear research.

"The lawyer told me" so Howard later recalled, "I should have a small board of three or four close friends so I could spend the money for research in any way I wished. The material he eventually sent me included a proposal for the formation of the Howard House Foundation for Ear Research. It was my belief that as a young surgeon—I was 38 years old at the time—it would be pretentious to memorialize my name. I also thought the word ear did not have a ring that was sufficiently scientific."

More than a year's discussion about the proposed foundation came to a head in 1946 when Oscar Trippet, Howard's lawyer, prepared formal articles of incorporation for what was called the Los Angeles Foundation of Otology. The founders, George Eccles and Gene Witter, joined Trippet and Howard as members of the original board. Four other friends, Drs. J. Mackenzie Brown, Alden Miller, Donald Tollefson and Russell Fisher, rounded out the board. In combination they took advantage of Howard's access to Hollywood's ablest film maker to produce a training film of new surgical techniques.

In future years the name of the Los Angeles Foundation of Otology would be changed to the Ear Research Institute and then to the House Ear Institute. There would also be fundamental changes in its personnel, governance, funding, housing, clinical research and educational program, as well as in its national and international outreach among otologists, the public at large and in its external relationship with a cluster of other institutions.

Even in its Lilliputian form, the foundation, as Russell Fisher recalled years later, "solved the problem Howard faced early in his career when he grasped the fact that the human value of his services to people of means far exceeded what he could or should charge for surgical operations that liberated them from their bondage to deafness. Howard would rather charge his usual reasonable fee and then make them aware of the foundation rather then to have his personal income soar skyward."

Eccles and Witter, the "invisible hands" that created the foundation, would steadily support its development. Eccles made possible the establishment of what is known as the George and Dolores Eccles Temporal Bone Laboratory, housed within the present-day House Ear Institute, whose importance to otology cannot be overstated. In 1961 Eccles provided funds so that Bill House could begin his bioengineering work on the cochlear implant—now used throughout the world.

Eccles seemed to understand better than most people the drive behind what became Howard's consuming dedication to the growth of the institute that was ultimately to bear his name. "The institute," so Eccles once remarked, "is for Howard what my First Security Corporation is for me—a cause, a way of life, an emotion, a challenge in the realm of art."

Many leaders in politics, commerce, finance and industry, as well as celebrities of stage, screen and television have been patients in Howard's office. Many have given freely of their valuable time, talents and support over the years to help promote the work of the institute. Countless leaders from overseas, including half a dozen presidents and ambassadors of foreign countries have also been patients.

With the help of his associates and devoted friends, Howard achieved something that had never been achieved before, for he built a private institute—firm enough to survive his demise—an institution devoted to research and training in otology where over 20,000 ear specialists from this country and abroad have taken courses and observed the work being done there. The well-endowed present-day House Ear Institute has no counterpart anywhere in the world.

23

The Seamless Web

While Howard's work was changing, his brothers were moving ahead in their own careers. Warren, demobilized from the army, settled in Amish territory in Indiana near the Fouts farm, where he was employed by the Parke Davis Drug Company which was marketing a veterinary product based on the hormones of pregnant mares. It was Warren's responsibility to persuade the Amish farmers to collect urine discharged from these mares for which he paid them by the gallon for what they collected in the receptacles he provided.

Initially, the farmers suspected this stranger with his strange request, but Warren eventually won their confidence. So much so that he later claimed he "needed a railroad tank car to transport the urine to the Parke Davis receiving station where it was used to make hormones." When synthetic hormones were developed, Warren moved back to the Los Angeles area where he opened several dog and cat hospitals and joined the veterinary service of Los Angeles County as an official in charge of all research animals.

Serving in the navy during the last part of World War II removed the leisure from Jim's growing up years. Just before V-J Day he married Ruth Smith and in short order they were the parents of three children, Danny, Tom and Richard. It was Ruth who helped Jim overcome the handicap of his dyslexia, and with financial help from Milus, he reversed the near-failure of his first stab at college education at Whittier College, sailing through his undergraduate courses at Whittier, and graduating in the top fifth of his dental school class at USC.

Bill, the middle brother, was in his third year in dental school when he married June Stendahl, a nursing student at the University of California. In 1945, on the eve of V-J day, he received his DDS degree and with his father's encouragement, he then entered USC Medical School, only to be stopped cold in his tracks for the official word came down that he would have to repay the U.S. Navy for the two years he spent in uniform while receiving a DDS degree.

Although he raised a storm because it meant he had to forfeit his place in the freshman class, his protests were in vain and he was commissioned a lieutenant j.g. and sent to the navy shipyard at Bremerton, Washington where he was presently joined by June. The postwar housing shortage forced the young couple to bring their firstborn, Karen, home to a quonset hut in Bremerton.

The shipyard's main activity after V-J Day was decommissioning ships and the large naval community was served by ten dentists who worked in the clinic, most of them regular navy officers, as was the captain in command.

These were the initial days of X-raying teeth, and distortion of certain aspects of the tooth structure was a problem dentists had to cope with—a reality that became a personal challenge to Bill. After immersing himself in technical literature, he designed modifications in the machines which resulted in clearer X-ray pictures and also devised a method whereby X-ray films could be instantly developed. An officer from the navy patent office presently called on Bill to say that patent rights to his improvements belonged to the U.S. Navy, because they had been made "on navy time, with navy personnel, and with navy material."

Other technical matters engaged Bill's interest. He reasoned that it would be possible to look directly at the upper teeth without using a mirror if the patient lay flat instead of sitting upright. This would enable a dentist to work easier, quicker and with greater precision. Bill developed the kind of dental chair he had in mind, then invited other dentists in the clinic to watch him drill the teeth of a patient who was lying flat on his back. "My God, Bill," an onlooker cried as if deputized to speak for the rest, "you can't do that when you get into practice. Women will think you are going to rape them." But years later, dental supply houses began to market dental chairs capable of being fully laid back, because other dentists agreed with Bill's analysis.

Bill's continued efforts to improve the technology of dentistry were derailed when he collided with existing navy regulations that set a quota of 300 fillings a month for each dental office. Navy dental officers would drill small cavities, each taking no more than 15 minutes to fill, and these would be entered on the captain's record against individual quotas. A large cavity which took considerable time to fill was either ignored or, what was worse, was disposed of by extracting the tooth. The system enabled regular navy dental officers to compress into a few hours work their required monthly number, after which they were free to read, sleep, play poker, gossip or simply stare vacantly into space.

At age 23 Bill was an idealist and was appalled by the skullduggery of the regular navy dentists. His father had impressed upon him the value of not extracting even an extensively decayed tooth until all means of saving it had been exhausted so Bill conscientiously tackled the big as well as the small cavities—though this meant going beyond the navy rule of one hour of work per patient.

Carefully Bill would clean out a cavity, put in a temporary filling and have the patient return for a second appointment. One day the captain in command reprimanded Bill for not meeting his 300 fillings per month quota. Bill explained he was filling the large cavities instead of extracting or ignoring them. "I don't care what your excuse is," the captain barked, "comply with navy regulations or you will be transferred to sea duty."

Bill was not one to stand in awe of high ranking official idiocy and pressed the justice of his own methods, with his reward being an assignment to an aircraft carrier as a dental officer. The ship, no grand symbol of America's imperial military power, was a small converted "victory ship" of Henry Kaiser's mass-produced model known for its addiction to much pitching and rolling.

The assignment was meant as a punishment, but the effects were the opposite. The small carrier presently became part of the navy task force that took part in the early post-war atomic bomb tests in the Pacific which Bill found "kinda interesting." In his capacity as the sole dentist aboard the small carrier, Bill was free to do whatever he thought would best serve the crew and so surveyed the teeth of all crew members, summoning to his office any enlisted man or officer who needed remedial or preventive dentistry—even if they were not themselves aware of the need.

Bill's two years of mandatory duty with the navy ended in August 1948. In anticipation of this he reapplied to USC Medical School and was again admitted to the freshman class, to start in September. They moved into a house provided by Milus in Whittier in order to save rent money. Two months after Bill started medical school, baby David was born, much to sister Karen's delight.

But this arrangement meant Bill spent an hour and a half each day commuting to and from the USC medical campus where his classes ran from eight in the morning until five in the afternoon. Arriving home after six, Bill would have dinner with June and the two infants, get to bed at seven, sleep until two in the morning, rise and study from two until seven, and then return to school. Often he would ask himself, "Why am I doing this, when I am already qualified to be a practicing dentist?" His struggle to survive the danger of sudden demise in some of his first-year courses was the source of a recurrent anxiety dream he had for years. "In the dream," he recalled, "I am back in the medical school, faced with imminent failure, with a wife and two infants to support."

Not everything was full of menace, for he found enjoyment in subjects such as anatomy because, he explained, "I was used to thinking in concrete terms." For the same reason, he looked forward to lectures Howard occasionally gave at USC on aspects of ENT or the anatomy of the head and neck.

The year before Bill entered medical school, Howard became—and for the next 20 years remained—the chair of what proved to be the historically important Subcommittee on Noise in Industry of the American Academy of Ophthalmology and Otolaryngology. He was appointed to that post by his friend, Dean Lierle of the University of Iowa Medical School and the chairman of the Academy's Committee on the Conservation of Hearing.

Howard had already won wide professional and public attention for his work in fenestration surgery and teaching of ear surgery and he had achieved leadership posts within professional organizations of the Pacific Coast, but his appointment to this new committee on noise in industry raised him to a sensitive plane of national prominence in his medical specialty, since their conclusions could potentially have major repercussions for environmental standards in the workplace, for compensation to employees based on claims of a work-related loss of hearing, and for the payouts on such claims by insurance companies.

Noise, a common cause of hearing impairment, is defined as an unwelcome sound. If your house is burning, the sound of oncoming fire trucks is music to your ears, but not for people awakened as the trucks roll by sirens wailing. Either way, however, the adverse effects of noise were not fully understood until the end of World War II.

For years it was suspected that hearing loss was job-related among blacksmiths, boiler makers, railroad workers and people who regularly fired guns or flew airplanes in open cockpits. Scientific confirmation was compiled by Dr. Aram Glorig who as head of the ENT section in a U.S. General Hospital based in England during World War II had carefully studied patients suffering from acoustic traumas due to explosions of mines, bombs, shells, and grenades. After V-J Day, the U.S. Army Surgeon General appointed him a temporary major general so he could head a program focusing on the hearing problems of returned veterans.

In 1946 Glorig came to Los Angeles for a one-month-long mastoid and fenestration course Howard was offering for the first time to otologists in groups of four, under the auspices of his new foundation. At the end of the course, Glorig resumed his work in Washington where he directed technical research and the development of centers throughout the country for the rehabilitation of army personnel and veterans suffering from hearing loss. Three years later Glorig accepted Howard's invitation to join the academy's Subcommittee on Noise. Then in 1952, also at Howard's invitation, Glorig moved to Los Angeles to be the research director of the Los Angeles Foundation of Otology and head up the subcommittee's newly established Noise Research Center.

The center's first move was to mount an educational

campaign aimed at insurance carriers and manufacturers to inform them of the adverse effects on hearing from excessive noise and to advocate not only the audiometric testing of employees, but also to measure noise levels in the work place and compute the length of time employees were exposed to noise. Next, the committee engaged an audiologist, Douglas E. Wheeler, Ph.D., to research the scope of the noise problem which he defined as: "How much noise, of what type, for how long, produces how much hearing loss in how many people?"

This vein of research suddenly became a compelling, national need when New York's Workmen's Compensation Commission made an award to a worker for a hearing loss caused by industrial noise, even though the claimant had suffered no loss of earnings. Other states followed New York's lead, and claims soon reached flood proportions. It was now a matter of survival for industries and insurance companies to bring the claims under rational control, based on reliable information.

In searching for answers to the relationship between noise and hearing loss, Howard and Glorig looked for an industrial firm that would permit hearing tests of employees who worked at high noise levels. Allis Chalmers Company agreed to cooperate and for the first time the results helped fix the relationship between noise levels and degrees of hearing loss.

Glorig, in a later meeting with Allis Chalmers executives, pointed out that farmers exposed to tractor noise often suffered a hearing loss, as compared to their wives who did not drive the tractors and experienced no hearing loss. To rectify this problem Glorig suggested that Allis Chalmers put a muffler on their tractors and reposition the exhaust pipe from over the engine to a place below and behind the seat of the tractor so farmers would be driving away from the source of the noise instead of driving into it.

The indicated changes were made and the new model was offered to the market on the wings of an extensive advertising campaign which featured the conservation of hearing. Although the medical and engineering concepts made sense, farmers perceived reduced engine noise as only meaning less power. In the absence of the familiar rattle and explosions, they concluded that the new-style Allis Chalmers tractors did not have the power for heavy-duty work and sales plummeted. Quickly the company reinstated the exhaust pipe in its former place and sales immediately improved. Unfortunately this arrangement still prevails on many kinds of heavy machinery.

The subcommittee work, however, went forward, and the full-time staff of the Noise Research Center was fleshed out with audiologists, bio-statisticians and an acoustic physicist. By 1957 the 50,000 audiograms supplied to the center by industry was a gold mine of information that expanded the horizons of knowledge about noise-induced hearing loss—which, in turn, gained for the center and its sponsoring subcommittee, an international reputation.

The center literally "wrote the Bible" for conservation of hearing in industry, with suggestions for companies in four matters: the control of noise at its source; the isolation of high intensity noise areas from other employees; hearing tests for new employees destined to work in high-intensity noise areas to establish a baseline for hearing tests to be repeated every six months; and lastly, providing ear plugs or ear muffs for ear protection. The standards formulated by the center were ultimately adopted by the Occupational Safety and Health Administration (OSHA) when that agency was created.

By 1949 Howard was nursing along the infant Los Angeles Foundation of Otology, making motion pictures of ear surgery, giving courses in mastoid and fenestration surgery, writing scientific papers, as well as serving as a

Clinical Professor at the USC Medical School and chair of the Subcommittee on Noise. His heavy professional schedule—which entailed many meetings away from Los Angeles—of course affected his family life.

During workdays Howard and Helen spent little time together for he left home early in the morning and often returned late after Helen and the children were asleep. Except when the matter was urgent, she never called him during the day and much of their contact during the week was via notes left on the bathroom washbasin. Saturday evening, and part of Sunday, were often the only periods during the week when the family was really "together".

Helen, a quiet person, accepted these realities as the price of Howard's growing professional eminence. Without bothering Howard, she would often decline social invitations that came their way and limited their entertainment at home or at the Jonathan Club to a circle of personal friends. She did enjoy going with Howard to meetings of medical societies, but always kept in the background.

In Los Angeles Helen was part of a small group of women who often lunched together which included Edith Lewis, Helen's intimate friend since grade school days. Helen was always careful to be home when school let out so her children never had to return to a vacant home. When sports became a big item in the children's schedule, it was she who carted them from one event to the next, cheering them on in their varied accomplishments. Her life centered around both Howard and the children.

In the spring of 1949 when Howard was in the tenth year of his practice, Dr. J. Mackenzie Brown proposed that he sponsor Howard as a member of the American Otological Society whose active national roster was limited to 100 otologists, each elected by the full membership. Howard thanked Brown for his generous offer, but maintained the effort was doomed to fail since there was no chance he could get past the predictable veto of Dr. Harris P. Mosher. Even though a decade had passed since the episode at Harvard, still Dr. Mosher maintained a frigid distance from Howard at any professional meeting they attended.

Brown assured Howard there was no need to worry about Mosher's animosity, but Howard was not convinced. He regularly attended national meetings of ENT organizations even though he was not a member because he believed there were always new things to be learned both from the formal presentations and from the face-to-face encounters with other practitioners.

The 1949 meeting of the Otological Society was held in New York's Biltmore Hotel and the secretary contacted Howard to say "Tomorrow morning I want you to stand outside the door of the ballroom where the society will hold its business meeting. I'll come out and get you when the members vote you in."

Howard did not follow those instructions, remaining in his room rather than be publicly embarrassed when the secretary emerged from the closed meeting to say, "You didn't make it."

Sure the business meeting was over, Howard entered a hotel elevator to go down to a scheduled presentation. The elevator stopped at the next floor down and who should step in but Harris P. Mosher himself.

Howard, as was customary at such encounters, once again tried to greet him, "Good morning, Dr. Mosher."

Instead of the usual vacant stare he expected, there was a twinkle in the man's eyes. "Well, Howard," he said, "they let you into the Otological Society, despite anything I could do."

Howard, unaware of his election, could only stammer back, "Yes, Dr. Mosher, they did. I'm very honored and I will always strive to adhere to the traditions of this great society."

"I know you will," Mosher replied and then, much to Howard's amazement, they walked into the meeting place together and sat next to each other while papers were being delivered and discussed.

At noon, Dr. Brown drew Howard to one side to say, "Let me tell you what happened at the meeting. The moment your name was brought up, Mosher jumped to his feet. I thought to myself, 'Well, here goes another tirade.' Instead, he spent five full minutes explaining why Howard House should be a member."

The memory of ten years of pain evaporated, and the pair were again as close as they had been when Howard left Mosher in Boston to go to Europe. From then on whenever Howard gave a paper at a professional meeting, Mosher was often the first to praise it.

Howard's last visit with this aging and infinitely complex titan occurred when the Otological Society held one of its annual meetings in Boston. Mosher, whose health was failing rapidly, invited about 30 members—Howard among them—to come to his home in Marblehead by chartered bus.

When the visit neared the end, Mosher called Howard over to the couch on which he was reclining. "When the others leave," he said, "let's talk."

Howard stayed, and at the end of the conversation, Mosher finally voiced what he had been aiming at all along. Clasping Howard's hand, he said with trembling lips, "Howard, I want you to know how proud I am of you."

It was a deathbed benediction.

24

Tears and Comedies

In 1951 when Howard was 43, Dr. Mackenzie Brown, who was retiring as chair of the ENT Department at USC, persuaded senior members that Howard, despite being junior to them, should be his successor. Howard was professionally qualified for the post and his organizational skills would be of benefit to the entire medical school—which faced an imperative need for a building program to give the school a home of its own. Howard accepted the role but also continued to attend to his private practice. He didn't shirk his new responsibilities, though, and his dedicated performance as a fund-raiser would later earn him the awed gratitude of the president of USC.

By 1954 Howard had performed some 5,000 fenestrations for hearing, and a similar number of mastoid operations for ear infections. In the years ahead, the number of major ear operations he performed would grow to 32,000, yet despite the total number—which included some cases of failure—he was never the object of a malpractice suit. Early in his experiences with fenestration surgery, however, he was summoned before the ethics committee of the Los Angeles County Medical Association to answer a strange charge.

Over the years Howard and his staff had developed various systems to make their procedures run smoothly. Whenever Howard judged a patient to be a candidate for fenestration or mastoid surgery, he would explain the nature of the operation, the prospects for success or failure, the length of hospitalization and convalescence, and the possible complications that could occur. He then urged patients to discuss these matters with their family or friends before finally deciding what they wanted to do.

However, when patients got home, it often happened they couldn't remember many of the technical details and so would then call Howard to clarify one or another point. Howard thought it would be helpful if he prepared booklets on mastoid and fenestration procedures, written in lay terms, which would contain all the information he had given orally. By adding a diagram of the ear, Howard hoped the publication, which could be read at leisure, would help prepare his patients for this delicate procedure.

The booklets he subsequently prepared were thus welcomed by his patients, but a nameless doctor filed a complaint against Howard with the ethics committee charging Howard with unethical advertising. Howard was staggered by a summons to answer the charge. He turned for advice to Dr. Brown, who though semiretired for several years, until his death in 1955, occupied space in Howard's office where he could see his patients. As a grateful student, Howard had invited his aging mentor to use these facilities gratis. In Brown's view, the interdicted booklets were the opposite of advertising for they demystified complex surgical procedures, giving patients necessary information if they were to make informed judgments about proceeding with surgery.

When the ethics committee met, Brown praised Howard, saying he should be commended for striving to provide a clear line of communication between himself and his patients. The committee members, for their part, dismissed the charges of unethical advertising and applauded the booklets themselves. Thus this innovative booklet was the first of many which Howard and his associates wrote and published on aspects of ear disorders. Soon otologists all over the country began to ask to use these helpful booklets in their own practice, and ordered them in bulk from the institute.

As Howard's practice expanded, so did his staff of nurses and secretaries. Also Howard began to hire, on a two-year basis, some of the younger doctors who had trained with him to work in the office and help teach new surgical techniques to other otologists who came to study. When Howard hired these associates he always explained that when they later established their own offices, they could take with them copies of their patients' records if the patients wished to continue under their care and they would be free to locate their offices anywhere they wished—even across the street from Howard's office.

One summer day in 1954 Lempert telephoned Howard from New York to say he was taking a two-week vacation— his first in many years. He and Flo were coming to Los Angeles where he had reserved a suite in the Beverly Wilshire Hotel. He went on to add, "I have a lot of patients in Los Angeles on whom I have operated and I would like you to see some of them. I will send you a list of their names so that you can invite them to your office."

Howard agreed and then to take advantage of this great man's visit, he asked Lempert to give a paper on fenestration surgery at a special dinner in his honor at the Los Angeles County Medical Association.

Howard's nurses contacted the 50 names on the patient list Lempert forwarded, asking them to come see Dr. Lempert on the appointed day. Howard himself took care of another preparatory touch. Knowing from his first meeting with Lempert in 1938 that he smoked a brand of large Dunhill cigars especially made for him at the then astronomical price of $100 for a box of 25, for years at

Christmas Howard had been sending a box to Lempert as a memento of his kindness. Now he ordered the same special brand and had the hotel deliver them as a welcoming present when his mentor checked in.

At two o'clock on the appointed day, Lempert's former patients filled Howard's large reception room and the hall outside. For the occasion Howard had also invited two Los Angeles otolaryngologists Lempert had trained in fenestration surgery in years past—Sylvan Goldberg and Victor Goodhill—colleagues Howard always respected with affection and respect who would make significant contributions to otology.

When Lempert arrived at Howard's office he happily bustled through the waiting crowd and was welcomed with cheers and applause. Five patients were already seated in the treatment rooms. After greeting his first patient, Lempert placed a special headlight that he had designed on his head—the same headlight Howard used—plugged it into the electric outlet and walked to the washbasin to scrub his hands. The instant he turned on the water he collapsed to the floor.

Howard thought he had suffered a heart attack. Some patients began to scream, and all were told to leave. Howard then felt Lempert's pulse and was relieved to find it had a regular, though weak, beat. Dr. Cryst, an internist, whose office was next to Howard's, arrived and examined Lempert, reporting that his heart was O.K. Lempert was coming to and began to complain of severe pains in his chest.

In the belief that he might have broken a bone when he fell, Don Blanche, an orthopedist in the building, was called and confirmed the fact that Lempert might have broken his shoulder. The elderly doctor refused to go to the hospital, but X-rays taken in Blanche's office revealed that the tubercle—a projection of bone from the upper part of the arm near the shoulder—had been pulled off completely on the right side and partially on the left side. Lempert had suffered a severe electric shock when he began to wash his hands while using a turned-on headlight. The shock caused a severe contraction in the chest muscles, which in turn caused the tubercle separation.

When Howard started to show the X-rays to Lempert, he said, "Don't tell me, the pain is so severe on trying to move my arms that my bones must be broken." He asked for a cigar. So Howard reached into Lempert's pocket, got one out, chewed off the tip, lit it, and put it in his mouth.

"You know, Howard," he said, "I have had a very rough life. Here I am in Los Angeles to have a good time and this accident happened. It is the story of my life." Tears came into his eyes. The orthopedist put Lempert's left arm in a sling and his right arm in an airplane cast but Lempert would not consider taking medication for his pain. "Medicine," he said, "is to give, not to take." All he wanted was to be helped to his chauffeured limousine so he could return to his hotel.

Sylvan Goldberg, Victor Goodhill and Howard accompanied him back to the Beverly Wilshire and during the ride they watched Lempert wince in pain with each bump on the road. At the hotel, when the limousine disgorged the four doctors, the doorman seeing the airplane cast (in which the arm is at right angles to the chest) asked Lempert in dismay, "What in the world happened to you?"

A weak but feisty Lempert answered, "They tried to electrocute me!"

With this rigid arm cast it was impossible for Lempert to pass though the hotel's revolving doors so the manager guided him and his helpmates through a side-door entrance. When Flo saw her ashen-faced husband being gingerly led into the suite by three doctors and the hotel manager, she cried out, "My God, Julius! What happened?"

A flustered Howard explained as best he could while they tried to find a comfortable chair for Lempert. When Lempert was trying to get comfortable in a soft French chair, but the chair's arm kept bumping the splint, so the manager summoned a hotel carpenter who promptly sawed off the chair arm.

Lempert instructed the medical trio, "Give me three nurses around the clock and a secretary because I am still working on my paper for tomorrow night."

Howard not only offered to leave some pain medicine with Lempert but also offered to spend that night caring for him, but Lempert refused both. Howard then announced he was going to cancel the county medical meeting the next evening. Again Lempert was adamant, he was not going to disappoint all the doctors who were due to be there.

Flo stepped in and suggested Howard could read his paper. "No," Lempert answered emphatically. Finally when Howard proposed that Lempert skip the dinner and arrive in time to read his paper, Lempert began to waver.

Howard recalls that memorable evening: "The next evening when I introduced Lempert to an overflow audience, I remarked 'Tonight you are witnessing the extraordinary dedication of a doctor who, in defiance of all the pain he has suffered, came here only because he did not want to disappoint you.' I then explained the accident, and meant every word of my tribute.

"Lempert's paper was a massive affair and he read it all. I stood by his side to turn the pages as he read because he couldn't use his arms. He began to sweat. I reached over to pull a bright red handkerchief from the pocket of his dapper suit. To my surprise and to the enjoyment of the audience, I kept pulling and pulling and like a magician's handkerchief, it kept coming and coming until I had a huge wad of red silk in my hand. I continued to turn each page and wipe his brow. Soon he asked for some water. I tried to hold the glass to his lips around the cast but water dribbled down his chin onto his shirt. I had to mop his shirt, chin and mouth, as well as his brow, before I could resume turning the pages.

"About half way through, Lempert asked for a cigar. I reached inside his coat, pulled out one of his big Dunhills and bit off the tip for him. With the glass of water in the other hand and not knowing what to do with the cigar tip, I finally just swallowed it. From that point on, the audience's laughter increased as I lit the cigar and held it while he took a couple of puffs. I was now juggling the glass of water, the cigar, turning the pages and mopping him with his huge red hanky. By the end of the hour, I was exhausted. The audience expressed their appreciation for both the fine lecture and the unexpected show by giving Lempert a long and well-deserved standing ovation."

Two weeks later Lempert had to return to New York where he had a whole year's surgery waiting for him. When Howard and the nurse, who was going along for the return trip to New York, arrived to escort the Lemperts to the train station, two extra cabs were needed merely to transport their luggage. Lempert always refused to fly saying, "If the pope blesses the plane before he flies, what chance does a little Jewish boy have?"

As a medical consultant to the Santa Fe Railroad Howard had been able to arrange a drawing room for the party—something that was hard to get. But even at that, it was impossible to pile three people and all their luggage into the drawing rooms, so Howard had most of it stored in the baggage car. Despite the gain in space it still seemed that a crowbar would be needed to wedge Lempert with his airplane cast into the room. The cross-country trip was bound to be an ordeal. As he said good-bye, Howard offered, "Dr. Lempert, I don't see how you are going to operate with that airplane cast. If I can be of help, just call and I'll be there."

In New York, Lempert insisted on going ahead with his scheduled cases. Doctors Meltzer, Morehead and Hoople would start the surgeries, then Lempert would enter the operating rooms wearing his airplane cast, which he placed on the chest of the patient. Using the dental drill, he would make the tiny, delicate fenestra opening, following which one of the assisting doctors would finish the operation. Howard would regularly call Meltzer to ask how things were going and invariably get the reply, "Unless you were here, Howard, you wouldn't believe it. Despite Julius' cast, he continues to make his usual, beautiful fenestration windows."

Lempert had triumphed over the constraints of his own anatomy. He could not know he was about a year away from the time when an accidental rediscovery of an alternative approach to the surgical treatment of otosclerosis would make his fenestration surgery obsolete.

During this same period Howard's life was marked by a series of personal experiences that bordered on the burlesque. One Sunday morning Howard was stricken with severe pain caused by a kidney stone. After being hospitalized, his doctor told him it might be necessary to open his back if the stone could not be removed from below.

Howard's room presently resembled Grand Central Station with myriad visitors, including Lloyd Bridges, the actor, and Dr. Carl Hansen, a visiting Danish ear specialist, who voiced his concern about the possible surgery Howard faced. Explaining that doctors in Denmark seldom operated for kidney stones, he passed on their finding that by giving patients four bottles of Danish beer within an hour—and then having them jump up and down 20 times stiff legged on a solid floor—in 90 percent of the cases the pressure of the urine and the sudden trauma of the jumping dislodged the stone without surgery.

After Hansen left the room Bridges, who had heard the conversation, thought the prescribed treatment was a "great idea." He absented himself and returned with four bottles of beer, apologizing that he couldn't locate any brewed by Danes. Bridges said good-bye and good luck, and Howard told the nurse that he wanted to rest and that no one, not even his family, was to come into his room.

The first bottle of beer was delicious. The second went down with a little more difficulty. After the third, Howard thought he would explode and finally he knew he would have to stop after downing only a half of the fourth bottle.

Climbing backwards over the bed rails, he took his first stiff-legged jump onto the floor and proceeded to almost faint from the pain. In no way could he manage 20 jumps. Finally he decided he could only make one big jump. Fortunately the toilet was close by and the door to it was open. There was no time to get a strainer as instructed and use it—he was a fire hose in action.

To Howard's surprise, the acute pain and pressure were suddenly gone and he returned to his bed and called the nurse who, on seeing him all smiles, said, "My, the rest did you a lot of good."

Howard explained that he had urinated, whereupon the nurse looked at the strainer and was disappointed not to see the stone. Unable to explain that because of the off-beat procedure he had gone through he had no time to use the strainer, Howard tried to look chagrined. A few punches on his back without a painful reaction suggested that he must have passed the stone, but X-rays showed the stone was still present, although its position had changed and it had rotated. This had allowed the backed-up urine to pass and hopefully the stone would pass by itself. If not, it could easily be removed from below.

Two months after undergoing the beer technique, Howard was due to go to Germany for a lecture tour. His doctor suggested he have the stone removed beforehand so Howard checked into the hospital. The normal procedure, done under a general anesthetic, entails the use of a cystoscope which is passed from below into the bladder and on into the ureter. The stone is grasped with a basket forceps, similar to a small basket on the end of a rod, and then removed.

The "Hazards of Being Howard" were at work so unfortunately there were slight abnormalities. As Howard later explained,

"When I awoke from the anesthetic, I saw the distressed faces of my two sons and my wife. My older son Ken said that everything was okay, *but* the doctor wants to talk to you 'right away.' Before the doctor arrived, I felt something must be very wrong; whereupon I raised the bed covers, looked below and to my horrified surprise, saw his surgical instrument still sticking out of me.

"The doctor, on his arrival, explained that nothing of the sort had ever happened to him before. After gripping the stone in the basket he had worked 45 minutes trying to get the instrument out, but stopped for fear that he might tear the ureter. He would try again the next morning to remove the instrument.

"It was no easy thing to deal with three legs. I spent a restless night trying to figure out what to do if the doctor did not succeed in removing the instrument. The next morning the doctor grabbed the instrument with both hands, gave a quick jerk and it came out. It wasn't exactly painless but everyone involved was pleased to see both the basket and stone, for there was always the possibility that the basket could break off in the ureter."

Other humorous incidents seemed to plague the ever-jovial Howard. Once on a flight from London to New York in a four-engine propeller plane, the passenger seated next to Howard was a woman of 65 who had never flown before and was very nervous. Howard, who can set his face in what is called a "sincere look"—which combined with his comforting voice explains why people tend to believe what he says—tried to quiet his companion by listing in advance what was due to happen on the take-off and in flight. There would be the roar of the engines, the creak of raised wheels, the flaps on the plane being adjusted and so on through the whole manual.

After supper, the passengers were made comfortable with pillows and blankets and the woman slept as the plane sped west through the night across the Atlantic. Shortly before daybreak, the far engine on Howard's side of the plane began to stammer and "feather down." On awakening at daybreak the woman looked out of the window, saw that one propeller was turning very slowly and shook Howard into consciousness crying, "Something is terribly wrong with that motor! We're going to crash into the ocean!"

Howard leaned over to get a better look through the window. "I see," he said, with majestic calm, "but don't worry. It's been a long trip and pilots rest their engines from time to time."

Fortunately in his practice he never invented such outrageous lies to calm a distraught patient, but it seemed appropriate here. The woman, like Howard's trusting patients, believed him and soon snuggled back into her pillow and went back to sleep. As for Howard, he was scared to death and didn't breathe easily until the pilot made an unscheduled landing in Boston for repairs.

During another episode at a College of Surgeons meeting in Chicago, Howard exhibited control that would have done credit to a Hollywood actor. Another friend in attendance at the meeting was his friend Dr. Joe de Los Reyes, a surgeon for the Los Angeles Police Department and a notorious prankster. At check-out time they met in the lobby and learned they were to be on the same flight back to Los Angeles. Both welcomed the chance to travel together.

At the airport Howard could not find his bags and gave his ticket to Joe saying, "Check me in while I locate my luggage." A few minutes later, Joe rejoined him to say the plane they were meant to be on was still grounded in New York, but he had transferred their tickets to a TWA flight that was leaving immediately. They had to run. In the dash across the tarmac, Joe had enough breath to say "You owe me $44. You had a coach ticket and the only seats left were in first class."

They scampered up the ramp and into the plane, the last passengers on the plane and the stewardess congratulated them for having just made it. "Unfortunately," she added, "there are no seats together."

Joe flashed his police badge. "I am," he said, "a Los Angeles police officer and I'm taking this prisoner back. We will have to sit together."

Howard was dumbfounded. So was the stewardess. She approached two men sitting together and asked in a voice that echoed the length of the cabin, "We have a police officer and a prisoner coming aboard. Would you mind separating so they can sit together?"

They acquiesced and as the pair walked down the aisle, every eye in the airplane was on Howard who had fallen into the role. As they passed one seat he overheard a woman say to her husband, "You can always tell a criminal just by looking at one."

Once the plane was airborne, the stewardess approached Joe and asked, "Officer, would you like to have a cocktail?"

"Yes," he said "I will have a martini."

"What about him?" the stewardess asked pointing at Howard.

"O.K." said Joe, "he can have one beer."

When she returned, she carried a tray with some tasty-looking canapes and a martini which she gave to Joe. Howard was given a glass and a bottle of beer with the cap off, but no canapes.

Presently the captain of the plane came down the aisle. Giving Howard a hard look he asked Joe, "Officer, is everything O.K.?"

Joe, who was happily munching his canapes, smiled warmly, "Mighty fine, Captain. Everything is under control."

Later the stewardess returned to ask if Joe would like another drink and he ordered another martini. Neither she nor Joe deemed it necessary to ask Howard whether he wanted seconds. Fortunately he was not denied a tray for dinner.

Later on Howard told Joe he had to go to the toilet and received "permission" to do so. When he reached the galley where the stewardesses were busy stacking trays, Howard tried to see if they would talk to him. Staring at him as though he were a wild man, they wordlessly backed up against the wall. Getting no response, Howard disappeared into the lavatory, but on reemerging made another attempt to engage the stewardesses in conversation. "My" he said, "you even cook and have running water and toilets aboard. It's my first airplane ride and it's amazing."

They stood mutely frozen and so he rejoined Joe, glaring down everyone he passed on the aisle. When finally the plane taxied to a halt in L.A. Howard headed for the exit with Joe coming right behind, his coat draped over an arm as if it concealed a pistol aimed at his back.

Stopping at the exit door for a final word with the stewardesses, Howard said, "I want to thank you for all you've done. In my whole life I never had an experience like this." He shook his head, "It's hard to believe they really pay you for having this wonderful job up here."

But not even in farewell were the stewardesses willing to break their stony silence. Howard proceeded down the stairs, and then turned around to see Joe talking to the same stewardess whose faces now were a picture of raw terror.

Jauntily Joe joined him and said, "I never had more fun in my life. I told them that you were one of the ten most-wanted criminals in the country. You had raped eight women and murdered two of them."

To this day Howard owes Joe the $44, with no intention of paying—ever!

The air seemed to hold special adventures for Howard—which was also a reflection of his extensive travels on professional business. On another flight from Chicago to Los Angeles where he and Aram Glorig had attended a medical meeting in Chicago, Howard left a sleeping Aram to use the lavatory. On opening the door, he saw a woman, about 25, seated on the toilet with her head lying on the basin. She did not move.

Howard found the stewardess and explained the door was not locked and that she should check on the condition of the woman. After he had returned to his seat, another stewardess approached to ask if he were a medical doctor and would he come look at the woman?

In the tiny lavatory space the stewardess sat on the wash-basin not knowing what to do with the immobile woman who was unconscious on the toilet seat. It was not a lavatory built for three but Howard ran through the list of possibilities—diabetic coma, heart attack, stroke. The stewardess mentioned that when the woman got onto the plane she obviously had been drinking a great deal and instead of eating her dinner she had drunk two cocktails.

Leaning over and smelling the woman's breath, Howard concurred. The diagnosis was obvious, but they had to get the woman off the toilet and back to her seat. He managed to put his hand under one armpit while the stewardess did the same on the opposite side.

"I'll count three," Howard said, "and we will both lift at the same time." They heaved on the count but nothing happened. She wasn't that heavy, but a second attempt didn't budge her. Finally Howard got a headlock on the woman and pulled up slowly, stretching her neck, but the rest of her body failed to follow.

This can't be! he thought, taking a fresh grip he then jerked her up with all his strength. There was a sudden explosive "PLOP!" and the woman came flying up at him with so much force that Howard hit his head against the door while she fell to her knees. It turned out when she first staggered to the lavatory, she had forgotten to put down the seat and had wedged herself into the aluminum bowl as tight as a cork in a wine bottle.

The stewardess asked Howard to sit on the toilet—the seat now down—and hold the woman on his lap while she tried to draw her girdle up to its proper position. It was an impossible task, so she proceeded to remove the girdle and her stockings and then the two of them managed to get the bundle of joy on her feet.

Howard then placed his arms around the woman's waist to start a parade back the narrow aisle to a vacant seat. He finally figured out a workable procedure—by kicking his one leg forward and then the other he managed to make some headway. Just then Glorig woke from a deep sleep and at first thought he was dreaming when he saw Howard kicking this woman along the aisle. After depositing the woman in her seat, the stewardess draped her with a blanket, and Howard returned to Glorig where, with some difficulty, he tried to explain that he was not fighting with this strange young woman.

As the plane approached Los Angeles, the captain told Howard that a man with a wheelchair would meet the woman—welcome news because he had envisioned himself kicking the woman across the length of the airport. When they landed Howard saw an anxious-looking young man waiting on the tarmac with a wheelchair and porter. "I thought to myself," Howard later remarked "that when he gets her home and takes a look, she will never be able to explain where she got such a huge, red ring on her bottom."

Not all Howard's adventures during these years were airborne larks, however. And some had serious consequences.

In performing the complex fenestration operation, occasionally the eardrum tears. When that happens, it will not heal and the patient's hearing will not improve. Once when Howard was operating on a beautiful, young 18-year-old girl, this misfortune happened.

"When I saw the torn eardrum," Howard later recalled, "I pushed my chair away from the table with a sick feeling in my stomach and a sense of despair. I knew, however, that I must at least try to repair the eardrum. After considerable troubled thought, I made three slits in the remaining portion of the eardrum so they would drop into the middle ear. The lining of the middle ear was 'freshened' to provide a raw surface on which I placed a small skin graft taken from behind the ear."

For the next three weeks Howard lived in an anxious state which ended in jubilant relief when the young woman appeared in his office to say she could hear "beautifully." This, so far as could be determined at the time, was the first successful repair of an eardrum with a skin graft.

Howard, who had but recently been elected to the American Otological Society, decided not only to deliver a paper but also a motion picture of this stumbled-upon repair technique at a meeting of the society. When he finished, there was polite applause at the end, but none of the usual questions and discussions that follow a talk on a new surgical procedures which made Howard conclude he must be the only one who had experienced the described mishap.

In the hallway after the meeting adjourned, however, Howard felt better when he was stopped by several otologists who pressed him with many questions about his new procedure. Finally it dawned on him these surgeons had probably hesitated to ask questions in the public meeting because doing so might imply that they, too, had torn eardrums during the fenestration operation.

Another challenging case where Howard tripped himself up during surgery also demonstrates his talent to improvise and soothe. Once an internationally known concert pianist came to him because her career was endangered by hearing impaired by chronic ear disease in both ears. Even though the infection had been controlled, a hole persisted in both eardrums with consequent partial disruption of the little ear bones.

At that time the only known way of restoring hearing in such a case was by using the "Pohlman Insert" named after Dr. Augustus Pohlman who was an otolaryngologist and professor of comparative anatomy at Western Reserve University Medical School in Cleveland. When Pohlman retired he accepted Howard's invitation to move to his office, again without cost, so Pohlman could continue his research on a unique method to replace damaged eardrums and ear bones.

The "Pohlman Insert" consisted of two silver bands, one of which fit tightly inside the other like an embroidery hoop, which in turn fit into the ear canal. Thin rubber was stretched between these two hoops to resemble a vibrating eardrum. A piece of cigarette paper was glued onto the rubber and a small hole was made in it so that a nylon fish leader line could be passed through the artificial eardrum.

One cupped end contacted the stapes and the other extended to the opening of the external ear canal so the patient could move the nylon back and forth until it contacted the normal stapes, thereby allowing the sound once again to travel across the ear to the hearing nerve.

The concept and device were ingenious, but short-lived, following the introduction of surgical techniques to reconstruct the eardrum and middle ear.

When the concert pianist arrived in Los Angeles, Howard informed her he would first operate on the poorer of the two ears. Under general anesthesia he removed the remaining eardrum and proceeded to install the Pohlman Insert.

Later that evening when he was making his hospital rounds, the pianist asked Howard why he had operated on her better ear. Not betraying his surprise that the nurses had obviously draped the wrong ear for surgery, Howard confidently told her that when she was under anesthetic he examined both ears more thoroughly and believed his best chance to improve her hearing at once would be to operate on the ear he chose even though it was the better ear.

The patient was effusive in her expressions of gratitude and was even more so three weeks later, when the insert which he was taught to make by Dr. Pohlman was set in place and she regained her hearing. Later the pianist returned for a repeat operation and insert on her second ear.

After this surgery she asked Howard whether he had any children and if they played the piano. He said he had three and planned to get a piano for them sometime in the future. Five days after this conversation, a truck came to a stop in the driveway of the House home and out hopped not only a delivery men but also the store manager who told Helen they were delivering a Mason Hammond grand piano for her.

Helen insisted there must be a mistake, telephoning Howard at his office—who was equally ignorant of the affair. Finally the mystery was cleared up because the records showed the piano was a gift from the concert pianist who had played many pianos in Los Angeles storerooms before finding the exact one with the right touch to be sent to the doctor who had restored her hearing—though she never knew of the initial mistake in the sequence of the operations.

Months later she was to give a concert in Boston and phoned Howard to say she was urgently in need of more rubber for her Pohlman inserts. Howard somehow could not tell her the rubber came from condoms and all she had to do was to go to the corner drug store and get a packet, so he asked one of his new nurses to go to the drugstore and pick up some condoms without also explaining to her their intended use.

The nurse flushed with embarrassment when the druggist looked at her with arched surprise as she told him to put them on Dr. House's bill. Only on returning to the office did someone explain this was a normal request for they used the rubber in the inserts. Howard cut appropriate one-inch squares and sent them air mail special delivery to Boston speculating that it was probably a novel way to send condoms across the country.

Late one afternoon in 1955 the nurse-receptionist in Howard's office received a telephone call: "I'm Mr. Curtis from Detroit. My ears are plugged and I must see Dr. House this afternoon."

Unimpressed, she replied that the doctor was very busy. Would Mr. Curtis care to make an appointment for another day?

No. The man hung up, but his secretary was on the phone minutes later. "Tell Dr. House," she said, "Mr. Curtis is the president of General Motors and he must give a talk tonight. His ear is plugged from flying and that affects his speaking voice."

Responding to this emergency, the nurse-receptionist said, "Oh! Have him come right over."

Curtis shortly arrived, a man in charge, determined to control his environment. He refused to submit to the usual hearing test saying he simply wanted his eustachian tube "blown out" as had been done for him by Dr. Jim Robb, his own ear doctor in Detroit.

Howard complied and did what the man asked, but without benefit. When he applied a tuning fork to Curtis's ear, the results indicated that Curtis' hearing nerve in the ear was not functioning, so Howard explained that the little blood vessel supplying the nerve of the inner ear may have gone into spasm, thus cutting off circulation. If so, to "blow out" the ear was like trying to fix a telephone when the wire has been cut.

Curtis hesitantly agreed to a hearing test which confirmed Howard's fears—Curtis' hearing nerve was severely damaged and he must immediately have emergency treatment.

"The more I talked," so Howard later recalled, "the more I could sense that he viewed me as though I were a country rube trying to outsmart him. So finally I suggested to him, 'Why don't we call Dr. Robb in Detroit now? I will explain the problem and you can talk to him.'

"I got Dr. Robb on the phone and reported what I had found. As his patient was due to be in Los Angeles for three days, I suggested starting him on intensive treatment until his return to Detroit. Dr. Robb asked to speak to Curtis again and told him, 'Do what Dr. House wants you to do.' But Curtis would do nothing of the sort. Instead he canceled all his scheduled meetings in Los Angeles and flew back to Detroit in the morning."

Howard heard nothing more from Curtis until he telephoned three months later wanting to apologize for his bad behavior. On returning to Detroit, Dr. Robb's test of his hearing confirmed Howard's diagnosis about the dead nerve in one ear. Also, said Curtis, he had not as yet received a bill.

"You never will," Howard replied. "I know that General Motors gives a million dollars a year to the Medical Association for medical educational purposes. Anyone who does that will never get a bill from me for medical services."

Curtis was pleasantly surprised that Howard was even aware of this—since most doctors were not. "When I appear before our annual stockholders meeting," he added, "I always have to justify giving the million dollars. It's hard to impress upon the stockholders the importance of good health care."

Nonetheless, Curtis urged Howard to send him a bill and when the latter refused, Curtis told Howard to "give him a call" if there was anything he could ever do for him. Something *did* turn up a year later.

In 1956, the Board of Trustees of USC bought eight acres of land near the County Hospital as the site of the new medical school. Howard had been picked to chair a "Kick-Off Dinner," marking the start of the drive for building funds. A week before the dinner, Howard received a call from a certain Mrs. Bishop whom he had never heard of, complaining of head noise. She said she could not come to his office because of her physical disabilities, but wondered if he could see her at the Ambassador Hotel where she was staying.

After office hours he went to see Mrs. Bishop, an elderly woman, in her suite. Not knowing whether she was passing through or a long-time hotel resident, Howard did note the beautiful antiques that cluttered the apartment and suspected the latter was the case. Beyond this, all he knew was that she was another mortal in physical discomfort who was in need of medical help and reassurance.

After questioning Mrs. Bishop about her symptoms, Howard examined her ears and conducted some simple tests, concluding the noise in her head was a case of tinnitus. He prescribed certain treatments for it and though he had not as yet had his supper, he spent some time with her, drawing pictures of her ear to explain her condition and assure her she was not suffering from a tumor, nor would she be going deaf. As he left the suite he told Mrs. Bishop, as was his wont with all patients, to contact him if she had any further need.

That week the kick-off dinner drew media interest and the Los Angeles press devoted space to Howard's role as the chair of the drive for building funds for the USC Medical School. He was in a final preparatory meeting of the dinner committee when they were interrupted by a telephone call from Mrs. Bishop who insisted on seeing Howard that evening.

Wondering what he could tell her about tinnitus that he had not already told her, he hesitated and then was surprised when she asked him over the phone if he liked lady fingers and brandy. He managed to say that he did and that he would call at her apartment later in the evening.

On his arrival, as she was serving him the promised lady fingers and brandy, Mrs. Bishop told him she was pleased with his clear explanation of her ear problems and that the treatment he prescribed had helped the ringing in her ear. She certainly felt better by understanding her problem, but why had he not told her about the fund-raising drive for the USC Medical School? Why had she learned about it only through newspaper accounts?

Howard was baffled but sat listening to Mrs. Bishop describe her beloved husband, now dead for 20 years. She was anxious to do something in his memory. Suddenly she stopped and asked Howard what the purpose of the building program was.

The purpose, Howard explained, was to provide classrooms for medical students. She then asked how high was the highest building in the plans. Ten stories, Howard replied. Just how much, Mrs. Bishop wondered, would it cost to put a floor in for a building of that height? Plucking a figure out of thin air, Howard said, "About $100,000 a floor."

"Well," she replied, "ten times $100,000 is one million dollars." Looking pleased she said, "That will be my contribution to the USC Medical School. I want it to go for the construction of the tallest building on the campus which is to be named after my husband. I also want you to know that I am giving the gift because of the way you came to me when I needed you. My attorney will call on you in the morning with a check."

Deciding Mrs. Bishop was senile and totally out of her mind, Howard assumed his best "sincere" manner, thanking her profusely for the prospective gift and dwelt on how the building would make a wonderful memorial to her husband.

What to his wondering eyes, the next day Mrs. Bishop's attorney called on Howard and actually gave him her check for a million dollars. The lawyer passed on one more request: Mrs. Bishop wanted the first spadeful of dirt on the construction site to be turned within six months.

Only then did a bedazzled Howard ask Mrs. Bishop's identity. Her attorney explained she was an heiress of the Union Carbide Company and that her late husband owned lumber and coal yards around the country. The lawyer added that Mrs. Bishop had one small quirk: she never let her checking account fall below a million dollars—because she could never tell when she might wish to do something quickly.

After the lawyer departed, Howard got the president of the USC on the phone. "Send someone over to my office," he said, "and pick up a million dollar check I am holding for the building fund." It all added up to a case of simple arithmetic. One house call plus one elderly woman who revered the memory of her deceased husband, plus one compassionate treatment of her tinnitus, equaled the gift which made possible the construction of what is now the John Edward Bishop building. Needless to say, it was a euphoric "kick" for the Kick-Off Dinner.

At the dinner held in the ballroom of the Biltmore Hotel, 21 "notables" were seated at the head table—all of whom Howard was to introduce. Many he knew by name, including his wife, Helen, who was seated next to him. As he went down the table, Howard skipped past her because he planned to introduce her last, but in the end he forgot. He was unaware of the slight until a friend called his attention to it just as the dinner was over.

The couple had come separately in two cars which enabled Howard to speed home where he pinned a penitent note to his wife's pillow which read: "You name it and I'll buy it." Then Howard jumped into bed and feigned sleep when Helen came home.

The next morning, he crept out of bed early and tip-toed into the bathroom where he spied a note pasted on the mirror: "A white Cadillac with red leather upholstery."

Two weeks later they were to attend a medical meeting in Montreal and Howard suggested they buy a car for Helen in the east and drive it to Montreal. Some doctor friends advised him that if he ordered the car from a dealer in Flint, Michigan, it would come equipped with a free air conditioner.

The dealer welcomed Howard's telephone order, but regretted not having a white Cadillac with red upholstery in stock. A special order from the factory would take a month.

Howard asked if it would help any if he called Mr. Curtis. Unconvinced, the dealer sarcastically said, "If you know Mr. Curtis it can't hurt."

So Howard proceeded to call and explain the problem in Flint, Michigan to Mr. Curtis who was delighted to be contacted—though he wished Howard had approached him directly without going to a dealer.

Some ten minutes later, the dealer telephoned Howard to say in a deferential voice, "Mr. Curtis, whom I have never talked to personally, called to tell me that the car would be delivered in one week." He personally offered to meet Helen and Howard at the airport when they arrived and take them to his showroom.

When Helen saw her new car she was thrilled—until she spotted its Goodyear tires. "That would never do!" Helen said, explaining to the befuddled dealer her fierce loyalty to their good friend, Leonard Firestone—who was Howard's patient and had served on the board of trustees of the Los Angeles Foundation of Otology—meant she could only drive on Firestone tires.

By now it was after five o'clock and the local Firestone distributor was closed for the day. The dealer contacted the distributor at home explaining the problem, referring to Leonard Firestone's connection with the couple.

That evening while the car dealer entertained this couple who could invoke the names of two of the supreme titans in the car world at his country club, the Firestone distributor returned to his place of business and replaced the Goodyear with Firestone tires.

As a placated Helen was being given the keys to her new car, she asked what the small initials "S.P." on the windshield meant. The dealer explained they stood for Specially Produced. For the special Cadillac to be produced in time for Howard and Helen's arrival in Flint, Mr. Curtis stopped the regular assembly line to give their Cadillac the right of way over everything else while each supervisor personally examined what went into the car. "Mr. Curtis," said the dealer, "can do anything."

The finished product was without a rattle or squeak and remained in continuous use for more than a quarter of a century. A brass plate on the dashboard announced, "Specially made for Helen House."

Mr. Curtis's power "to do anything," however, was not absolute. Although he could stop an assembly line to give the right-of-way to an SP car, because of the deafness in one ear, he could not determine the direction of sounds when he was duck hunting which resulted in a gruesome and tragic accident—and a fatal wound to a close friend while they were hunting.

25

The Setting and the Rising Sun

Toward the mid-1950s, Howard received a call from his friend, Dr. Joseph Goldman, chair of the ENT department at New York's Mt. Sinai Hospital to say that a member of his staff, Dr. Samuel Rosen, who had been working on a new type of operation known as stapes mobilization to restore hearing to otosclerosis patients, would soon be contacting Howard.

"Howard," Rosen said when he telephoned, "I've been developing something that may interest you and I'd like you to see the effects with your own eyes. Can you come to New York?"

"When?" Howard asked.

The reply was, "Right away."

As Howard listened to Rosen's description about the new operation, an electric chill rippled up and down his spine. If the evidence continued to back the success Rosen had with the first handful of cases, the event would usher in a new surgical approach to otosclerosis and the Lempert age of fenestration surgery would be eclipsed. Immediately Howard rearranged his schedule and flew to New York.

Rosen had hit upon the technique by accident, he explained. While performing fenestration surgery on a patient, he had tested the extent to which the stapes was fixed in place by otosclerosis. When the pressure of the instrument he used loosened the stapes, the patient erupted in a joyful shout, "Doctor, I can hear!"

Rosen called his new technique "stapes mobilization," which in some respects could be considered a sophisticated and surgical method of the "self-mobilization" method used by that 19th-century English Lord who had jiggled a silver rod vigorously on his eardrum to loosen the otosclerosis-locked stapes in his ear—which enabled him to hear for a few months before he would repeat the precarious procedure that also scarred his eardrum.

Now Howard watched Rosen perform this stapes mobilization operation and witnessed the patient's joyful reaction when the eardrum was put back in place: "I can hear! I can hear!"

The mobilization procedure Rosen worked out promised to overcome the known problems of fenestration surgery—which was a delicate, complex operation with a protracted recovery period. So much anatomy was impacted in such a small space in which the surgeon operated that the slightest anatomical structural variation—in the location, for example, of the facial nerve—could have ruinous consequences for the patients if the attending surgeon was not at maximum alert at every step. Stapes mobilization had its own risks, but they were of a lesser magnitude and the recovery period was generally brief.

As Howard ended his New York visit, Rosen gave him a set of the unique instruments he had developed so Howard could practice with them—first on cadavers and then on patients. Back in Los Angeles, Howard proceeded with headlight, magnifying lenses and an otoscope to mobilize the tiny stapes, wholeheartedly experimenting with the new technique, though he was also troubled by the fact that many of the mobilized stapes became fixed again and the hearing regressed. It was clear to him, as it was to Rosen, that ways must be found to prevent such refixation. Only then would the concept of stapes mobilization gain wide acceptance.

In the winter of 1955 Rosen was scheduled to deliver a paper before the National Triological Society. The text, covering 200 stapes cases, included those where surgery had been performed by a handful of cooperating otologists—Howard among them—who sent Rosen copies of the relevant records, who in turn generously acknowledged their contributions.

Some time after Rosen's paper was presented at the Triological meeting, Howard received a phone call from Dr. Kenneth Day of Pittsburgh, president of the American Otologic Society, proposing the idea of having Julius Lempert and Sam Rosen on the same program at the forthcoming meeting of the Society. What did Howard think? One would present a paper on fenestration and the other a paper on stapes mobilization.

Howard concurred, adding that it would generate an interesting discussion pro and con.

At the meeting itself, when Lempert gave his paper, he decried the "terrible thing Rosen was doing to patients through his stapes mobilization operation." Rosen, mindful of his own immense debt to Lempert, tried in his own presentation to turn away the older man's wrath.

Sitting in the audience, Howard mused that Lempert's fierce attack on Rosen was similar to the blind hostility Lempert himself had experienced earlier in his own career. His thoughts on the point were suddenly broken by the voice of Kenneth Day who, without forewarning, called on Howard to start the discussion of the two papers.

As he walked to the lectern, Howard wondered what he could safely say amid the cross fire between his two friends. Opening the discussion by remarking on Lempert's work—now recognized as a dependable technique to restore hearing—he went on to discuss Rosen's work—which he had seen—and which incorporated Lempert's technique to raise up the eardrum and expose the middle ear. Howard then mentioned the several stapes mobilizations he himself had performed which combined Lempert's ear canal approach with Rosen's concepts and instruments. Some patients suffering from otosclerosis had been helped by this new method while others experienced short-lived benefits because of the refixation of the stapes. Only time could render the ultimate judgment on the worth of Dr. Rosen's innovative surgery in dealing with otosclerosis.

Lempert, the brilliant innovator of new surgical techniques, seemed unable to accept the inexorable nature of progress in science that comes as practitioners seek different ways to deal with medical problems. At the end of the session Lempert invited Howard to lunch where he launched into a two-hour diatribe saying the stapes mobilization surgery could never work and if Howard encouraged this movement he would be "setting otosclerosis surgery back 50 years."

Howard could only repeat that it was too early to tell what the final result would be, but he reminded Lempert that "Change is constant and happy are those that can change with it." The two men parted as friends and remained so, but not so with Rosen for Lempert was devoured from within by personal bitterness toward Sam Rosen and his work.

Meanwhile, it was left to Howard to develop a project which never got off the ground in Lempert's hands. Like Lempert, Howard always told his patients prior to surgery they had a two percent chance that their hearing would be worse than before and a one percent chance that they could not hear even with the most powerful hearing aid. Howard was particularly bothered by these two out of the hundred where an operation would go well, but three weeks later the patient, on testing, would have a nerve-type hearing loss that was permanent and inexplicable.

Years before when Howard saw Dorothy Wolff's temporal bone work at Washington University in St. Louis, he had suggested that her research would be enhanced if a patient's history was available. Subsequently the idea of a temporal bone bank gained prominence after the death of Margaret Sullivan, the actress, when it was learned she had bequeathed her temporal bones to Lempert who had performed fenestration surgery to help her hearing.

Convinced anew that a temporal bone bank would fit in with the work of the Los Angeles Foundation of Otology, Howard began promoting setting up a program whereby patients would be asked to pledge their temporal bones to the foundation after their deaths. Through this temporal bone acquisition program the cause of their hearing impairment could be studied under the microscope and compared with the patients' life histories.

The impetus for this push came from a case where the surgery failed. The patient, an elderly woman, had a fenestration operation which unfortunately resulted in a dead ear. It was Howard's bleak duty to gently inform her three weeks later of the complication. He risked outraging the woman by what he said next—which was also the first time he had said anything of the sort to a patient.

"I'd like," Howard said, "for you to consider willing your ear bones to our foundation on your death. We simply don't know why or how this happened to you and only through research can we find the answer. A study of your temporal bones could conceivably shed light on how your misfortune could be avoided in the future. It won't help you or me, but it might help members of your own family, because otosclerosis is hereditary."

Howard later said that if the woman had been offended by the suggestion, he probably would not have had the nerve to put the same request to other patients, but the gracious woman responded enthusiastically and following her death, her family honored her pledge. Hers was the first temporal bone to be acquired in the foundation's new bank and from this modest start, the temporal bone bank was destined to grow into a major instrument for otologic research.

A main source of support for research in otology came from Collete Ramsey of New York whose hearing had been restored by Lempert. She subsequently established the Deafness Research Foundation (DRF) in 1958—with Howard as a founding board member—to provide funds for ear research.

The DRF appointed Dr. John Lindsay of the University of Chicago to develop a National Temporal Bone Bank program at five university centers with government funds. The program followed the lines of the one at the Los Angeles Foundation of Otology and Lindsay visited Howard and secured copies of the pledge forms signed by patients who bequeathed their temporal bones to the foundation. The DRF then distributed the copies nationally to otologists for use among their patients. Though several small-sized temporal bone banks were established afterward, they failed to survive. Currently significant banks are housed at Harvard under Dr. Harold F. Schuknecht, at Johns Hopkins under Dr. George Nager and at the University of California at Los Angeles under Dr. Victor Goodhill.

26

Bill Joins Howard

During these years Bill House had finished his internship at Los Angeles County where he remained for his ENT residency. With the advent of sulfa drugs and antibiotics, many doctors had felt the specialty of ENT—which had largely been confined to treating infections—would soon die out for the lack of patients. This was the theme of Dr. Lymon Richards' presidential address to the Triological Society at the end of the 1930s. It was not foreseen how the new drugs would make possible major advances in ENT surgery, free of the old haunting concern about infections.

ENT as a specialty had fallen so low as a career choice among medical students that in 1953 when the County Hospital invited applications for the four first-year ENT residencies then available, only two interns applied. Bill was one of the two, despite the earnest advice of his classmates not to "enter a dying field."

No full-time doctors were on the ENT service, and interns and residents—as in Howard's earlier cases—worked with the voluntary faculty. The unstructured residency allowed Bill to focus on matters of greatest personal interest and because he was on call every other night, he gained rich experience with all kinds of head and neck diseases and injuries.

"I remember," Bill later remarked, "that in the hospital library I found reports on 15 different ways to reduce a fractured jaw, and I tried them all. Had a full-time attendant doctor breathed down my neck and said, 'This is the way I do it, and this is what I want you to do,' I would have been stifled. Instead I could find out on my own how best to meet the challenges in a great sweep of cases."

Bill, like Howard before him, set out to master anatomy through dissections on cadavers. His wife, June, a trained surgical nurse, would often assist him while he explored the fine anatomical points of the head and neck.

Not that everything moved along smoothly in his residency. His past experiences as a dentist, plus his tendency to buck authoritative rules when they were contrary to what he thought was right, led to a jurisdictional clash at the hospital. Specifically, the hospital's dental service claimed the sole right to treat fractured jaws.

Bill at first did not challenge that monopoly, but moved into action when he saw how patients with fractured jaws whom he admitted at night would not be treated by a dentist until the next day, and then only to X-ray the fractures. Worse, when patients were admitted on a Friday afternoon, a dentist would not see them until Monday, and the longer the fracture went unreduced, the greater was the chance for infection.

Under his own title of right as a licensed dentist besides being the ENT resident, Bill proceeded to intervene in these cases. Whenever an emergency patient showed up with a fractured jaw, Bill would set it in a procedure that took no more than 15 minutes. The patient could then either stay overnight in the hospital or be treated as an outpatient.

Virtue, however, was not its own reward for an inflamed protest was made by Dr. Paul Hamilton, head of the dental service, to Dr. Alden Miller, head of ENT service. "Look!" he exclaimed, "your resident, Bill House, is doing things that our dental interns are doing, and we don't like it!"

The protest sent Miller scurrying over to see Bill, and ask him what he was "doing".

Bill explained that when he was on ENT duty he would set fractured jaws instead of waiting for a dentist to come around to do it.

Miller eyed the intern and said, "Look, Bill, for the sake of peace in the hospital, don't do anything further to upset the dentists."

An indignant Bill rejoined, "Well, *I am* upset. Besides the longer these patients wait to set a fractured jaw, the greater the chance of infection.

"Bill, be reasonable," responded Miller. "Do what they say."

Defiantly Bill shook his head, "I won't stop until they put their dentists on call so they will set jaws when they should be set."

It was through this disturbing clash between the older and the younger man, that Bill's rebellion would have a positive effect. Because of his insistence, the head of the dental service placed dental interns on regular call so they could deal promptly with fractured jaws. Bill taught them what he knew about how to treat all facial fractures and a precedent began which continues to this day where dental interns and ENT residents regularly work together.

The last year of Bill's residency in ENT was spent at Children's Hospital where he continued to dissect cadavers in order to improve his surgical skills. In focusing on the temporal bone, he used instruments Howard gave him and he also spent Saturdays watching Howard do ear surgery.

He was keen on learning what it takes to be an accomplished surgeon and later Bill said, "What it takes to excel in surgery is similar to what it takes in sports—a commitment to a continuous improvement in pursuit of excellence. An ace sports person works on every detail of the game. When they make a mistake they ask, 'What went wrong? What did I do?' Just as a really good athlete thinks about all the possible plays well beforehand, so does the top-notch surgeon think through every step that ought to be taken—and does this kind of thinking while merely looking out of a window or driving home.

"It always amazed me to see surgeons spend a fortune on golf lessons and not be equally concerned about the learning processes of their work. A surgeon such as Howard knows in advance exactly what procedures are going to be followed as well as being prepared to adapt and meet emergencies that might arise. If you don't take advantage of a bad experience by learning from it, there is no way you can enhance good judgment."

As Bill was trying to decide what to do at the end of his residency in July 1956, some events set the stage for that decision. After finishing his residency at Harvard, a Dr. John Shea II became Rosen's student, studying his technique of stapes mobilization just as Howard had done. When Howard published an article detailing some of his improvements on stapes mobilization, Shea came to Los Angeles for what was meant to be Howard's one-month course in ear surgery, but in the end Shea stayed six months. Howard would have welcomed him as an associate for he judged him to be a "brilliant young man" with "excellent surgical hands" as well as a "bold imagination."

One night as the two were reviewing the day's surgery, Shea turned to Howard and said, "Why don't we take out the stapes entirely and put something else in its place over the little window?"

Howard shook his head, "I would be fearful," he replied, "of exposing the inner ear that widely."

"Why?" asked Shea. "You do it every day in the fenestration operation and then put a skin flap over the opening." "Yes," Howard agreed, "and we put that flap over very quickly."

"Well," said Shea pensively, "maybe we can work out something."

Howard never discouraged anyone with new ideas. "Any idea," he used to say, "is better than no idea and too many people have no ideas."

After Shea returned to Memphis to start his practice, he reviewed the medical literature and found old case histories where stapes had been removed and replaced. The operations were unsuccessful because they did not have antibiotics or adequate magnification.

A few months later Howard and Helen, with the red-upholstered white Cadillac, arrived in Montreal for the 1955 meeting of the Triological Society where Howard was to moderate a panel on stapes mobilization, with Rosen, Meltzer, Hooper, Goodhill, Shambaugh, Kos, Schuknecht and Farrior taking part.

Before the discussion got underway, Shea approached Howard to say, "I've got something to show you," handing Howard an audiogram of a patient before and after a new kind of stapes operation he had performed, which he called a stapedectomy. Shea also had slides showing the steps of the operation as well as the hearing tests before and after which indicated excellent hearing result. Following up on his own idea, in order to avoid the problem of stapes refixation that often followed mobilization, Shea had removed the stapes entirely, covered the oval window with a piece of vein from the wrist and installed a plastic stapes.

Letting the implications sink in, Shea looked intently at his former mentor and said, "I'd like to report this procedure, and get it into the literature."

Knowing what to expect and hoping to forestall a scatter-pattern attack by the assembled doctors on Shea's operation, Howard countered with a tactical proposal. "John," he said, "this looks great! I'll tell you what I'll do. At twelve o'clock sharp, I'll say there is time for only one more discussion. Put up your hand and I will call on you. You can present your new approach and then I will immediately adjourn the meeting."

True to the plan just at noon Howard recognized Shea who spoke for four or five minutes. Victor Goodhill, who would later be the author of a widely used textbook on otosclerosis, recalled that Shea's comments in those few minutes stirred a tidal wave of anger and excitement that billowed up from the audience.

Notes began to converge on Howard from all sides of the room saying: "Don't stop the meeting." There were also sharp warnings to be voiced about what Shea was up to as well as earnest questions to be asked.

Howard, however, with the immediate end in view of getting Shea's innovative work into the literature, waited until Shea finished speaking and then declared, "The meeting is adjourned." The rap of his gavel stopped further discussion and prevented an inflamed attack on young Shea's work and the stapedectomy operation which was to revolutionize otosclerosis surgery.

This new approach completed the eclipse of Julius Lempert, for as stapedectomies increasingly became the technique of choice among otologists, Lempert—who used to have a year-long backlog of patients awaiting fenestration surgery—saw his patient load shrink to a trickle. Whereas in times past he had spent prodigally on research and on entertainment, now he was forced to come to terms with an economic pinch.

It was a painful experience for a surgical genius who had at so many turns been hurt by life itself. Whenever Howard was in New York he made it a point to call on Lempert, just as he had once always called on Mosher when he was in the Boston area, but with each visit, he found Lempert had further deteriorated physically and mentally. His last visit occurred on the eve of Lempert's death in 1958 and the old surgeon failed even to recognize Howard, questioning him vaguely about how things were going in Miami. Shortly thereafter, at Flo's request, Howard participated in delivering the eulogy at the memorial service for her husband.

The second event that impacted Bill's last year of residency began with an earlier trip Howard made to Germany where he had seen the work of Professors Zollner, Wullstein and Litman—whose pioneering research was to change otologic surgery dramatically. As head of the ENT Department at Freiburg University, Professor Zollner was studying ways to reconstruct the eardrum and ear bones. His former assistant, Professor Wullstein was now head of ENT at the University of Würzburg and the work of these two pioneers made possible tympanoplasty surgery (the reconstruction of the eardrum and ear bones) with the restoration of hearing in chronically infected ears. Wullstein also worked with Litman, a Ph.D. employed at the Zeiss factory, in developing a constant focusing device that made possible the Zeiss operating microscope universally used in ear surgery—and later in other specialties such as eye, orthopedic, vascular and neurosurgery.

Returning to Los Angeles with enthusiastic reports about the work of Zollner and Wullstein and the new surgical microscope, Howard persuaded Wullstein, who spoke English well, to visit the United States and present his tympanoplasty technique plus the surgical microscope at this same Montreal meeting. Before returning to Germany Wullstein came to Los Angeles to visit. Bill volunteered to drive Wullstein around town and thus had a chance to talk at length with him.

As a result of these encounters Howard, along with Shambaugh in Chicago and Dr. Charles Kinney of Cleveland, obtained one of the first Zeiss scopes shipped to the United States and thus Bill was among the first in the country introduced to the new surgical microscope.

The fantastic clarity and detail of what he saw—the tympanic membrane, malleus, incus and stapes and their relationship to the facial nerve—bowled him over. "It was," he later said, "like walking into the Grand Canyon and seeing that marvelous panorama for the first time."

In one fell swoop he shelved his interest in maxillofacial surgery in favor of otology. Howard made it clear he would welcome Bill as an associate and so it was arranged when Bill completed his residency in June 1956. That this would be no routine association among two doctors sharing the same facilities was prefigured by Bill's first remark to Howard when their formal association was agreed to. "It seems to me," he said, "that you and the doctors of your era," (meaning the older generation of leaders in otology) "have pretty much solved the problems of the middle ear. My own aim will be to tackle the problems of the inner ear."

Howard encouraged Bill to pursue this objective and assured him he could draw on the available resources of the foundation in support of his projects. Still Howard could not help smiling to himself. Until Bill included him with "the doctors of your era," Howard had thought of himself as part of the young guard. Certainly at 48 he was a long way from being an antique.

Conversations between Bill and Howard on otologic subjects became acts of collaboration. When Bill would begin a conversation with a radical "Why not?" or "What if?" Howard could answer from the depths of his clinical experience. Things said at such times were always purposeful for their aim was to reassess existing methods and explore the road to future advances in otology.

The effects of these conversations between the two half-brothers transcended the 15 year disparity in their ages and the fundamental differences in their personal styles. In retrospect, it seemed to both that an invisible hand had been preparing them all along to be joined as a team so that each could ultimately attain a major goal that perhaps would have escaped their individual reach if each had stood alone.

27

Visions of a New Era

Bill's use of the phrase, "the doctors of your era," was a respectful salute to Howard and his notable mentors and colleagues who had initiated or perfected new surgical techniques to deal with problems of the middle ear and temporal bone. All had benefited from new antibiotic drugs, innovative methods to test hearing, better X-rays, improved surgical instruments, superior photographic methods, the introduction of the dental drill and now the operating microscope.

At the same time, the rising number of new Ph.D. specialists in audiology made major contributions of their own to knowledge about the hearing mechanism. Their research findings were a boon to clinicians eager for insights that might guide their hands when they had to intervene surgically in an otologic system that was treacherously small and complex. The research scientists and clinicians in otology, taken together, fit a judgment voiced in a different connection by Bernard of Chartres, the twelfth-century classical scholar and church leader:

> We are like dwarves seated on the shoulders of giants. We see more things than the ancients and things more distant; but this is due neither to the sharpness of our own sight, nor to the greatness of our own stature, but because we are raised and carried aloft on that giant mass.

From the day of Bill's formal association with Howard, he and the other doctors in the office searched for new ways to do things better in ear surgery and their interests branched out on many fronts simultaneously. They were aided by the fact that as Howard became increasingly busy with otosclerosis patients, he diverted to them a stream of patients with infected ears and balance problems.

Added to this, in Bill's case, other factors contributed to his search for ways to improve ear surgery. His dental training had taught him that a stream of water, when attached to a suction tip, could be directed more accurately to achieve two purposes: to remove bone dust produced by the burr and to prevent overheating of the delicate area. Bill proceeded to develop what is now known in otologic surgery as the House Irrigation-Suction Device.

This, however, was only the beginning. Soon afterward he linked up with Jack Urban, an event which was to be of supreme importance to otology. Though Urban was not a college graduate, he was a genius when it came to mechanical engineering, optics and photography. While working for General Motors, he conceived the idea of raising and lowering car windows and convertible tops electronically. Later working for Lockheed, he made important contributions in missile instrumentation and in the development of sophisticated cameras for military surveillance. Beyond this he also designed the spectacular circular motion picture used at Disneyland's Cinerama.

Urban, however, was depressed by the thought that his defense work was eventually aimed at "destroying people" so when he met Bill, who explained the problem he and Howard had encountered with the marvelous surgical microscope they had imported from Germany, he was happy for a challenge that would benefit humankind and graciously donated his creative services to develop and improve surgical instruments.

Though the new microscope was a remarkable surgical tool, it was of limited use as a teaching instrument because only one person could see through it at a time. What was needed, so Bill felt, was an observing tube attached to the microscope that would provide the same image to a viewer as appeared to the operating surgeon while not interfering with the maneuvering of the microscope or drawing any light away from the surgeon's eyes.

It was just the kind of problem Jack Urban thrived on and in response he created what is now known as the House-Urban Observing Tube which is a wonderful teaching aid widely used in medicine and in many industries. He then proceeded to develop the House-Urban camera to take still, motion picture and television pictures through the operating microscope. Further, Urban invented a device that shaved and sucked out tissue in the removal of ear tumors—which was also soon being used by orthopedic surgeons to remove cartilage fragments from a knee joint.

Later, when Bill became interested in the electronics of hearing, Urban, as always, continued to work without charge to develop the electronics of the cochlear implant. Then, because much of what he designed proved to have an industrial as well as a medical use, Urban was able to leave the weapons industry to establish the Urban Engineering Company. Later he would be honored by the American Academy of Otolaryngology—the first lay person to receive an award for his contributions to otology—but which would be the first of many honors bestowed on him from around the world.

While Bill was engrossed in his varied interests, Howard decided to create a permanent ear clinic to be known as the Otologic Medical Group (OMG). This would replace the previous arrangement where Howard engaged qualified doctors to work with him for two years before they opened their own offices and allow them to develop a permanent group of specialists.

The first person brought in on a permanent status in 1958 was Dr. Frederick H. Linthicum, Jr., whose primary interest was children's otology and the histopathology of the temporal bone—a subject in which he would gain world-wide prominence among otologists.

Dr. James L. Sheehy, the next addition to the set-up, had been highly recommended by Dr. Robert McNaught, Howard's close friend and Chief of the ENT service at Stanford Medical School, who described Sheehy as "the finest resident" he had ever trained—a superb clinician with a passion for structured orderliness.

The terms Howard proposed to Linthicum and Sheehy when they joined the newborn OMG were the same as those offered Bill and the others, including Howard's son, John, who later became members of the OMG. The terms recalled Milus's advice when Howard was offered a post with the Moore-White Clinic. Each doctor would be compensated not only by a salary but by productivity. Thus the junior associates were offered a good starting salary for the first two years, but it would be up to them to build their own practice by becoming masters of a subspecialty in otology.

Like Howard, these new doctors would get all the income they generated, less overhead costs. They would also volunteer part of their time for research and teaching at the Los Angeles Foundation of Otology—now the House Ear Institute—and at the USC Medical School. Agreements reached were sealed by a handshake, based on a clear understanding of what they entailed. Howard never signed a contract with an associate of the OMG or the House Ear Institute.

Every Monday was reserved for a "working dinner" attended by the nurses and doctors which gave them a chance to discuss case problems, ways to improve office and patient management and matters related to the foundation. As the OMG grew in size, these Monday night sessions eventually became a valuable teaching program with participants coming from beyond the members of the OMG core group which would include Fellows of the House Ear Institute, visiting doctors, residents from medical schools and audiologists. By the early 1980s attendance grew to 30 or 40 people under the chairmanship of Dr. James Sheehy, and discussions about unusual or difficult cases were taped and published by Dr. Mike Glasscock's *American Journal of Otology* for distribution to otologists worldwide.

The ceaseless exchange of insights among members of the OMG told the scope, depth and significance of their practice, while also enlarging the foundation's agenda for applied clinical research. Once Bill, for example, noted that many patients with mastoid operations returned regularly for a cleaning of the open mastoid cavity, so he devised a way to do mastoid surgery without creating the open cavity— a method that came to be known as the "intact canal wall technique." After performing a few such operations, he turned the project over to Sheehy who perfected the technique to a point where it is now in common use among otologists.

The cumulative weight of the papers published by OMG doctors, along with the lectures and courses they offered based on their own research, increasingly influenced the work of their fellow specialists in the United States and around the globe. Meanwhile, the growing influx of patients to the OMG impressed upon Howard the need to build a professional building of his own.

An area across from St. Vincent Medical Center on the corner of Third and Alvarado seemed an ideal site. On the assumption that he would predecease his wife, he wanted the projected building to be a source of income to Helen, so the structure he commissioned was designed in ways where it could be readily converted into seven independent offices for rental. Meanwhile, Howard formed two corporations—one to own the land and the structure, the second to own the equipment and furnishings within the building which would be leased to the OMG. Bill, Linthicum and Sheehy held one share each in the second or equipment corporation. Stock in it would ultimately be sold on an equitable basis to other doctors as they became associates of the OMG.

While the building was under construction, Howard gave three-year leases for the extra space to some medical friends, but the OMG practice continued to expand so rapidly that the group needed the leased-out space—and took it over at the end of three years. The pressures of an ever growing practice continued to increase the demand for ever more space.

Added land neighboring the OMG building was gradually acquired for purposes that included parking. The original building was enlarged three times to provide a total of 20,000 square feet, yet the tight fit between the need for more space to accommodate the influx of patients and the space actually available, was like trying to wedge two feet into a single shoe. The solution still lay in the future.

28

Family Matters

Changes, meanwhile, were underway within the extended House family. In 1957, Milus Marion House, the pervasive "presence" in the lives of all his sons, received a rare tribute. At a Los Angeles dinner in his honor, with national leaders of his profession on the dias, he was hailed as the person who had made the greatest contribution to dentistry in Southern California in the previous half century. A year later, Milus, at the age of 80—a man who did much for human well-being—died suddenly of a heart attack.

He had lived long enough to have the pleasure of seeing how the careers of Howard and Bill had evolved in the field of otology. Warren, too, was doing well in his chosen field of veterinary medicine though he had faced some heavy times. Warren had married and had three children—Pamela, Michael and Debra—but Michael had been killed in an automobile accident. The marriage ended in divorce and Warren was given custody of his two surviving children. Several years later he happily remarried. Mary, a welcome addition to the House family, was unfortunately widowed early when Warren's life was snuffed out when his car was struck by a drunken driver.

Although Jim had joined Milus in the Whittier dental practice in Whittier, his true career lay in dental education and in 1953 he began to teach at the USC School of Dentistry. A decade later he accepted a position as full-time professor at the Indiana University School of Dentistry where later he went on to become chair of the department of prosthetic dentistry. In moving his family to Indianapolis he facilitated having one of Milus' wishes fulfilled for Milus had hoped that someday his teaching materials, articulators, molds and skull collection could be permanently displayed back at his alma mater. Jim organized this, helping distribute some of this collection to the Smithsonian while the remainder was placed in the Milus M. House Memorial Museum at the Indiana University School of Dentistry.

Meanwhile Howard's family was growing and achieving—in true House style. Ken, the oldest, was a fine athlete and had been an all-league high school basketball player as well as Los Angeles High School tennis doubles Player of the Year. When he began college, in order to stay in tune with Ken's life, Howard tried to lunch alone with him one day a week. This worked so well he continued the practice with John when he started college.

One day when Ken was lunching with his father and mulling about what he would choose as a career, he began discussing a psychology course he was taking. The professor was very stimulating and the study of the subconscious was a fascination to him. Maybe, suggested Ken, if he personally helped people with their emotional problems, they could lead happier lives. He was uncertain, however, as to whether his interests should take him into psychiatry—which would mean going to medical school—or into clinical psychology.

Many of Howard's patients were also his personal friends. To help expose the still-undecided Ken to various careers, Howard picked some of the most successful people he knew in one or another line of work and then arranged to see them, bringing Ken along.

At one of these encounters Ken put a blunt question to "Dutch" Kindelberger, president of North American

Aviation. "What job satisfaction do you get from your work?"

Kindelberger looked intently at the youth, then turning to Howard asked, "Should I tell him the truth?"

Howard's head nodded and so Kindelberger admitted that he didn't get an iota of satisfaction from his work. He was trained as an engineer—which was enjoyable because it was creative—but he did not enjoy his presidential role: "One day I have to fly to Washington to sell our products; the next day I have to fly back to Los Angeles and face the stockholders who demand to know why the company is not doing better."

Their discussion brought Kindelberger to introducing Howard and Ken to their personnel director, a psychologist. This person, too, said he found little satisfaction in his post. It had been far different when he used to work with just a few employees in a small branch of the company, helping them with their psychological problems. As he rose to be a vice president with his chief duties centering on negotiating union contracts, the satisfaction he had found working with people was lost.

Howard then took Ken to see the chair of the department of psychiatry at the USC School of Medicine, Edward Steinbrook, who had both a Ph.D. and an M.D. degree. Steinbrook told Ken he had first trained to be a psychologist, but soon saw he could be more effective with patients if he were a psychiatrist, so he went to medical school, became a psychiatrist and was currently studying to become a psychoanalyst.

Then with the help of Jim, Howard's brother, they found a clinical psychologist whose office was over a corner drugstore. Climbing the stairs to a little reception room, they were greeted by the psychologist and soon Ken was asking his usual questions. Finally they had found someone who thoroughly enjoyed his work because he helped many people with their personal problems. When Ken asked how he handled patients who were psychotic, he replied that he referred them to psychiatrists and also said that if he were Ken's age and could do things all over again, he would certainly go to medical school and after receiving an M.D. degree, go into psychiatry and psychoanalysis. In that way he could serve the needs of anyone who walked into his office.

This encounter with a very happy figure who had a simple practice in a not-too-elegant scene set the course Ken was to follow. As he walked down the stairs he turned to his father and told him there was no need to look farther. They could cancel the other appointments because he knew what he wanted to do: go to medical school and become a psychiatrist and psychoanalyst.

And so he did, receiving his M.D. degree from USC followed by a residency at County Hospital. Later he married Joan Bertotti, and together they have raised two children, David and Nicole. Currently Ken has a successful private practice as a psychiatrist and psychoanalyst in West Los Angeles, but he also followed the House tradition by teaching at USC County Hospital.

In order to make his mark in the competitive House-world John succumbed early to the pervasive family pressure. Although as a child he had loved trains and had declared widely his intention of becoming a railroad engineer in order to give his father and mother free train rides, he changed his mind on the day Helen took him to see "the train of tomorrow"—with its diesel engine—which was being exhibited near the USC School of Medicine.

John looked at the "tall building" of the school—five stories in all—and when Helen told him his father had attended USC Medical School and taught classes there, he informed his mother he was not going to be a railroad engineer after all. He was going to be a doctor like his father. After that he never changed his mind again.

Where Carolyn was concerned, Helen and Howard followed the advice he often gave parents of hearing-impaired and deaf children: they should find something the child could do better than anyone else on their block and then build up that talent. All the House children loved to swim in the pool that had been installed in the backyard of their home.

As a good safety precaution Carolyn had been taught to swim the moment she could walk. By the time she was in grade school her swimming ability began to attract notice when, at the Jonathan Beach Club, she came in a close second to Gail Human, who was nationally ranked as an age-group swimmer. At that same meet John had won in his event and afterwards Gail's father, the organizer of the meet, asked Howard and Helen who was coaching Carolyn and John. When they admitted the two had no coach, Mr. Human urged Howard to join the Los Angeles Athletic Club so they could work under the tutelage of the nationally known Peter Daland, who also coached the USC swimming team.

The first time Daland watched the two youngsters swim a few laps he remarked, out of his long contacts with champion California swimmers, that he might have two potentially good swimmers on his hands. As a prophet he would be doubly confirmed for John went on to become the captain of the USC freshmen swimming team and in his senior year, when he was captain of the varsity team, USC won the NCAA national championship for the third time in a row.

Carolyn's development as a swimming star was meteoric. Practically every month she passed another milestone. Her parents had always assumed she must have had a very strong heart to have survived her premature birth—and now her heart plus her determination began pulling her through one after another of the grueling tests of swimming competition. Still her parents were wary when Peter Daland wanted to enter Carolyn in the National Women's Swimming Meet in Topeka, Kansas. Howard thought that 1500 meters was too long a race for a girl of twelve, but he caved in under the importuning of Carolyn, John and their coach. Carolyn came in fifth in the race. Two years later, at the National Women's Swimming Meet in Indianapolis, she became the American record holder in the same 1500 meter freestyle event.

The following spring John and Carolyn were in the tryouts held in Detroit for the swimming team that would represent the United States at the 1960 Olympics in Rome. Helen, Howard and Ken were present to cheer them on. The tryouts were the first and only time—due to a lack of funds—that there would be only two contestants instead of three in a single event on the final U.S. team. Because the pool water was cold Howard, in his role as an ad hoc trainer, rubbed wintergreen oil on the bodies of the Los Angeles Athletic team to warm them up before they competed—and in the process became known as the "Earl of Wintergreen."

Carolyn, to the astonishment of coaches who wondered what Howard had rubbed on her to make her go, came booming into second place by half a length in the 400-meter freestyle. All Carolyn could excitedly say as she jumped up and down, "I'm going to Rome! I'm going to Rome!"

John entered in the 400-meter individual medley. The first place winner in the race was clear, but the judges could not decide who was second and who third. Ten minutes passed before they reached a verdict: John missed second place by six-tenths of a second—and that meant no berth for him on the U.S. Olympic swimming team. His parents and siblings urged John to go with them to Rome, but he refused. "I don't want to go to Rome that way," John said. "I wanted to make it on my own—but didn't. So I'm staying home." And he did.

In the summer of 1960 Carolyn arrived at the Olympic village in Rome with the rest of the American team and within a few days Helen, Howard and Ken showed up. Carolyn celebrated her 15th birthday while they were there and it seemed that the entire American contingent in the Olympic village turned out to celebrate. It was a tribute from the cream of American athletes to a special one of their own—someone who overcame great obstacles to be in their company. What she had achieved in her quiet, private battle against impaired vision could never be denied her— despite what happened when the elimination trials began.

In nighttime events, during American competitions, Carolyn's coaches were allowed to place a white towel at each end of her lane in the pool so she could better see where she should turn. A formal request to the Olympic authorities to permit the same arrangement was refused. On the night of the elimination trials in Carolyn's specialty, Elsa Conrads, the Australian champion, was in her neighboring lane. There was the bark of the starter's pistol, a plunge into the water, silence until the contestants surfaced and then the thrashing noise of the race.

When Carolyn realized the Australian was forging ahead, she stepped up the pace of her own strokes, only to hit her head against the end of the pool on the first turn—all because there was no towel to help tell her where the wall was. Out of caution she lost ground on each turn and failed to qualify for the finals. She bounced back from the defeat with the same resilience that enabled her to overcome other bumps along the way. A year after Rome, when she was 16, she held seven American records and set the 800 and 1500 meter freestyle world records.

After attending USC, she got a position in Washington,

D.C. with the International Eye Foundation. One evening, Carolyn had double dated with her friend Susanne Kos and her date, Richard Helmuth, a young architect in a Washington firm. Carolyn's own escort had been arranged by Susanne. In a throw of fortune's dice, when Richard subsequently telephoned Carolyn and asked her out, she hesitated, contacted Susanne and received her go-ahead blessing.

On their first date Carolyn and Richard were surprised to discover he had been in the stands observing a national swimming meet when the little, blond 13-year-old Carolyn had won the 400 meter freestyle. In the fullness of time, after Carolyn and Richard were engaged, they returned to California to be married. They now make their home in Newport Beach and where Carolyn teaches and coaches swimming and is Mom to their two children, Karen and Brent.

The House family was extended still further when John, upon graduation from the USC Medical School in 1967, married Patti Roberts. Their three children—Hans, Chris and Kurt—when added to the children of Ken and Joan and of Carolyn and Richard—gave Helen and Howard seven grandchildren, all living nearby.

Howard and Helen enjoyed the role of patriarch and matriarch of the clan. In Helen's case, the enjoyment would be cut short.

29

Bill in Motion

In the 1950s, the Los Angeles Foundation of Otology was little more than a desk and part-time secretary in Howard's office. Its personnel, aside from Howard, included his associate doctors—Bill, Fred Linthicum and James Sheehy. The doctors taking courses offered by the foundation were taught in the office, hospital operating rooms and the County Hospital morgue. All clinical research by Bill, Linthicum, Sheehy and Howard was done during the evening and on weekends—with Linthicum concentrating on children's problems and Sheehy on chronic ear disease.

Bill's clinical research interests were more broad-based and he never focused on just one problem at a time. One of his projects dealt with the problems of the facial nerve— which resembles a telephone cable with hundreds of individual fibers, each carrying electrical impulses to a specific facial muscle. These nerve fibers—a stunning piece of multi-purpose engineering—not only allow us to laugh, cry, smile or frown; but also carry impulses to the saliva glands, provide taste in the tongue and pain in the external ear canal. As the facial nerve leaves the brain stem, it passes through the temporal bone in a course full of twists and loops until it exits from the bone at a point below the ear where it spreads to the various muscles on that side of the face.

Unlike other nerves which have room to swell when inflamed, the location of the facial nerve in a small rigid bony canal prevents it from doing so. If swelling occurs in Bell's Palsy, the nerve function can be temporarily or permanently damaged. Up to this point, if pressure here was not relieved spontaneously or with medication, the common practice was to relieve it by surgically opening a portion of the bony canal through which the nerve passes, leaving the rest of the nerve under pressure.

In Bill's view this procedure was not good enough. So the former "troublemaker" in the U.S. Navy and USC County Hospital developed an approach to the canal—now in wide use—whose aim was to open the whole of the bony canal so as to obtain a total exposure of the facial nerve.

A small shelf of thin bone in the internal auditory canal had been previously described by others, but it was Bill who fixed it as a signpost, marking the boundary line between the facial nerve and the balance nerve. Bill proved that by adhering to that line, it was possible to expose the entire course of the facial nerve. He called the shelf "Bill's Bar" and both the name and the technique passed into international use in connection with operations on Bell's Palsy and certain balance problems.

Other young surgeons who trained with Bill further perfected this type of surgery, as was notably true of Ugo Fisch of Zürich. Later, his nephew John House developed what is now the accepted international standard method for determining degrees of facial nerve paralysis.

While Bill worked to expose the entire facial nerve, he wondered if through the same approach he could do something about the problem of vertigo—or a loss of balance—in Ménière's disease—named after the French doctor who first described it in 1861. Marked by intermittent attacks of acute vertigo, the symptoms generally include accompanying nausea and vomiting, a fluctuating type of hearing loss (usually in one ear and often characterized by a loss of clarity), a roaring tinnitus and a sensation of fullness or pressure in the ear. Any of these might last from a few minutes to hours. An estimated 3.5 million Americans now suffer from this problem.

The cause of the attacks that go with Ménière's is unknown, but is commonly ascribed to an increase in the pressure of the inner ear fluid. In a normal ear, the fluid—consisting of only three drops—is constantly being produced and absorbed in what is known as the endolymphatic sac, and which is thought to act as "the kidney" of the inner ear. Anything that interferes with the absorption or production of these fluids produces the symptoms of Ménière's—a condition similar to glaucoma of the eye where pressure on the fluid in the eye produces visual impairment.

In some patients the disease clears spontaneously. In others, attacks occur with increasing frequency and severity in spite of medical treatment. When Bill reviewed the literature about Ménière's, he found that most operations for it caused the destruction of the balance and hearing mechanism in the inner ear. He began to wonder whether there was a way to avoid this extreme trade-off where both hearing and balance in one ear were destroyed in order to spare a patient the miseries of Ménière's.

In his research he came upon an article on Ménière's by the celebrated Dr. George Portmann of France who reported on two cases of Ménière's in 1924 where he had tried to preserve the hearing and prevent attacks of vertigo by incising the endolymphatic sac of the inner ear for drainage. Intrigued by the logic of the approach, Bill wondered why Portmann did not continue along the line he was on and determined to begin cadaver work in order to follow through on Portmann's lead.

Bill soon understood why his predecessor stopped where he did for he found the endolymphatic sac was extremely difficult to get to without damaging the vital structures lying next to it. One after another route of entry that Bill tried failed. Suddenly one evening while dissecting a cadaver, he suddenly dropped right into the endolymphatic sac. Triumphantly he called his wife, June, who was aware of the difficulties he had been having to say, "Hey, I finally got into the sac!" Her immediate reply was, "With whom?"

More dissections convinced him that by using known landmarks, the sac could be entered in most cases. At first Bill merely opened and drained the sac as Portmann had done—which helped some Ménière's patients, but there was a high recurrence of attack symptoms. To produce a more lasting effect, Bill developed a tiny tube—known as a "shunt"—to connect the sac and the spinal fluid space, using the underlying theory that when pressure in the sac increased, the fluid would pass up the tube, acting like a safety valve which opens automatically when there is too much pressure in a water tank.

The development of the shunt greatly improved the treatment of Ménière's where prior medical treatment failed. A patient helped in this way was astronaut Alan Shepard whose role in the space program was threatened because of Ménière's. He had been grounded after one space mission, but when NASA physicians read medical reports about Bill's new shunt operation, they arranged for him to operate on Shepard who came to Los Angeles and was admitted into St. Vincent Medical Center under an assumed name.

Shepard later returned to the NASA program and was chosen to lead a mission to the moon. Bill and June, as guests of NASA at Cape Kennedy, were inside the control room witnessing Shepard's space vehicle blast-off for the moon—which Bill, knowing of Shepard's problem, found to be among the more stirring experiences of his life. Long after the space vehicle was out of sight, Shepard repeatedly addressed Bill, "You still there, Doc? The tube is working just fine!"

In the early 1970s the institute conducted the largest Ménière's study ever done to try to determine the cause of the disease. Over a five-year span 120 patients volunteered for monthly tests to measure their hearing, speech, balance, metabolic function, blood composition, allergies and psychological well-being. Data from the study failed to show why one patient suffered from the disease and another did not, nor why approximately 52 percent responded to medical treatment and the others didn't. The institute's research continues under Fred Linthicum.

Bill's work with the shunt, meanwhile, came under sharp attack from eminent critics on both sides of the Atlantic, but he also had eminent supporters. In the continuing controversy over the shunt technique, the authoritative voice of George Shambaugh sounded on Bill's side. "Despite reports in the literature to the contrary," Shambaugh wrote in his textbook on ear surgery, "to seek surgical treatment in Ménière's disease when all medical and allergic avenues have been exhausted, is still sound and will remain so until the etiological factors in the disease are more clearly established."

Bill was always encouraged by Shambaugh and always had the firm support of his brother, Howard. He would need Howard's support as never before when he turned his attention to still newer and more radical techniques and concepts.

30

Bill on the Eve of a Storm

Tumors on the hearing nerve—known as acoustic neuromas—are wart-like growths that constitute six to ten percent of all brain tumors. Unlike cancer, they do not spread (metastasize) to other parts of the body and their potential power to cripple and kill lies simply in their growth. The work of two noted neurosurgeons, Harvey Cushing and his student, Walter Dandy, had enabled alert clinicians to diagnose acoustic neuromas if they were large.

The surgical procedures they helped to perfect called for an approach through the back of the head (suboccipital) to raise a part of the brain in order to get at the tumorous growth. A forty percent mortality rate was associated with this type of surgery and the patients who survived often paid a very high price in morbidity—deafness, facial paralysis or numbness, speech impediments and inability to coordinate arm and leg movements. Only a minority of the patients in surgical cases returned to normal and productive lives.

Acoustic tumors—which often start with tinnitus, a slight hearing loss and later a balance disorder and facial weakness—grow slowly. Even when a patient was diagnosed at an early hour, neurosurgeons knew the chances were the patient would outlive the tumor and succumb from other causes, so the pragmatic thing to do was keep the patient under observation until it was clear the tumor had grown to the extent it was producing crushing pressures on nearby nerves and the adjacent brain stem. Only when the tumor was life-threatening would a neurosurgeon feel justified to run the high risks of morbidity and mortality associated with surgical intervention.

As a resident Bill had never seen a patient with an acoustic tumor, though he had read many articles on the subject and knew the early symptoms. In the autumn of 1957 while Bill was developing a surgical approach to expose the full length of the facial nerve, a patient came to his office who was to have a fateful import on Bill's future— and on the future of neuro-otology. A robust fire fighter in his early 30s, the patient was married to an attractive young woman who was by his side. He had only a slight tinnitus and hearing loss in one ear, but X-rays showed some enlargement of the internal auditory canal, suggestive of an early tumor.

The neurosurgeon to whom the patient was referred, informed Bill that the fire fighter did have a small acoustic tumor and that surgery should be delayed until the tumor's size justified it. Bill and the neurosurgeon continued to observe the patient for about two years, by which time he could no longer work due to dizziness and a persistent headache. The patient was hospitalized and prepared for surgery.

Bill was on hand to witness what was virtually an all-day procedure involving the back of the head approach. It took several hours merely to expose the tumor. The patient tolerated the procedure well until a fragment of the tumor close to the brain stem was pulled away. At that point there was a flash flood of bleeding, as well as other complications, because the tumor was located next to the brain centers that control breathing, blood pressure and heart functions.

"The scene that followed," Bill remarked years later, "filled me with a sense of doom and horror that I shall never forget." The neurosurgeon tried to put clips to stem the flood of blood which obscured the surgical field. When the ghastly operation was finally ended, the patient's blood pressure remained very high, but he had no spontaneous respiration and died several hours later.

The neurosurgeon explained that, "It's always the last piece of tumor that kills the patient." He added that the risk of fatality in the case of patients with large tumors was very high. Bill silently observed to himself that in his view surgery six months earlier might have allowed the patient to live. By waiting they had only decreased his chances for survival.

Bill returned from the hospital and stormed into Howard's office to tell him about the young fire fighter's death. In the voice of a person possessed, Bill vehemently proclaimed, "This is terrible! There must be some other way to get at these tumors when they are still small and remove them without such severe morbidity and mortality. I've just got to find a better way!"

Within two years of the fire fighter's death, Bill and Howard had diagnosed four more acoustic neuroma cases which were referred to a neurosurgeon. Following surgery, one was fortunate enough to have only a total facial paralysis. One died and the other two, besides their facial paralysis, had additional balance and neurological problems. Bill began to dread seeing patients with nerve loss in one ear. If they had an acoustic neuroma, they faced a bleak future.

As someone who tended to find his ideal in his difficulties, Bill set out to discover how to get at acoustic tumors when they were still small. Coincidentally he was developing the middle fossa approach to the facial nerve in connection with surgery for Bell's Palsy and an awareness began to grow that by adhering to the same middle fossa approach by an incision from in front and above the ear, he could externalize the tumor on the hearing nerve. This would eliminate the need to lift the brain as in the Cushing and Dandy technique—with all its associated hazards. Furthermore, his ability to spot the facial nerve by the signpost of "Bill's Bar" enhanced the prospects for effective surgery on acoustic tumors with much less chance of injury to the facial nerve and consequent facial paralysis.

Bill's concept met with sharp opposition from most neurosurgeons, but one of the few who did not flatly reject it was Dr. John Doyle who had worked with him on Bell's Palsy. Another who seemed open-minded was Dr. Theodore Kurze, chief of neurosurgery at both the USC County Hospital and at St. Vincent Medical Center.

It was one thing for Bill to be convinced that his procedure worked on cadavers, but something else entirely to apply it to a living person. The high mortality and morbidity rates associated with the back of the head approach had come to be accepted as "normal" by neurosurgeons. A first-time failure with Bill's radical new procedure, developed not by a neurosurgeon but by an otologist, could brand him as an upstart whose headstrong ways caused needless loss of life.

The team of Bill and Doyle scheduled a small tumor case for surgery on February 15, 1961. Despite the natural unease—this being the first use of an operating microscope in neurosurgery—the operation was successful. The patient not only survived—thus spared from the pronounced morbidity that went with acoustic neuroma—but there was little or no damage to the facial, balance or hearing nerves. Between February 1961 and May 1962 eight more operations for acoustic tumors were carried out by the team of Bill and John Doyle. There was one flaw: if the tumors were very large, few could be totally removed.

A gnawing conviction kept growing in Bill's mind—perhaps it would be possible to remove the tumor totally if they were to approach it through the mastoid and the inner ear. There were certain advantages to this and improved chances for preserving the facial nerve because the surgery would be easier and safer since it could be done with the patient lying down, instead of strapped into a chair in an upright position using the Dandy method. The proposed new procedure, called the trans-labyrinthine approach, had been tried in Germany in 1904, but had not been successful for familiar reasons: no microscope, rudimentary instrumentation, no antibiotics or blood transfusions and inadequate knowledge of the anatomy of the ear.

Although Bill was convinced the end was clearly in view, there were still successive surgical steps that had to be worked out. His driving passion was to achieve a breakthrough in medicine that had been deemed impossible by "authorities" in the field. As he worked in the cool and antiseptic air of the morgue, one thought kept him intent on his goal: If, through his dissections on what had once been a human being, he could learn how to remove acoustic tumors without the high mortality and morbidity rates associated with orthodox surgical methods, then the nameless person represented by the cadaver would become one of humanity's benefactors.

At last Bill reached a point where he knew by heart the complex steps that marked the avenue of the approach. True, the process would sacrifice the balance mechanism and any residual hearing in that ear, but the gain was worth the cost. Besides, the loss of the balance mechanism in one ear would be compensated for by the opposite ear and the remaining mortality and morbidity rate would be far less.

At the Monday night meetings of the Otologic Medical Group, Bill kept the doctors informed of the progress he was making in his dissections. He had in his associates a core of informed critics who, by their questions and suggestions, helped clarify his own thoughts about what he was doing. Doyle, however, appeared skeptical from the start about the prospects for success with the new approach because it forced a surgeon to operate through a "keyhole"—an allusion to the limited space for surgery. Theodore Kurze was also kept abreast of the new developments and, for the time being, did not object to what it entailed.

One thing was self-evident: A mastery of the anatomy, the surgical microscope and of Jack Urban's micro-instrumentation was imperative in trans-labyrinthine surgery. Only so could the surgeon hope to save the facial nerve, avoid damage to the surrounding brain structures and yet remove the entire tumor.

31

In the Eye of the Storm

By 1963, Jack Urban had pioneered for the foundation the first black and white television camera for the surgical microscope—one that did not interfere with the position of the microscope or the surgeon. Bill, Doyle and Kurze agreed that Urban's technological marvel warranted offering a course on acoustic tumors at St. Vincent Hospital. As well as being a two-day course featuring two operations for acoustic neuromas and a lecture, it would also be the first time a microsurgical procedure would be televised live to a group of observers.

Later Bill recalled, "There were neurosurgeons and otologists in our viewing room, as well as residents from different medical schools. I knew that Doyle as well as Kurze favored removing large tumors through the back of the head approach, rather than through my ear approach, but still Doyle and I were to work as a team on different stages of the operation. However I was not prepared for what happened. As I was starting the procedure, I could hear the commentary Doyle was making to the group, telling them he did not agree with the new approach. If the patient died, he would take no responsibility for the case.

"Returning to the operating room, Doyle helped with the tumor removal, but decided in the final phase of the procedure to leave a piece of the tumor along the brain stem. Recalling the old admonition, 'It's the last piece that kills the patient,' I was very glad to see the case closed before there was a confrontation in the operating room. The patient did well, though he had partial facial paralysis."

That evening, Bill and Doyle's review of the day's events was marked by angry recriminations. Should the next day's surgery be canceled and the course ended? The two decided to go ahead with the agreed-upon schedule. Fortunately the next patient also did well, but the breach between Bill and Doyle seemed irreparable.

Bill still favored his team concept where an otologist and neurosurgeon would work together, but the problem was finding a compatible teammate. Howard—who was ceaselessly on the lookout for finely tuned surgical talent of any kind—called Bill's attention to a young neurosurgeon named William Hitselberger. The two met.

Hitselberger—or "Hitz" as he was called—a Harvard Medical School graduate who was thoroughly trained in neurosurgery, had not yet passed his specialty board. Bill warned that if they worked together he might be viewed as an enemy alien by the neurosurgical hierarchy. Hitz replied that he had seen Bill's surgery and would welcome a chance to be on his team. As for the neurosurgeons who were opposed to what Bill was doing, Hitz was not awed by them and was prepared to walk alone if that enabled him to be of greater help to patients with acoustic tumors.

The words were music to Bill's ears, the more so when Hitz suggested they be cross-trained in ways where each could function in the area of the other's specialization. The consequent innovation—the integration of the neurosurgeon and the otologist—was in contrast to the traditional division where the otologist would diagnose the tumor and the neurosurgeon would perform the surgery. The professional relationship between these two colleagues continues to this day.

After Hitz and Bill began to work as a team in the operating room of St. Vincent Medical Center, a neurosurgeon practicing in Fresno wrote to ask if he could observe their surgery. The pair happily replied they would contact him as soon as they had another acoustic tumor scheduled for surgery, thinking this interested Fresno doctor might encourage other neurosurgeons to converge on the hospital and watch the new technique.

The Fresno neurosurgeon visited St. Vincent several times to observe Bill and Hitz at work, but then, to their surprise, he suddenly informed them that he had an acoustic neuroma and would like them to operate on him. They agreed, but an uneasy thought rippled through their assent— if anything happened to this doctor as a patient, it would set back acoustic tumor surgery many years. The patient, whose name was Hector McKinnen, fortunately recovered from the surgery with virtually no facial weakness and later became a valuable ally when Bill and Hitz were in need of as much help as could be mustered.

By 1963 when Bill and Hitz had performed 52 acoustic tumor surgeries, they decided to publish a monograph which would comprise a complete history of all the cases—a time-consuming project, but they both found in preparing the manuscript they gained valuable insights when they carefully reviewed each case to determine what could be learned from it.

At the time George Shambaugh was the editor of the *Archives*, and on receiving the 50-page monograph Bill and Hitz had prepared, he called Bill to say the report was so forthright, comprehensive and important he had decided to devote an entire issue of the journal to it. Bill walked for a while without touching the ground. Suddenly, however, the handsome spread in the *Archives* ushered in not the dawn of a bright new day, but the onset of a storm which threatened Bill's career as a young surgeon.

Kurze and Doyle held strong professional convictions that Bill and Hitselberger were engaged in a deadly gambit. To stop them from going any further, they jointly convinced the members of the neurosurgical committee of St. Vincent Medical Center that the trans-labyrinthine procedure should be placed under the committee's direct control—which meant that the committee would review the case of any patient admitted to the hospital with an acoustic neuroma and have the sole right to decide whether the trans-labyrinthine or sub-occipital approach should be followed.

Though Bill was a member of the hospital's executive committee, he was not present on the day the neurosurgical committee proposal came before it and was approved. The next morning the chief of staff called Bill to say that his and Hitselberger's right to operate on acoustic tumor patients was suspended until investigations were made.

Reeling under the shock of these words, Bill told the chief of staff that they had two cases scheduled for the following week. What were they to do? He couldn't call the referring doctors and the patients to say the scheduled surgery would be delayed indefinitely. In discussing this decision with Howard and Hitselberger, Bill, in an embattled mood, said that if the negative view of the neurosurgeons prevailed, it would be best for him to resign from St. Vincent Medical Center and go elsewhere with all his cases. He realized there were doubts about the trans-labyrinthine approach. It was new, risky and might fail. All he asked was that it be given a fair trial.

So far the evidence indicated that this new approach, coupled with microsurgical techniques, dramatically reduced the mortality rate and many of the serious consequences of the sub-occipital approach. In Bill and Hitz's monograph they cited statistics that showed they had cut the ten-year average mortality rate in California from 43 percent to thirteen percent. Bill agreed with Dandy, a noted authority, who had said it was inappropriate to remove a tumor only in part merely to give a patient a few more years of life and added that surgery should be undertaken early in the development of an acoustic tumor in order to remove it totally.

Throughout Bill and Hitz's early cases, Howard had stood squarely behind them. He had the prestige, the seniority and the political clout to fight their perilous battles which were fast approaching in medical circles. Far from being an innocent in the ways of medical politics, Howard could never forget how major figures in the ENT field had once treated Lempert, denying him a fair hearing and dismissing his great work as being that of a charlatan. He knew that despite the "idealism" in the creed of the medical profession, specialists may be inclined to use every weapon at hand to protect their turf and foresaw the trouble Bill was inviting because of his intention as an "ENT person" to proceed with a new approach for acoustic tumors, when surgery for such tumors was long viewed as the domain of neurosurgeons alone.

What Howard anticipated materialized when the nationally respected Kurze emerged as the leader of an attack on Bill by neurosurgeons. The Sisters of St. Vincent Medical Center and the executive committee were beside themselves with anguish over the storm on the rise all around them. At the "final meeting" to resolve the conflict— with Kurze, Howard, Bill and others in attendance—the sisters opened the session with a prayer. When the prayer was over and the bowed heads were raised, the controversy between the opposing camps was promptly brought to a boil.

"If Bill House," said Kurze, "is allowed to do his kind of tumor operations in this hospital without first clearing his cases with the neurosurgical committee, I will resign from the hospital staff rather then compromise my principles about what should not be done by an ENT person in acoustic neuroma cases.

Howard countered with his own ultimatum, addressing Kurze and the sisters, "If Bill is not allowed to use his technique to remove acoustic tumors in this hospital, then I will resign from the staff."

So there it was—a "High Noon" stare down between two surgeons in white, with each of the adversaries firmly holding to their beliefs as to what was best for the patient. The distressed sisters broke into the confrontation to say they would go into an executive session—the last thing they wanted was the very showdown they had witnessed, but making discerning decisions was part of their training. Emerging from their session the sisters announced that Bill would be allowed to operate with Hitselberger on acoustic tumors, using the trans-labyrinthine approach.

Bill later acknowledged that if it were not for Howard's forceful intervention, the decision reached would no doubt have been adverse to him. True, eventually he would receive the American Medical Association's highest award for achievement in medicine and would be recognized internationally as "the Father of Neuro-otology," but at the time of the showdown, Bill lacked the personal status to withstand unaided the attacks by neurosurgeons as esteemed as Kurze and others. Even if he moved to some other hospital, he would be blocked by neurosurgeons who shared Kurze's convictions. In speaking of this episode, Howard often wonders aloud how many young doctors with brilliant ideas are rebuffed by their seniors with the result that their ideas can never mature for the benefit of humankind.

Kurze, for his part, was incensed by the decision. True to his words, he resigned from the staff and never admitted another case to that hospital. He took his stand on a point of principle, but his anger, unfortunately, overwhelmed his better judgment. As chair of the department of neurosurgery at USC he discharged Hitselberger from the USC faculty on grounds, he explained, that he did not want medical students and residents to be exposed to the work of "such an incompetent neurosurgeon."

In spite of this, Hitselberger passed his boards. The atmosphere itself, however, remained inflamed, and neither he nor Bill could understand why they should be singled out for continuous attacks—despite the demonstrable fact that their own approach to acoustic tumors had drastically reduced both the mortality and morbidity rates. In an effort to break through the ranks of the opposition, Bill got what is now the House Ear Institute to sponsor a five-day international symposium on acoustic tumor diagnosis and treatment featuring televised demonstrations of the surgery.

The invitation, aimed high at leading neurosurgeons, otologists, neurologists and audiologists, attracted distinguished surgeons including Lord Moran, the preeminent British neurologist and Winston Churchill's physician during the war; Professor H. Olivecrona of Stockholm, the foremost neurosurgeon in the world in acoustic tumor surgery; C.S. McCarty of the Mayo Clinic; J.L. Pool of Columbia University and author of a book detailing 76 cases of his acoustic tumor patients; Henry Dodge, who had established himself as a leading neurosurgeon in Los Angeles; and others.

The conference had three important results. One was the dissemination of more concrete knowledge on the procedures of trans-labyrinthine approach. Second, all participants were brought abreast of the advances that had been made in the early diagnosis of acoustic tumors. Third, the meeting stimulated neurosurgeons across the country to use microsurgical techniques for, in fact, it was the first time the neurosurgeons present gained a direct sense of what could be seen through the microscope and it posed new challenges to their surgical techniques.

Dr. McCarty, then head of the department of neurosurgery at the Mayo Clinic, took Bill aside to ask if he really believed the operating microscope was all that valuable in intracranial surgery. Bill responded that in his opinion those who did not learn the techniques of microsurgery within five years would not be practicing modern neurosurgery. The prediction was to come true.

Though the colloquium stirred worldwide interest among neurosurgeons, Bill and Hitselberger's approach for acoustic tumors remained controversial. Over the next few years their technique steadily improved, their operating time was reduced to three hours and the incidence of mortality and morbidity steadily diminished.

At one point, however, they were subject to a protracted lawsuit for the "wrongful death" of a patient who died after trans-labyrinthine surgery. The suit had been delayed until close to the hour when the statute of limitations was due to expire. Lawyers for the estate had been advised by a "nameless" neurosurgeon that in time the trans-labyrinthine approach would be completely discredited. They could then win the case by proving that Bill and Hitselberger had failed to use the accepted sub-occipital approach on the patient.

The ensuing trial dragged on for four weeks. It was a strained experience, but a number of neurosurgeons came forward to testify on behalf of the defendants. The most telling testimony was that of Hector McKinnen, the Fresno neurosurgeon who lucidly explained why he had chosen them for his own acoustic tumor. The jury decided in favor of Bill and Hitselberger.

In 1968, some three years after Bill and Hitselberger had offered their first course on acoustic tumors, they again presented their course. The atmosphere was considerably different the second time around, because many of the neurosurgeons by then were using microsurgical techniques.

By 1981 when the institute published a two-volume book detailing the team's first 700 cases, the mortality rate had fallen to 0.4 percent. "We had succeeded," Bill laconically remarked, "in moving the decimal point two places, from 40 percent to 0.4 percent."

By 1989 members of the OMG had performed in the aggregate over 2,000 acoustic tumor operations—a record not equaled anywhere else in the world. Taking all the cases together, the mortality rate for acoustic tumor operations has been reduced to around one percent and on a consecutive series of 200 cases at the OMG where Doctors Brackmann, De la Cruz and John House were the surgeons, there were no deaths at all.

The greatest successes in avoiding post-operative complications have occurred when the tumors were small. Larger tumors still present problems. What was gained in consequence of Bill's pioneering work prompted Dr. Glasscock, a former OMG fellow and editor of the *American Journal of Otology*, to say that "the three giants in the field of acoustic tumor surgery in this century have been Harvey Cushing, Walter Dandy and William House, the last being the leading authority on acoustic tumor surgery today. He has firmly established his place in medical history."

Unfortunately that judgment did not place Bill and Hitselberger beyond the reach of more lawsuits. One of these also ensnared George Shambaugh who had come to Los Angeles to be on hand when Bill scheduled a new approach he had developed for what was originally thought to be a large blood type glomus tumor in the ear of a young woman. It turned out to be an aneurysm of a malpositioned internal carotid artery.

Shambaugh was gowned and standing next to Bill at the operating table, following the operation through the viewing tube. "George," said Bill under his breath, "have you ever seen anything like this before?"

"No," said Shambaugh, "but you sure have a big problem on your hands."

"I know it," Bill answered.

The critical and unexpected problem was eventually overcome with only minimal harm to the patient. Shambaugh returned to Chicago. As a reward, Bill presently found himself the defendant in a malpractice suit for five million dollars on the grounds that due to his careless surgery he had permanently crippled the patient.

It didn't matter that prior to the trial the patient was seen with only a slight limp. When she was wheeled into the courtroom, she was a well-coached, crumpled bundle of humanity—a young woman with little control of her speech, head, arm, hand or legs. On the second day of the trial, Howard's wife Helen followed the girl to the rest room and noted that the girl spoke clearly and walked well until she again got into her wheelchair.

The judge instructed the jury not to be swayed by sympathy for the plaintiff and that they should only weigh the question of whether the medical evidence introduced at the trial confirmed the accusation of incompetence, of negligence and malpractice. The jury awarded the patient $140,000 in damages and when polled, they explained they felt sorry for the girl. At the same time, they unanimously agreed that she was lucky to be alive, precisely because her medical and surgical care was the finest to be had anywhere.

The costs of the award were covered by malpractice insurance, but that was a secondary matter to Bill who saw in it a gross perversion of justice. Outside the courtroom, he approached the lawyer who won the suit. "Listen," Bill asked, "if you had a glomus tumor, who would you go to to get it removed?"

"Why I'd go to you," said the lawyer. "After all, you are the best in the business."

To Shambaugh's surprise, the same lawyer filed a one million-dollar suit against him on two counts: he had invaded the patient's privacy—though all OMG patients prior to surgery give their written consent to allow other doctors to observe the surgery for education purposes—and by talking to Bill during the procedure, he was practicing medicine in California without a license. Neither accusation was covered by malpractice insurance.

The lawyer eventually reduced his original asking price of a million dollars to the sum of $2,500, which Shambaugh rejected, but as long as the suit was on file in California, Shambaugh could not risk entering the state for he could be served with legal papers summoning him to appear in court. The case dragged on until Bill and Howard called the matter to the attention of the California State Bar Association. After conducting their own investigation, they informed the lawyer they would initiate disbarment proceedings against him if he persisted in his harassing suit. It was promptly dropped.

Many neurosurgeons now use microsurgical and temporal bone techniques and have formed teams with otologists as Bill always proposed. Together, they have saved a great many lives and have made more lives worth living by greatly decreasing the post-operative complications of facial paralysis and imbalance.

Bill's own moment of vindication came in 1984 when he was invited to New York to present his work on acoustic tumors before the American Society of Neurosurgeons, formerly known as the Harvey Cushing Society. Cushing had always been one of Bill's heroes and he concluded his presentation by saying, "I have always felt that Dr. Cushing might have welcomed the fact that I carried on the work he had started some 80 years earlier."

32

The Cochlear Implant

All during these days of controversy Bill had been busy on another front—with the usual difficulties of trial and error, the usual strong opposition in medical and in other circles and the usual grim determination on his part to stay with his innovative work until he found a proper response to the challenges he faced. The curtain on the drama of Bill's work on the cochlear implant was first raised in 1961.

"A dream in science," Bill House once wrote, "is a vision one can never achieve because as each goal comes near, more exciting ones beckon toward ever farther horizons." He was referring to the fact that he and Howard were part of a changing era where new surgical techniques led to striking changes in otology—from the life-saving methods used without regard to the preservation of hearing to methods to restore hearing. Among the many personal contributions Bill made to those changes, his greatest satisfaction was from his pioneering work on the "cochlear implant" when he helped totally deaf adults and children leave the world of silence and enter the world of sound.

The cochlear implant is not an organ transplant. It is an electrical device that stimulates the hearing nerve by converting sound into an electric current which is passed through the skin behind the ear. Electrodes carry the current into the cochlea of the inner ear, and the hearing nerve then carries it to the brain, thereby creating the sense of sound.

When Bill first began to work in 1961 on a cochlear implant, an estimated ten percent of the population, or 22 million Americans, suffered from some kind of hearing impairment—which meant that it was affecting more people than cancer, blindness, nephritis, tuberculosis, diabetes and heart disease cases combined. Totally deaf individuals in the United States, according to conservative estimates, number some 400,000 people. Though hearing impairment is the most common human handicap and often can be helped by medical, surgical or hearing aids, less then one percent of all medical research funds go for research in hearing.

The two main types of hearing loss are *conductive* in nature and *sensorineural*—or a combination of both. Conductive disorders centered in the middle ear engrossed the interest of Howard and other otologists of his generation. These involve changes in the ear drum and disturbances to the middle ear bones from trauma, infections or fixation of the stapes. They can be corrected either by surgery or by hearing aids.

Sensorineural (nerve) disorders centered in the inner ear, which captivated Bill's interest, include problems with the cochlea such as damage to the hair cells and to semicircular canals which influence balance—as in the case of Ménière's disease. These also include neural or acoustic nerve problems often attributed to aging, genetic factors, noise exposure or other causes. The normal hearing nerve, which is slightly larger than the lead in a pencil, contains 30,000 fibers (neurons) and these tiny hair cells in the cochlea create an electrical current when sound goes into a normal ear that is then transmitted to the brain. When these hairs are damaged or lost, there is no mechanism to carry the electrical impulse they generate to the brain.

The combination problems are those hearing disorders which involve the central nervous system caused by problems of the brain stem or other parts of the central nervous system. The afflicted individual may hear speech but have trouble understanding it, they may hear but be unable to speak (aphasia) or may have balance disturbances.

As is often true in the history of medicine where things hover in the air for decades and even centuries, knowledge that electricity could stimulate the hearing nerve goes back to Alessandro Volta (1745-1827), the Italian physicist who passed an electrical current through his head and noticed that he heard sound. Volta saw in the phenomenon the first ray of hope that sound might someday be restored to the deaf.

Bill's personal interest in restoring hearing through electrical stimulation of the inner ear dates from the moment he read a newspaper item concerning a totally deaf patient of Drs. Djourno and Eyries in Paris who heard sound when his inner ear was stimulated by electricity. The two had implanted an electrical wire in a deaf patient, but it functioned only temporarily. The doctors never followed through with their innovative work. This came to Bill's attention while he was working with Doyle, the neurosurgeon, on Ménière's disease and acoustic tumors. The two discussed this news item and Doyle remarked that his brother Jim was an electrical engineer.

Bill was intrigued and asked Doyle to query his brother about the possibility of picking up the electrical output of the inner ear during a surgical procedure. If electrical engineers could design the necessary device, it could be tested when the cochlear nerve was exposed during surgery for some other disease. Jim Doyle undertook the project and several weeks later gave Bill a speaker device which was designed to pick up cochlear microphonics.

The team gave it a first test during surgery on a Ménière's patient, placing an electrode over the exposed cochlear nerve so the electrical pickup was turned into sound. The astonishing result was that one could actually hear the distortion of sound that occurred due to the inner ear hydrops (the abnormal accumulation of fluid in the inner ear).

Bill had a hard time containing his excitement. When the operation was over, he spoke at length with Jim Doyle about stimulating the inner ear of totally deaf people. Jim became equally excited by the prospect and said he would build a series of electrical stimulators for a clinical trial run. But where could they find the resources to carry out such a project?

Bill spoke to Howard about what he and Jim wanted to do and the need for funds to finance the preliminary work. Howard pointed them to George Eccles, a generous benefactor of the foundation. When Eccles heard Bill and Howard explain what they wanted to work on, he promptly wrote a check for $10,000. He knew from personal experience that any degree of sound the device could engender was far better than living in sonar silence. With Eccles's gift, the foundation became the first sponsoring research agency for the cochlear implant.

Since stapes and chronic ear operations are performed under local anesthetic so patients can answer questions during surgery, stimulators were built to determine what they could hear once electrodes were placed on the surface of the inner ear. Amazingly, tests showed that with such electrical stimulation patients not only had excellent pitch discrimination, but could also ascertain increases or reductions in loudness.

Bill then moved on to try this stimulation on a patient with very severe bilateral otosclerosis who had had a fenestration in one ear which was now totally deaf. When stimulated, he too, had sensations of sound. This patient was jubilant about the prospect that he might regain some hearing through electrical stimulation and agreed to participate in the experiments that had to precede the development of a permanent implant system.

With Jim Doyle working out the details of a system in line with the anatomical specifications Bill laid down, they settled on a multi-channel device to provide better understanding of speech because different levels of the cochlea pickup different levels of sound. The implant had to be made of gold wire, because as Bill knew from his work in dentistry, gold is well tolerated by tissue and its flexibility makes it suitable for surgical manipulation.

Spending endless nights in the dissecting room searching for the right path where the device could be inserted, Bill finally discovered that an electrode system could be slipped into the round window of the cochlea for twenty millimeters (about three-quarters of an inch) without causing any damage. Jim finally produced a device that consisted of a five-electrode system with a sixth ground wire aimed at duplicating the normal stimulation of the neurons in the hearing nerve, thereby reproducing the function of the hair cells.

Six months later the team was ready to test the surgical procedure on a cooperating patient. The first operation went smoothly and Bill implanted the internal receiver above and behind the dead ear. The next day this receiver was connected to an external source of electrical stimulation and at once the patient actually had the sensation of sound, though he did not understand words spoken into his implanted system. It was clear the problem of total deafness that had plagued humankind since creation was not going to be solved overnight.

Bill and Jim continued to work daily with the patient, but on the sixth day Bill became alarmed for redness and swelling began to develop around the implanted area. The patient, who was a plastics worker, may have developed an uncommon sensitivity to plastics such as the silicone rubber used to insulate the internal receiver device. He was given antibiotics to stop the infection, but Bill decided rather than risk serious complications it would be best to remove the coil and electrodes.

This was done under local anesthetic. The end of the experiment left a very disappointed patient, otologist and engineer, yet the few days the patient wore his device made it clear that the implant program had a future. The $10,000 grant from George Eccles had by now been exhausted.

What happened next between Bill and Jim Doyle caused an irrevocable breach—in advance of the later breach on other counts between Bill and John Doyle, the neurosurgeon. "Unknown to me," Bill later explained, "Jim Doyle was looking for added funding. A story in the local press told of a major breakthrough in hearing whose potentialities could be realized if funds were invested in Jim's firm.

"People Jim had contacted called me to say that Howard's and my name and that of the foundation had been used in connection with the reported breakthrough. There were also inquiries from patients who wanted their hearing restored with this new miraculous device and even brokerage houses telephoned, asking if they should buy and recommend stock in Jim's firm.

"Howard and I were shaken," said Bill. "At a meeting with Jim, we emphatically stated that this kind of commercial exploitation would have to cease. Jim replied that he had talked matters over with John, who believed he could carry on the medical aspects of the implant program. I was no longer needed.

"I then asked Jim to give us the circuits and the information on the project for which we had spent Eccles' grant of $10,000. He refused saying, 'I'm not going to give you this material. There was no written contract between us and as far as I am concerned, it's mine.'

Bill continued, "It was one of the most depressing moments I ever had in medicine and, like deep wounds, it did not close without a scar. I respected Jim as an exceptionally clever engineer. By working together we could develop what I believed was a very promising program. Now I would need to start all over again."

Jim and John Doyle did pursue the program for another few months in collaboration with Dr. Fred Turnbull, an ENT doctor. The result, a publication in medical literature, was based on the work that had been done previously. Jim also filed for a patent on the basis of the previous work, which became—so far as anyone can tell—the only basic patent in cochlear implant research.

Bill began to discuss the implant project with Jack Urban with whom he had been working for several years on other matters. "Jack Urban's sole desire," Bill later said, "was to help the totally deaf patients he met. I always had an unbounded respect for his technical abilities and now I came to love him as if he were my own brother."

In the 1960s the transistor gained widespread use in implants such as the heart pacemaker. Improved materials were also being developed which were not rejected by the body. During this period other investigators were doing some encouraging work with cochlear implantation in animals. Robin Michaelson, an otologist in Redwood City, and Blair Simmons of Stanford gave promising clues regarding electrical stimulation of the inner ear. Simmons had implanted a single electrode into the eighth nerve of a cat in order to get single-neuron recordings.

Bill maintained contact with both surgeons over several years, besides monitoring the increased data coming from other research centers where wires were being implanted into the various brain cells of animals. By 1967, Bill and Urban had worked out the details for a new approach to the cochlear implant. Instead of putting an induction coil beneath the skin, a button containing an induction coil was placed on the outside of the skin behind the ear, with direct electrical contact to Urban's newly designed implanted electrode wires.

In early 1969, conditions were ripe to try it on three specially chosen patients—Charles Ricca, Charles Graser and Mabel Niedwicki. All had heard in the past and each had willed their temporal bones to the foundation. They were implanted, over a period of several months with a five-electrode system.

Six weeks after Mabel Niedwicki's implant, some granulation tissue developed around it and the implant was removed. Years later, she was successfully implanted with the single electrode system which she wore for 13 years up to the time of her death. Her account of what life was like during her years of deafness before she received a successful implant and what life was like afterward, explains in its own way why Bill and Urban—and the otologists Bill later trained—became passionately engrossed in the work to be done in perfecting the cochlear implant.

"When I was deaf" Mabel Niedwicki recalled, "I was in a department store shopping one time. A woman behind me must have been saying 'Excuse me, excuse me,' but I couldn't hear her. Finally she shoved me and I was knocked to the floor. I wanted to go home and be safe between my four walls. I wouldn't go shopping alone after that. I always had to wait for my husband to accompany me because I didn't have many friends. How could I call my friends when I couldn't use the telephone? I got tired of explaining to everyone that I was deaf. I was so isolated.

"When I was deaf, I was extremely tense. I was so intent on lip-reading and trying to understand what the person was saying, that my body quivered. When I was out, I worried that I had left the garbage disposal on at home—I've burned out a few disposals because I couldn't hear them running.

People used to talk to my husband so he could relay the message to me, but now they look at me and talk to me. Now I have confidence in myself. I go where I want when I want. When I'm driving by myself, I can hear sirens and I pull to the side of the road. I wouldn't drive without my implant. My husband is thrilled that I can tell him when the phone is ringing. I can have simple telephone conversations.

"I've been deaf so long that I really forgot what everything sounds like. Every day I learn sounds all over again—voices, the ocean, the vacuum cleaner, the disposal. My husband is helping me with music. I'm learning to recognize violins, clarinets, trumpets. The only problem I had with the implant occurred at an airport, going through the X-ray security check. The warning lights lit up like crazy. My husband explained that I was wearing an electronic hearing instrument, but the security people weren't satisfied. They took me into a separate room to examine me. Finally they understood."

Charles Graser, then a 43-year old high school librarian, had good results from the start. Some years previously he had lost his hearing completely from a mycin drug. Bill and Urban knew that whoever was selected to receive a cochlear implant had to be willing to work tirelessly with doctors and engineers to help perfect the electronics of the implant system. Graser, in that respect, was one of those "made in heaven" patients whose commitment to a research program was of central importance to the advances made in it.

With Graser participating, Urban and Bill began a long series of evening sessions in Urban's shop to determine the type of electrical stimulation that should be used in a cochlear implant. The tests were subject to elaborate safety measures.

Bill had asked various authorities in otologic neurophysiology for guidance on the type of electrical stimulation that should be used. From the answers he got, he concluded that everyone was in the dark on the point. So he and Urban agreed they would ask Graser—and later patients—how any particular electrical stimulus sounded to them. They would use whatever sounded good. Research animals could not answer what words they could hear.

"The test sessions," Bill recalled, "usually ran from about six until nine in the evening and Jack and I would sit around for another hour or two trying to figure out what we had learned from Graser's responses. What we were seeing didn't make any neurophysiologic sense to us. More devices were designed, but they often proved worthless after a few hours of testing."

At the end of a year and a half of experiments, the best features of the devices that had been tested were put into one unit for Graser—the world's first wearable cochlear implant. Graser could now walk out of the laboratory and perceive on his own the sensation of sound. Recalling that when his father mastered a difficult case and provided a patient with a new set of dentures that actually fit, he would take the patient to a restaurant and enjoy watching him eat corn on the cob with relish, Bill set up a counterpart celebration with Urban and they invited Graser and his wife, Barbara, to dinner at an Italian restaurant where they enjoyed Graser's delight as he heard the tapping of his fork on a plate and the clinking of glasses in an exchange of toasts. He savored the din of the restaurant and was comfortable with the environmental noise.

For the next six days after that dinner, Bill regularly called Barbara regarding the condition of her husband. He was wearing his unit from the time he got up until he went to bed and constantly asked his family about the various sounds around him. Bill later remarked that, "everyday I said a little prayer asking that the sound continue."

Bill and Urban continued to see Graser and his wife on a weekly basis. After two months the foursome celebrated the first 1,000 hours of use. "As I look back on that moment" Bill said, "the joy I felt when that 1,000-hour bench mark was passed was equaled only by the time when my wife June and I were at Cape Canaveral and felt the ground shake under our feet as we watched Alan Shepard take off for the moon."

As the months went by a crusting of the skin began to accumulate behind Graser's ear around the button of the implant where it passed through the skin. Urban, with his usual flare, in order to solve this new problem designed an electromagnetic induction system that eliminated the button put through the skin.

Graser, when offered the benefit of this new development, decided that he did not want to risk the loss of his new-found hearing, preferring that the new system be tried out on his opposite deaf ear. A single electrode and coil were placed in Graser's other ear, with positive results.

By 1973, Bill and Urban had implanted eleven systems in patients. Bill was careful not to make any inflated claims about who could benefit from a cochlear implant—or for that matter—what could actually be heard by means of one. Events underlined the fact that a general acceptance of the cochlear implant would take much longer than the one or two years he had envisioned on his own timetable.

33

Art in the Practice of Medicine

Since his days at the Moore-White Clinic, Howard distinguished between the science and the art of the practice of medicine and always endeavored to pay as close attention to the fine points of the art as he did to the science of a surgical procedure.

With each new development in otosclerosis, for example, Howard reexamined the records of all his patients—long before the advent of computers—and contacted those most likely to gain better hearing by innovative methods. Charity Ritter was one such patient who, when first examined by Howard, was told nothing could be done to help her hearing, but she would be contacted should future developments change the picture. Nine years later she was surprised that he remembered his promise. Today she hears.

Other patients, such as George Eccles, took advantage of successive advances in otosclerosis surgery which Howard brought to their attention. In Eccles's case, after his initial fenestration, he underwent five stapes operations—each with a fresh technique to improve his hearing.

Currently OMG otologists treat over 10,000 new patients annually, along with 30,000 patients who return for checkups. Patient records are all computerized, as is the research at the institute which provides a rich data bank for studies. By retrieving this data, the doctors often gain new insights into balance and hearing disorders, as well as the rate of success or failure with particular kinds of medical or surgical treatment. Past claims thus come to be revised and past hunches often are confirmed.

Dr. J.C. Ballantyne, one of England's foremost otolaryngologists and the editor of the *British Journal of Otolaryngology*, noting the staggering number of 33,000 ear operations Howard had performed personally by 1983, in addition to treating many thousands of patients who did not require surgery, observed that while otolaryngologists such as himself operated on the head and neck as well as the ear, Howard had confined himself to otology. "Today," he said, "many surgeons the world over do stapedectomies and many of these have been trained by Howard. Yet if I needed stapes surgery and wanted to be absolutely certain of a successful 'clean ear' after an operation, I'd still go to Howard House."

Howard had his share of instances where the things he thought would work in surgery did not. He dwelt on these failures in his lectures and writings, adding, "The way you deal with patients in failed cases is your best defense against malpractice suits even though you are blameless as a surgeon."

In surgical cases that failed, he would ask the patient to consider pledging his temporal bones to the institute, promising to contact the patient if anything innovative came along that might help. "Meanwhile," he would say to the patient, "you are flying on one wing and we must watch your only hearing ear; a card will be sent to you each year as a reminder for your checkup." Howard would thus make patients with poor results members of his "team," and many of them not only willed their temporal bones but also contributed funds in support of the institute's research work.

After Howard had shifted from fenestration to stapes surgery for otosclerosis—which requires using instruments with exceptionally delicate hooks—he unfortunately found himself in that rare instance where his new hook had a concealed flaw. When a surgeon with such a defective hook starts to lift the tiny stapes bone, the slight stress can break the hook from the shaft. That happened to a young woman during an otosclerosis operation and to Howard's dismay the broken hook dropped into her inner ear and came to rest on the sensitive balance center. Any attempt to remove the metal piece would cause a dead ear and a balance disorder. Howard completed the surgery but got little sleep that night and needless to say after this he advised doctors to always test new hooks before using them.

Finally after an uneasy three weeks the patient returned for her post-operative visit. When she walked into his office she was radiant with happiness because her hearing was restored. Howard affected a mock-serious air. "Did you know," he said, "that you are a real bone-head? The bone of your stapes was so hard, it broke off the delicate hook I was using and it fell into your inner ear. The fragment will show up any time you have the ear X-rayed. We will get an X-ray now so that you can see the metal piece."

The young woman's reaction was out of a storybook. She flushed with embarrassment and apologized because her hard bone broke the delicate instrument and when she left his office she stopped at the front desk and insisted on buying a new instrument for Dr. House.

Patients bound themselves to Howard because he always explained their problems in words they could understand and treated them in ways which conveyed the impression that he viewed their cases as worthy of his most concentrated attention. Some patients were specially appreciative of his gift for laughter.

Once Keenan Wynn, the actor, came in suffering from a noise-inflicted hearing loss. Howard fitted him with ear protectors and hearing aids, but admonished him to forgo the noise of the racing cars and motorcycles he favored.

"But they are my hobby. What do I do for recreation?" Wynn asked.

"Take up canoeing," Howard laconically replied.

Wynn enjoyed telling others of this ridiculous advice, but understood full well that he should turn to quiet forms of recreation.

Though Howard spoke to his patients about the research work at the institute which might one day help their problems, he could never bring himself to ask any of them to contribute financially to its support and always claimed he was not a fund-raiser. Many bystanders disagree, saying he is one of the best because of his low-key manner with patients and friends. He did, however, ask some patients to serve as trustees of the institute and others rendered it unique and valuable personal services.

As the 1950s gave way to the 1960s, the board of trustees was invigorated by the important addition of two men from the corporate world. Leonard Firestone had regained his hearing in one ear through Lempert's fenestration surgery, but found Lempert's raw manner regarding fees off-putting, to say nothing of the pain he had experienced because of the rough way Lempert removed his bandages. When Firestone was returning to his Los Angeles home, Lempert referred him to Howard for follow-up care.

When stapes surgery replaced the fenestration, Howard suggested this innovative operation to Firestone—who still had vivid memories of the negative ordeals of Lempert's surgery. Howard convinced him this stapes surgery would have none of the after-effects associated with fenestrations, and so the operation was scheduled and in fact Firestone regained his hearing. Surprised to find that Howard charged him only his standard fee, Firestone asked Howard if there was anything he could do for him. Howard said yes, he could accept an invitation to be a member of the board of trustees. And so he did.

Through his extensive associations in the corporate world, Firestone brought many executives with hearing problems to Howard's office including Herbert Hoover, Jr., the son of the former president, who had suffered a hearing loss in both ears at the age of four when he fell from a swing and was knocked unconscious for several days. None of the many doctors who were consulted in later years could help him. At 14 his father sent him to work with his friend, Thomas A. Edison, to prove that impaired hearing did not prevent a fruitful career and also to have Edison design a hearing aid for him.

Hoover's hearing loss was getting worse when Firestone brought him to the institute. Howard knew that Herbert Hoover Sr. wore a hearing aid and had a hunch that this might be another hereditary case of otosclerosis. An examination of Herbert Jr. showed he was a suitable candidate for surgery.

During the operation, Howard came upon eccentric features he had never seen before. The childhood fall from the swing had partially detached the stapes arch from its foot plate and otosclerosis had fixed the foot plate, which accounted for the progressive loss in hearing. To Howard's added surprise, a similar fractured stapes arch and otosclerosis was also found when his second ear was operated on.

When Herbert, Jr.'s hearing was restored in both ears, Howard had in him a very grateful patient and in the aging Herbert Hoover, Sr., an appreciative father for what Howard had done to liberate his son from this life-long affliction. Herbert Jr., readily accepted an invitation to join Howard's board of trustees.

Many leading figures in the entertainment world have been Howard's patients and helped in many ways to support the institute. One of the first of these was Nanette Fabray MacDougall, star of stage, screen and television. At the time of her visit in 1966 to Howard's office, she was accompanied by her husband, Randy MacDougall, the author of many memorable screen plays and president of the Screen Writer's Guild of America.

Nanette first became aware of a hearing problem when she was starring on Broadway in the early 1940s. Over the next decade Dr. Rosen had performed the stapes operation on both of her ears and her hearing improved, but the stapes refixed—as mobilizations often did—the hearing regressed and she returned to wearing hearing aids.

The problems of the hearing impaired now became her "cause," and she was the first celebrity to publicize her hearing problem and was untiring in her efforts to educate the public regarding the plight of the hearing impaired and to encourage people with hearing problems to speak up. She served on the President's Council for Deaf Education through five administrations and testified many times in Washington urging the appropriation of funds for ear research.

At one point in all this, Nanette heard of the new procedure, stapedectomy, which had replaced stapes mobilization in the surgical treatment of otosclerosis. After she and her husband consulted Howard about it, she agreed to have the new stapes operation. The results were successful. Later, Dr. Sheehy operated on her other ear, again with productive results. Aware of all Nanette had done on behalf of the hearing impaired, Howard asked her to serve as a trustee on the board of the foundation—which began her long and fruitful association with the foundation.

Florence Henderson, also a well-known star, was among the many leading performers who was referred to Howard by Nanette. In speaking about her own career which was threatened by a hearing loss, Florence put the realities of the case in the form of a succinct sentence: "No hearing, no song and dance; no song and dance, no work."

Florence's hearing loss was due to otosclerosis—which was repaired with surgery. She, too, has been very helpful in fostering the institute's work. As has Mary Martin, a shining star of the great musicals of the post-war era. Once while Mary was in Chicago performing in "South Pacific" she developed wart-like growths on her vocal chords known as singer's nodes—which produced hoarseness. Mary was referred to Dr. Paul Hollinger, who comically said the nodes might be due to the way she hit high C. He explained she could resume her singing style once the nodes were removed.

An operation was performed and when she recovered from the anesthesia, she wrote on a piece of paper, "Was it C?"

Hollinger wrote back, "No, the whole scale."

A successful operation to remove the nodes should have calmed her fears regarding her voice, but it didn't. After she resumed her performances she had Hollinger stand in the wings of the stage and between numbers spray her throat with a soothing liquid known by the exotic name of Schmugra Oil. When the "South Pacific" company moved on to San Francisco, Hollinger arranged with Dr. Shirley Baron to continue Mary's throat treatments. Then when the company moved on to Los Angeles, Dr. Baron referred Mary to Howard who was still doing throat work at the time.

After Howard examined her throat, he told her that Hollinger had done a "great job" and no further treatment was necessary. But Mary doubted if she could get through a night's performance unless her throat was regularly sprayed. Would he please come to the theater and stand in the wings where he could administer the same treatment she had in Chicago and in San Francisco? He said he would be happy to do so, and went through the procedure the first night.

On the second night, after spraying her throat, Howard suggested he see the show from out front with his family. He would come back stage at the first sign of trouble. Mary was still unsure, but made it through the rest of the show without further medication. On the third night, Howard urged her to dispense with the spray even at the start of the performance. The doubting Mary again sparkled in her usual enchanting style, and her self-confidence was now restored. On Howard's 75th birthday, she joined Nanette Fabray and Florence Henderson, saluting him with a favorite song from South Pacific: "I'm in Love with a Wonderful Guy."

Dolores Hope, the wife of Bob Hope, was a different case. After she dove into her swimming pool she came up with an ear that felt "full." She had never met Howard, but called and was told to come at once to his office. Examination revealed a huge perforation in her ear drum with a slight infection and damaged ear bones. To Howard's surprise, she had essentially normal hearing. Questions followed. Did she ever have any difficulty in the ear before? No. Had anyone ever told her that she had a problem with her ear? No. Howard treated the infection which cleared up the "fullness," and fitted her with ear plugs to keep water out.

A concerned Bob Hope called Howard, who told him a future operation might be necessary but for now she was to protect her ear and treat it with medication. The problem, for the moment, did not seem serious. When later Dolores returned to Howard's office, she had Bob in tow because she thought he had a hearing loss. Bob did in fact have a slight nerve impairment, but he did not want a hearing aid. Instead he faithfully adhered to the regimen Howard prescribed to help prevent further hearing loss.

Certain pills were part of the treatment and they figured in a story Bob later told Howard. "One day when I was on a plane with President Reagan, I had finished eating and I took a couple of my ear pills. The President noticed them and said, "I take those same pills. I'll bet Howard House is your ear doctor too."

When Dolores Hope brought Bob into the office, Howard took the opportunity to examine her ear and again could not believe what he saw. The perforated eardrum had healed and despite the problem with the little ear bones, her hearing remained good. From the standpoint of a medical textbook, she had "an abnormally normal ear." Both she and Howard were delighted by a result that had been achieved simply by medical self-restraint.

The friendships formed in this way had long-term spin-off effects. Dolores became a trustee of the institute and Bob served on its national council. In addition, he has served as the master of ceremonies for the institute's annual fund-raising dinner since its inception.

Phyllis Diller, the comedienne, was yet another one who suddenly had an uneasy feeling of "fullness" and loss of hearing in one ear. She had never before had any hearing problems and so dismissed the experience. Two weeks later she had an acute attack of dizziness and called her friend Nanette Fabray, who arranged for her to see Howard at once.

Howard determined she had had a spasm of a blood vessel which severely damaged the hearing nerve. His treatment entailed a series of three intravenous histamine injections over a three-day period—each injection taking an hour or so. This was to be followed by twice-a-week injections and other medications taken by mouth for a three-month period.

As Phyllis was due to leave for an extended tour, Howard showed her how to practice self-injections on an orange and then gave her syringe needles and a vial of histamine to take with her. But Phyllis could not steel her nerves to inject the orange, let alone herself. For starters.

In the course of her tour, she reached Houston on the day she was due for a shot. With vial and syringe in hand she went to the emergency room of a nearby hospital for the injection. Not so fast. There are procedures. She must first fill out a questionnaire bearing on the most intimate details of her private life. When she was at last brought before a doctor and extended the vial and syringe toward him, his response was a rasping question: "What is this stuff?"

"It's a treatment," she said, "prescribed for my dizziness and hearing loss."

"How do I know it isn't dope?"

"You've got to take my word that it is histamine, or you can call Dr. Howard House in Los Angeles to confirm the truth of what I am telling you."

The doctor finally got around to giving her the injection, for which she had to pay $50. On her way out of the emergency room, she swore she would never again go to a hospital for a routine shot. In Dallas, her next stop, she bought a dog collar and leash, put on a fur coat, placed the dog collar around her throat, gave the attached leash to her secretary and headed for the office of a veterinarian.

When she reached the door of his office, she dropped to her hands and knees and barked her way across the threshold. "My dog," explained the secretary to the startled veterinarian, "needs an injection of histamine."

The veterinarian recognized the "dog" to be Phyllis Diller and immediately gave her the injection. All he asked for his services was her autographed picture which he proudly placed on the wall of his reception room between the pictures of Fido and Lucky. Phyllis regained her hearing and became a devoted friend of Howard and of the House Ear Institute.

The exact cause for a sudden hearing loss has so far escaped the grasp of research scientists and for that reason there is much controversy over how to treat the affliction. Some doctors advise bed rest, others recommend surgical intervention and still others suggest no treatment at all because in certain instances the hearing returns spontaneously. In Phyllis Diller's case Howard adhered to the "do something and do it now" school, even if the efficacy of injections of histamine is not based on conclusive scientific proof—no more than was Simon Jasberg's use of pork strips to stop a massive nose bleed.

A disagreement about such procedures flared one evening when Howard spoke about sudden hearing loss in a talk he gave to the medical staff of the Good Samaritan Hospital. His "do something" views were challenged by a general surgeon—a personal friend—who strongly argued that Howard's approach had not been scientifically tested. The precise way to deal with the matter was to separate patients suffering from a sudden hearing loss into two groups. One would be injected with histamine, the other with placebos. If more of the first group regained hearing than the second, it could be said the treatment made the difference.

The discussion ended on an inconclusive note. A few days after the meeting Howard received a distress call from his surgeon friend/critic who reported that just as he was nearing the end of an operation, he suffered a sudden hearing loss in his right ear. Howard told him to come to his office as soon as possible. When the examination confirmed the surgeon's fears, Howard, with a nurse standing by, prepared to give him an injection.

"What's that you are going to give me?" asked the surgeon.

"I don't know," replied Howard.

"What do you mean you don't know?" he responded.

Howard returned, "I'm following the advice you gave at the hospital the other night, so I've set up a blind experiment. My nurses alone know who I'm injecting with placebos and who with histamine. They will keep track and let me know the results several months from now."

The surgeon paled. "So what *are* you going to give me?" he demanded, "Histamine or a placebo?"

A benign-looking Howard said, "Doctor, how unscientific of you even to ask."

Howard relented when he saw the alarmed look on the surgeon's face and explained he could never do a blind study on any patient. Each one deserved the treatment which in his judgment offered the best chance for having his hearing restored. The surgeon received an injection of histamine and two days later regained his hearing—becoming a "true believer" in Howard's approach to the baffling problem of sudden hearing loss.

Such real-life humor Howard found thoroughly enjoyable. Sir Terrence Cawthorne, the noted British otolaryngologist, also delighted in the droll moments, which partly explains the intimacy between the two and the fact that they were frequent traveling and lecture companions. In 1967, Cawthorne was president of the Royal Society of Medicine and Howard was his guest of honor at their international conference. The program focused on new ways to restore lost hearing and included Howard's first film on stapedectomy surgery.

The film was shown before an audience of doctors and their wives after cocktails, but before dinner. "I hope" Howard said introducing the film, "that the sight of a few drops of blood does not upset anyone. The film is in color."

The lights were dimmed, the film started and within a few moments a loud crash was heard. A woman in the back of the room had fainted at the first sight of some blood. The lights were turned on and she was carried out of the auditorium.

Howard restarted the film, only to be treated to a domino effect. Three other women fainted in quick succession. Each time the lights went on again, the fallen were removed and Howard continued the film, wondering when the next crash would occur.

Later at the banquet, Howard apologized to the diners, while the women who had fainted, apologized for the stir they had caused. Cawthorne, who witnessed the disaster, affecting envy of Howard's record, said, "I am jealous of your score of five bodies. The best score in fainted women I have ever achieved was two." Then, holding the stiletto in a velvet-gloved hand, he thrust home, "Perhaps I should try not make my own operations so bloodless."

Another real-life comedy entailed the claims of miraculous cures made by a Hollywood chiropractor whose name happened to be Howard J. House and who advertised in the newspapers and on a sidewalk sign in front of his bungalow office that he could give the human body any shape a patient desired—a flat stomach, slender hips, clear skin, bigger breasts—besides which, the treatment would be "fun."

Howard P. House, M.D. and Howard J. House, D.C. sometimes received mail intended for the other, but that was the least of the things that got mixed up between them. When doctors would refer their patients with hearing problems to Howard, M.D., some patients would mistakenly see the Howard, D.C.—who did not forward them to the intended address as he did misdirected mail. Instead he would explain that their hearing loss was due to toxic material in the body and recommended a series of high colonic irrigations—or enemas.

The patients were surprised by the intended treatment and would later tell the story to their regular physicians, who would call Howard, M.D. and ask, "Since when are high colonic irrigations a cure for hearing problems?"

Explanations about mistaken identities followed, but in Howard's view, what really bothered him were not the doctors who called, but those doctors who didn't. To preserve the evidence of what he viewed as slapstick comedy, Howard had someone photograph the sidewalk sign under the name of Howard J. House, Chiropractor and then displayed the framed photograph in his own office. In addition, he regularly exchanged a specially printed Christmas card with the chiropractor: Merry Christmas Howard House to Howard House.

Howard J. got so busy treating hearing impaired patients with high colonic irrigation that he changed his sign to read: "Dr. Howard J. House D.C. and staff—Dedicated to Restoring Hearing and Ear Hygiene." This caused even more confusion. Nor would the situation be helped by emphasizing the difference in the middle initials. Howard, M.D. obviously did not want to be known as "P" House or "Payne" House. The confusion ended only when the "other" Howard House passed away. Howard, M.D. observes, "My practice has zoomed since then."

Part of Howard's "feel" for comedy forms a bridge to the different ways Howard and Bill bore themselves in adversarial situations. Bill adhered to the conviction that the shortest distance between two points is a straight line and simply would not negotiate with his critics as Howard could and did. Had he not plunged forward on the straight line of his own convictions, in defiance of his critics, he would never have become the "Father of Inner-Ear Surgery."

Bill was fortunate in having Howard nearby to shield him from attacks. Yet Howard often remarked that it was Bill who made basic contributions to otologic surgery, while his own, though not small, were confined to refinements on points of detail.

Where otology as a whole was concerned, the contributions Howard made as a builder and conserver of institutions has no match among his contemporaries. Without him, there would not be an Otologic Medical Group and a House Ear Institute. Through him the OMG developed into a cooperative ear practice and the institute is available to break new ground in treating hearing and balance disorders and to pass this knowledge on to other otolaryngologists throughout the world through courses and the medical literature.

While Bill in his own style, achieved what he set out to do, so did Howard. Bill was to be honored, as Howard was, by leading medical societies throughout the world, but he never headed a major professional organization or chaired any of their key committees. Howard, on the other hand, because of his skill in group diplomacy—and his "feel" for the needs of institutions as institutions—was raised to successive leadership posts in his profession.

In 1951 Howard was elected to his first important position—secretary-treasurer of the Pacific Coast Oto-Ophthalmological Society. He was not unmindful of the personal professional advantages that went with the high visibility of such a post; for years, it had largely been a one-person operation.

Howard changed the dynamics of the society by delegating more work and more responsibilities to more doctors. The effect of the increased participation raised the institutional importance of the society in the eyes of its 500 members. Five years later, Howard was elected president of the Society. Whenever possible, he repeated his managerial formula of subdivision and delegation in the elected or appointed posts he subsequently held in the major national professional organizations in his specialty. (Among others, he served as president of the Triological Society, 1962-1963; the American Otological Society, 1966; and the

American Academy of Ophthalmology and Otolaryngology, 1971-1972.)

Among professional societies in the field of otolaryngology, the Collegium, the oldest, is at the summit of international prestige. Today, its elected membership world-wide consists of roughly 250 otolaryngologists and Ph.D. scientists representing 38 nations in all hemispheres. Howard was elected when the quota was fixed at ten surgeons from each country, though it was eventually increased to 20 from the United States because of large number of ENT specialists in this country. Many members are heads of ENT departments in university medical schools throughout the world. Bill House and Fred Linthicum are currently members. To have three members of the Collegium come from the same private institution—The Otologic Medical Group with its link to the House Ear Institute—has no counterpart elsewhere in the world.

Once again however, not everything was flawless. In the 1960s and 1970s the institute showed signs of internal strains, some due to growing pains.

34

En Route to a Watershed

In 1959 when the OMG was formed and subsequently moved into the building Howard built at Third and Alvarado, a room was set aside in it for the use of the Los Angeles Foundation of Otology. In 1956 patients were asked to will their temporal bones to the foundation for microscopy study. Now, however, there were many innovations to be taught, and Bill House, Fred Linthicum and James Sheehy—as original OMG members—joined in expanding the educational work of the foundation.

The recent innovations included the use of the operating microscope and the unique instruments Jack Urban designed in collaboration with Bill House. There were also fresh techniques in stapes surgery for otosclerosis and tympanoplasty for chronic ear infections to be taught, plus operations for Ménière's disease and acoustic tumors and the beginning of the cochlear implant program for total deafness.

Between the start of the 1960s and the watershed years of 1974-75, many institutional developments eventually warranted changing the foundation's name to that of the Ear Research Institute so that the public could better understand the purpose of the foundation. The first was creating the George and Dolores Eccles Temporal Bone Laboratory as a counterpart to the pre-existing temporal bone bank program.

Dr. George Keleman, an internationally recognized research scientist in temporal bone histopathology who had left his native Hungary in 1940 and joined the faculty of the Harvard Medical School, was commissioned to work with Fred Linthicum as the first director of the Eccles Temporal Bone Laboratory with full-time technicians assisting the preparation of the acquired documented temporal bones for study. Dr. Keleman was 72 years old when Aram Glorig and Howard invited him to come to Los Angeles.

As a close friend of Hans Brunner—with whom Howard had studied in Vienna—he managed to secure for the foundation Brunner's wonderful collection of temporal bone slides and the original copies of his four volumes on temporal bone histopathology. Keleman's presence was a tribute to the foundation, for not only had he received honors and awards from a dozen countries, he was also a member of 30 otolaryngological societies around the world—including the Collegium—and served in an editorial capacity for 13 major publications and had published 200 professional papers. He continued his research in the laboratory until his death at the age of 93.

Research in the Temporal Bone Laboratory led to important findings about hearing and balance disorders. Each temporal bone takes nine months to prepare before it can be cut in sections, 1/1,000 of an inch thick—much thinner than cigarette paper—yielding between 400-600 sections from a single bone. Every 10th section is put on a glass slide and stained for microscopic study by the doctors and compared with the patient's history and findings during life. Specimens removed from the ear during surgery are also prepared and studied in the laboratory.

A second institutional development of the time was the development of a formal relationship between the foundation and the USC School of Medicine. All OMG members had served the school as voluntary faculty members teaching otology (as had Howard since 1939). Even after Howard relinquished the position of chair of its ENT department to Dr. Alden Miller in 1961, he gave 15 lectures to its students each year.

In 1962, USC's president asked Howard to consider a formal link between the two entities. After discussions, the OMG members and the trustees of the foundation, recognizing that such an association provided academic accreditation for the foundation's ear courses and other mutual scientific advantages, agreed to the affiliation but retained for the foundation its own distinct identity as a freestanding body. Practicing ENT specialists, faculty and residents from an ever-widening worldwide circle took the foundation's accredited course offerings. In fact, it was the only place in the United States—or the world—which offered advanced training in inner ear otologic surgery.

A third institutional development dating from the 1960s entailed the creation of two fellowship programs—clinical and research. Clinical fellows were selected from ENT specialists who had completed their residency programs and obtained California licenses. To this day these are funded jointly by St. Vincent Medical Center and the OMG. During their year of training, the fellows observe and assist OMG doctors in diagnosing and treating ear problems by medical or surgical means and also participate in the foundation's research projects and in the publication of the results.

Research fellows, on the other hand, are largely selected from foreign doctors who do not have Californian licenses and are funded independently or by their universities or governments. They spend from three months to three years observing OMG doctors in surgery and in the clinical care of patients, take courses, do extensive temporal bone dissections and undertake specific research projects.

Most doctors invited to become members of the OMG come from the ranks of the clinical fellows. Even John

House, Howard's son, first served as a Clinical Fellow before he was voted into the OMG in late 1974. Not all the doctors who joined the OMG remained with the group. Several OMG members, for example, resigned the group practice in favor of setting up smaller offices for themselves. Others became chair of various ENT departments or received full-time teaching appointments in medical schools.

Other institutional developments occurred as doctors from around the globe in increasing numbers converged on the Otologic Medical Group and the foundation to observe what their members were doing. To replace the random manner in which they were made and to make these encounters more profitable for the individual doctor, a formal Visiting Doctors Program was established in 1968 so that a personalized schedule could be prepared in advance to match the special interests of each visitor.

Meanwhile, the dual growth of the OMG practice and the expanding work of the foundation compounded the pressure on available space in the OMG building. To meet this ever-increasing demand, Howard steadily purchased adjoining properties, so that eventually they owned three and a half acres. A point was reached when the foundation could no longer be managed in an ad hoc way, nor financed solely by voluntary contributions from grateful OMG patients. Obviously there was a need for year-round fund-raising efforts, better budgetary controls on expenditures and supervision of the foundation's daily routines. So in 1967 Glenn R. Snyder was appointed the first full-time managing director of the foundation—a post he held for the next seven years.

A major change in the structure of the foundation's leadership occurred two years later, following the death of Oscar Trippet—the lawyer for the Moore-White Clinic who had served since 1962 as chair of the board of the foundation. He was succeeded by Mahlon E. Arnett, president of Bullock's Department Stores.

Arnett had long suffered a hearing loss and wore hearing aids—which he bought in much the same way as a customer might buy a pair of shoes in his stores. Once after a stockholders' meeting where he mentioned his hearing problem, two women came up and advised him to go see Howard House who had successfully operated on them so they no longer needed to wear their hearing aids.

Taking their advice Arnett regained his hearing after Howard performed a stapedectomy. When he received the $600 bill for the surgery, he called Howard to say the amount was grossly inadequate compared to his joy at being able to hear again. Howard explained that was the standard fee then, but Arnett would not be put off. "I would like to do something for your foundation," he said. "I am sending it a check for $3,000."

Howard thanked him for the proposed gift, but had something else on his mind. "Would you consider coming on our board to fill a vacancy created by the death of Herbert Hoover, Jr.?"

He would and later became chair of the board. One of Arnett's intimate friends, Charles M. Hart, president of the Hart Insurance firm, agreed to be vice chair. Another long-time friend, David E. Agnew, accepted Arnett's invitation to join the board as secretary-treasurer and chief financial officer. Agnew, a graduate of Harvard Law School and a leader of the Los Angeles Bar, first met Howard in 1969 when he brought his youngest daughter to him for care. Out of gratitude for Howard's help, he agreed to assume the taxing job of secretary-treasurer of the foundation.

The question tended to loom up periodically as the foundation grew in significance: Why did so many busy people give not only money but time and energy to help Howard achieve the goals he set for the foundation and the

House Ear Institute? What qualities drew people to him even when he had to tell some of them that nothing more could done on their behalf?

Nanette Fabray has suggested, "There is a 'star' quality to Howard. I have seen him walk into a room—a completely self-possessed person—and without saying a word, he is noticed by everyone and his presence is felt." She added that Howard, through his contagious enthusiasm for what he was doing "offers powerful people in competitive realms a unique chance to be his collaborator in a great scientific venture whose reward would simply be the sense of doing something wonderful for the rest of humanity."

In 1971, the foundation established a Vestibular Testing Laboratory under the direction of Fred Linthicum. Disorders of the vestibular, or balance systems, produce symptoms ranging from occasional mild unsteadiness to persistent, violent episodes of vertigo accompanied by nausea, vomiting and severe head noise (tinnitus). Determining the cause of these symptoms—unlike the routine tests for some other medical problems—is not always easily done. Innovative tests at the vestibular laboratory entailed the measurement of involuntary eye movements (nystagmus) which occur in vestibular disorders. Together with other diagnostic steps, these procedures eventually became a standard way to help determine the cause and management of patients suffering from dizziness.

That same year the foundation established a film production studio because Bill House believed they should film a series of lectures and surgical demonstrations which could then be made available to doctors, universities and medical societies on a rental or purchase basis to defray the production expense. After much preparatory work, the first of these films was made in 1971, followed by five more the next year. It was reasoned that a doctor in the comfort of his home or his office could observe these films and be brought abreast of the latest advances in otologic surgery. This early film project, though of great educational value, was later reluctantly abandoned when it proved to be very costly.

Also that year the foundation established an Electrophysiologic Testing Laboratory. There was a direct connection between the need for such a laboratory—which could measure minute electrical currents generated in the nerves of the inner ear and brain cells—and Bill's work on the cochlear implant.

The laboratory came into being one year after Dr. Derald E. Brackmann had joined the OMG Group following his residency in otolaryngology at USC County Hospital. Since every OMG doctor has a special niche for research under the auspices of the foundation, Brackmann declared his interest in what is known as electrocochleagraphy (measurement of cochlear function) and was subsequently sent to Bordeaux, France to study with two French scientists, Michel Portmann, M.D. and Jean Aron, Ph.D.— pioneers in this field.

Returning to Los Angeles, Brackmann became the director of the electrophysiologic laboratory, besides engaging in his regular OMG practice. However the work in the laboratory grew from a research project into an accepted clinical tool, for among other things, it made possible the first use of brain stem audiometry to diagnose acoustic tumors, as well as tests for hearing in babies. Through this work, Brackmann later consulted with colleagues at the University of Utah Medical School who had an interest in developing their own cochlear implant project.

The international outreach of the programs offered by the foundation grew in range and depth as the foundation evolved into the Ear Research Institute and then into the House Ear Institute. Its seminars, conferences, symposia and regular courses were attended not only by otologists from every Western European country, but from most of the Eastern Bloc countries, the Middle East, the Pacific, Japan, India and eventually mainland China.

Its expanding outreach throughout Latin America was due in no small measure to the missionary educational work of Dr. Antonio De La Cruz, a Costa Rican by birth who, after serving as a clinical fellow, was invited to join the OMG in 1972. With his fluency in Spanish and with his fund of energy that always seemed to be in "overdrive," De La Cruz traveled far and wide in Latin America to give lectures and conduct seminars on the new techniques developed by OMG surgeons. Doctors in the audiences he addressed subsequently often arranged to come to Los Angeles for further courses. In a kind of capillary process, many Latin American magnates and political leaders with hearing problems—including six presidents—were also drawn to him at the OMG for treatment.

In a profession that is all too often scarred by the unhappy effects of back stabbing, the reaction to the institute by members of the Collegium—which stands at the summit of world prestige among otologists—is all the more remarkable. Among the French members of the Collegium, for example, the institute was the object of a cherished tribute from Dr. Michel Portmann, the director of the Portmann Foundation at the University of Bordeaux which bears the name of his celebrated father, Dr. George Portmann. Once while Portmann was in Los Angeles as a guest of the institute, he remarked, "This institute is the most important place in the world for otologic research."

This view was echoed by Dr. Imrich Friedmann from London, the world's foremost authority on electron microscopy of the ear. In an address to the trustees of the institute he remarked, "I have watched your organization develop into a very great institute—a mecca for all of us."

Dr. Carl Axel Hamburger of the Karolinska Institute in Stockholm, the source of the Nobel Prize awards in medicine, put aside his professional reserve when he addressed an institute symposium. "One day," he said in a reference to the OMG association with the institute, "you will see a Nobel Prize from this group."

Dr. J.C. Ballantyne, the editor of the *British Journal of Otolaryngology*, said, "No country in the world has anything like the institute which Howard House founded and built with his associates. In contrast to the way things go elsewhere, it has not depended on government support and does not take its direction from any governmental agency. Its great work is due solely to private effort and private funds."

One could add that none of the fundamental clinical advances in the surgical treatment of hearing and balance disorders made in the United States since the 1930s were due to government-sponsored research. All were made from private offices and individual clinicians who privately financed their research—Lempert in fenestration, Rosen in stapes mobilization, Shea in stapedectomy and Bill House in inner ear surgery.

With all these international connections, Howard found himself the recipient of various professional honors bestowed outside the country. In 1968 he was awarded an honorary degree in medicine by the Karolinska Institute in Stockholm and became an Honorary Fellow of the Otologic Society in Australia and of the German Society of Otorhinolaryngology. This was followed in 1970 when he was made an Honorary Fellow of the International College of Surgeons, in 1973 he was granted the same honor by the Royal Australian College of Surgeons and in 1975 he was made an Honorary Fellow of the Royal College of Surgeons of England.

Of all the honors, however, it was the one from the Karolinska Institute which left the deepest mark on Howard's memory—due in part to the fact that its Old World pomp and circumstance went hand-in-hand with a desperate and ludicrous personal battle Howard quietly fought in the grand tradition of the "Hazards of Being Howard."

The saga began with a telegram Howard received from the president of the Karolinska Institute informing him he had been nominated for the honorary degree which was followed up with a letter requesting the size of his hat and ring finger because a special ring and top hat went with the honorary degree in medicine. When Howard mailed back the measurements, he added that his hat size was seven and one-fourth inches—provided his head "did not swell in the meantime from such an honor."

The morning after Howard and his family arrived at the Grand Hotel in Stockholm a woman called from the lobby and asked for "Dr. House."

"When you are in Sweden," said the voice, "I am at your disposal."

"Good," said Howard, without allowing his fantasies to run riot, "Come up—meet my wife."

The beautiful young woman who presently appeared at the door turned out to be one of the top graduating students in the Karolinska Medical School. She explained that it was a cherished distinction for students to be chosen to look after the needs of doctors who were being awarded honorary degrees.

The morning's schedule began with a stop at a hatter's shop to determine whether the hat that had been made for Howard actually fit. En route to the shop, Howard noticed that his escort seemed to be looking frequently at his head. Finally she turned to him in the manner of a medical student taking down the case history and asked, "Doctor, what problem do you have that causes your head to swell? I saw the letter you wrote in which you referred to that possibility, but none of the medical books I've consulted contain any references to the type of difficulty you mentioned."

Howard tried to explain that it was like saying "busting your buttons," but that caused more confusion and explanation.

From the hatter, the pair drove to the clothier where Howard was measured for rented formal clothes for that evening's festivities. He was assured it would not be necessary for him to return for a further fitting, rather the white tie ensemble would be at his hotel by two o'clock. The next stop called for lunch with the other recipients of honorary degrees and a brief rehearsal of the award ceremony.

Later when Howard put on the formal, heavy woolen clothes that were waiting for him at the hotel, he noticed the pants did not come with suspenders but were held up by an elastic waistband. He and the family left the hotel and drove in an official limousine to Stockholm's Town Hall for the ceremony. The area around the hall was festocned in holiday style with flags serving as a background for an honor guard resplendent in their finery. Their vehicle came to a halt in front of the Town Hall, immediately followed by the queen, the crown prince and other members of the Swedish royal family.

The moment Howard stepped out of the limousine, disaster struck. He was so hot in the heavy woolen clothes from the uncommon heat of the day—a high 80° for Stockholm—that the elastic waistband on his pants became very loose. The pants dropped to his knees as he stepped out, almost causing him to fall right in front of the royal family. He desperately yanked them up under the long coattails before the picture he presented as a "flasher" was generally noticed. Newton's law of gravity tormented him from that moment on, while Helen and his family were beside themselves with laughter.

The rest of the ordeal went like this: The only way he could keep his pants up was to put his left hand in his pocket and his right on the outside of the pants while he puffed his stomach out. Helen and the children went off to their assigned places near the ceremonial stairway down which Howard would walk. He was to bow to the royal family, then turn and bow again to the president and the faculty of the institute. All this required much stealth in shifting his hand to keep his pants up and on. When standing or walking, both hands were folded in front of his stomach.

The problem grew more acute during the ceremony before the royal family and a large audience of Swedish notables, faculty and a solid sea of white-capped senior medical students from the Karolinska Institute. Howard was the first of the honorees to be called to the podium where a citation was read, handed to him, a ceremonial top hat placed on his head, a ring placed on his finger and a rolled diploma placed in his hands—all punctuated by handshakes—while a Swedish cruiser in the harbor split the air with a salvo. Every step, except for the salvo which shook the Town Hall, called for another frantic maneuver requiring a quick shifting of his hands from his pockets to his stomach.

Once the awards were made, his son Kenneth came to him with what he hoped would be his father's salvation: he had located a small safety pin. Howard snapped it shut in the heavy folds of the pants to take up some of the slack. Just as he completed the task, the chief actors in the affair were led on a ceremonial march into a beautiful dining room where the honorees were seated at the head table. Here the president of the institute introduced the honorees all over again. When Howard stood, his pin snapped open.

After each course in the eight-course dinner, there was also a collective standing for another toast. The pin now stuck into Howard's flesh each time he stood up or sat down.

At the end of the dinner, the president of the institute leaned over to Howard to whisper, "The orchestra will soon start to play a medley of Viennese waltzes. You are to take the lady on your right and lead her down to the dance floor for the first waltz."

The lady on Howard's right was the wife of a German chemist who had been the recipient of an honorary degree. When the moment came for him to lead the lady to the ballroom floor, the only avenue of escape from his embarrassing predicament was to take her into his confidence. He told her about the problem with the elastic in the pants of his rented clothes and that he could only hold the pants up by keeping at least one hand in his pocket. If he danced that way with her, she should not think it strange.

She was not only understanding and sympathetic, but added, "Neither I nor my husband dance."

To Howard's relief this turned out to be true. Later, the honorees were asked to stand together for a group picture while being serenaded by the student glee club. Howard remained in a cold sweat, hands firmly folded in front of him, holding both his citation and diploma. It was only when Helen got a large safety pin from someone in the glittering assembly that Howard's ordeal was finally over and he could enjoy himself by dancing the evening away.

In contrast to Howard, Bill House had not yet received any professional honors in recognition of his own work, though in the 1960s he had been elected a member of the elite American Otological Society. He continued to press ahead with his applied research on many concurrent fronts and was convinced that 1973 would be "the year of the implant."

Unfortunately, this was not to be. As the year wore on, the obstacles Bill encountered made it plain that acceptance of the implant would take much longer than the one or two years he had projected on his own timetable.

The impediments in Bill's way differed from those that marked his innovative surgery for acoustic neuromas. Leading research scientists were not hostile to the idea of an implant, but simply believed their own approach—which differed from his—was the right way to proceed. Robin Michelson, for example, continued to work with his cochlear implant on animals using ten electrodes—a far more complex system than the original five electrodes Bill and Urban used before they replaced it with a single-electrode system. Michael Merzenich, a highly respected neurophysiologist at the University of California Medical Center in San Francisco, was convinced that their single-electrode system was naïve and that the multiple-electrode system was the only way to perfect the cochlear implant.

In early 1973 Bill received a telephone call from Frank Sooy, head of the ENT department at the University of California Medical Center and another figure in Howard's network of personal friends, asking if Bill and Howard could come to San Francisco for a meeting with Merzenich because the multi-electrode system on which he had been working with Michelson had been perfected for animals. Merzenich admitted it was not yet ready for application to humans, but thought it might be soon and he believed Bill and Urban should cease any further implants with the single-electrode system in humans because their multi-channel system would soon be available.

On the plane back to Los Angeles Bill discussed the substance of the meeting at length with Howard, expressing his conviction they should go ahead with their own program. Howard accepted this judgment and continued his backing for it—an indispensable support for its survival as was his earlier backing of Bill's work on acoustic neuromas.

Scientists are supposed to be very open-minded, but at times what they cannot explain they tend to deny. Certainly the cochlear implant results were not to be explained on the basis of any conventional neurophysiological information about the inner ear. Over the years, Bill personally had avoided making any statements as to how he thought the cochlear implant actually worked, but he vividly remembered that at the 1973 meeting of the American Otological Society when the discussion turned to cochlear implants, a distinguished scientific associate voiced his firm conviction that the single-electrode cochlear implant which Jack Urban and Bill were trying to perfect would be of no use to the patient. They should abandon any further work on it. "If I tell you," he said, "that a lead balloon will not fly and then you go out, suspend the balloon and it drops to the ground, what have you learned?"

Bill pointed out that he had flown to the meeting in a giant aluminum balloon and was sure that not too many years previous the most distinguished scientists in the world would have said such a thing was impossible. Bill admitted the limitations of the implant as well as the amount of auxiliary therapy a patient had to undergo in order to claim the maximum benefit from it. But he was buttressed by the recollection of the energy he had spent when he tried to get neurosurgeons objectively to assess the merits of his translabyrinthine approach to the acoustic tumor. The memory of these earlier battles and the ultimate acceptance of his concepts gave him the courage to press on into the watershed years that were ahead.

35

The Watershed Years: 1974-1975

In January 1974 the trustees of the Los Angeles Foundation of Otology voted to change its name to the Ear Research Institute. They wished to call it the House Ear Institute, but Howard objected, saying he did not as yet wish to be memorialized by perpetuating his name over his associates at OMG. The Institute at that time had a staff of 16, an annual budget of $1 million, and three important laboratories. It was far from being the original small venture designed to teach otologists new surgical techniques.

Otologists and audiologists associated with the Ear Research Institute regularly contributed seminal papers and reports to leading medical journals. In 1974 alone they authored 22 articles which appeared in medical journals—a figure that would compare favorably with the annual productivity of research-oriented departments of major medical schools. In addition, the five-year study of Ménière's disease directed by Jack Pulec was completed in 1974. A major book, *Micropathology of the Temporal Bone*, was published under the imprimatur of the institute, as was the study of the extent to which sodium fluoride therapy initiated by Shambaugh slowed the progression of otosclerosis. Still further, new studies were begun on disorders of the facial nerve and on the causes and relief of tinnitus.

Meanwhile, plans were made to establish a new Electron Microscopy Laboratory—destined to spur further the institute's major contributions to otologic knowledge. Electron microscopy magnifies up to 300,000 times greater than can be seen with the naked eye. The advantages of this type of magnification over the conventional microscope is that it illuminated the surface of solid objects instead of merely transmitting illumination through them and presents the specimen as a single whole rather than in cross-sections alone.

Prior to 1974 an institute review of the published work of major electron laboratories elsewhere showed that the bulk of the reports only involved animal tissue. Not more than a handful of the reports were concerned with hearing and balance disorders in humans. Still fewer correlated the preoperative examination with the postoperative analysis of specimens in the laboratory. The institute was in a unique position to use the technical features of electron microscopy to expand sharply on the understanding of the auditory system—because the laboratory could draw on specimens from the large volume of ear surgeries performed by OMG doctors from which a complete case history was made available.

Three of the foremost authorities in the world on electron microscopy of the ear served as consultants to the institute— Drs. Imrich Friedmann of London, David Lim of the College of Medicine at Ohio State and Fritsof Sjoestrand, originally of Stockholm and subsequently of the University of California. The organizer and first director of the laboratory, Dr. Malcolm D. Graham, was an OMG doctor interested in this new field of research. Subsequently he joined the faculty of the University of Michigan Medical School as a professor of otology and the laboratory is now under the direction of Dr. Linthicum.

During 1974 Barbara Walters' interview with Bill and Howard on the "Today Show" had an unforeseen political spin-off. The program focused on the cochlear implant and many viewers wrote to the National Institute of Health (NIH) requesting further information about this procedure. On learning that the NIH was doing little in this particular field, the letter-writers sent their questions on not only to their representatives in congress and their senators but also to Casper Weinberger, then head of the Department of Health, Education and Welfare (HEW).

This barrage of letters from private and congressional sources converging on Weinberger caused bureaucratic wheels to turn. Weinberger wrote Bill and Howard asking them to come to Washington to meet with the under secretary of health and with the chief of the National Institute for Neurological Diseases and Strokes, a component within the NIH in which hearing programs were centered.

At that Washington meeting Casper Weinberger was present for the opening ten minutes, during which he was briefed on what the cochlear implant entailed. Before rushing off to another meeting, he said he wanted a study made to determine if the NIH should support cochlear implant research and that the study should be on his desk in four months.

Thus a subsequent meeting was arranged by the NIH and held at its headquarters in Bethesda, Maryland where Bill and Howard were present, along with Blair Simmons, Robin Michelson and a group of NIH advisors, who included Collette Ramsey, head of the Deafness Research Foundation, Harold Schuknecht, Nelson Kiang and others from Harvard and MIT who were engaged in neurophysiological research on the inner ear.

An attack on Bill's cochlear implant program, which started the discussions, took its tone from the proposition that the new style House-Urban implant, consisting of only one electrode, would not produce any useful results for the patient. So another Bethesda meeting was proposed to be held within six weeks, this time in San Francisco with a larger group of invited experts on hand where it might be possible to settle the issues that were dividing the various camps concerned with cochlear implants.

At the two-day meeting in San Francisco, Robin Michelson's multi-electrode cochlear implant was strongly favored by Merzenich and Robert White of Stanford. Jack Urban and Bill spoke favorably of their single electrode system and Bill, for reinforcement, brought along Charles Graser, his first implant patient and very successful user of the single electrode implant.

Graser was able to present some of his favorable experiences with the implant, but as he could only give his "impressions" of what he heard, his impressions were not acceptable as scientific proof. "A resolution that was adopted over very strong objections" so Bill later recalled, "asserted that the participants had reached a consensus to the effect that no more single electrode implants should be made.

"Afterwards Frank Sooy, who was moderating the meeting, said to me, 'Well, Bill, it really doesn't matter to you whether or not we passed this resolution, because you are obviously going to go ahead and do what you want to do anyway.'

"I told him that was true, but was still firmly convinced that the resolution itself was unfortunate. Through its failure to endorse any kind of implant, less emphasis would be placed on what to me was a very promising development in the rehabilitation of a totally deaf person."

Before the meeting adjourned, the participants approved Bill's suggestion that all patients currently having cochlear implants should be reviewed by an independent source to determine what benefits, if any, they were getting from their implants. The number to be reviewed was not great for the program Bill had developed with Jack Urban by now had only eleven functioning patients, while Michael Merzenich's program, based on Robin Michelson's multi-electrode device, had three and White's program with Simmons had one. This proposal was forwarded to the NIH within a month, and a NIH contract for the indicated evaluation was awarded to the Pittsburgh Eye and Ear Hospital under the direction of Dr. Bilger.

In the midst of this uncertain and sometimes discouraging environment, Bill was treated to a happy surprise. At the annual meeting of the American Medical Association in July 1974 he received the Distinguished Service Award, the highest honor the AMA bestows on a doctor. The text of the award noted that he had "combined the private practice of medicine with basic and clinical research, as well as graduate and postgraduate education." It then cited him for three specific achievements at the Ear Research Institute: The "development of the shunt operation for the treatment of Ménière's disease; research leading to better diagnostic methods and new surgical procedures to remove acoustic neuromas and the cochlear implant project to help patients with total sensory deafness regain some sensation of sound electronically."

All the while during this turbulent year an administrative and financial crisis was brewing in the institute. Unfortunately the various programs which enhanced the institute's utility and celebrity were revisited on the institute in the form of budgetary deficits. The gap between income and expenditures was bridged only by drawing on dedicated reserves to pay current bills. There was an obvious imperative to set priorities for the allocation of resources and restrain the tendency to try to do at once everything that seemed worthwhile.

Howard, as president, had figuratively come to live for the institute. There was, however, a physical limit to what he could do for it unaided. He needed help, the more so after Glenn R. Snyder was relieved as managing director of the institute—a post he had occupied since 1967. He was held technically responsible for the way budgetary expenditures "got out of hand," including the costs of educational films, but it would be difficult for any administrative employee, to withstand the pressure of powerful OMG members who insisted on the need for one or another new piece of equipment for their applied research.

Restraints were all the more difficult when the source of pressure was Bill House, whose authentic genius enabled him to triumph over so many skeptics and to contribute so much to the worldwide renown of the institute. There was a fundamental problem here that could not be solved easily and would later lead to painful strains in the management of the institute once Howard retired as president and Bill was elected to that position.

The able business and professional members among the trustees of the institute thus found themselves with a management problem they would have quickly spotted and met head-on if something like it had crept into their private affairs. Perhaps because many of them were Howard's patients, their personal gratitude to him, intermixed with awe for the scientific attainments of Bill and other OMG members who worked within the institute, made them hesitate to intervene in the way the institute operated.

When the disarray in the budget could no longer be ignored, the trustees finally felt forced to intercede and they engaged the firm of McKinsey and Company to assess the institute's place and value in the world of otology and recommend measures to set right what was out of joint in the management of the institute and so restore it to budgetary health.

The McKinsey study team, directed by Robert Attiyeh, presented its report to the trustees in July 1974. After reviewing the nature and extent of the hearing losses in the American population, they stressed the importance of the institute's redemptive role in the general picture, but then called for "a more formal structure for research planning, . . . an order of priorities regarding other needs of the institute, . . . a reorganization of the board of trustees into a more formal structure of standing committees," and "increased technical, financial and administrative support for the OMG doctors who were themselves voluntarily contributing each year to the housekeeping costs of the institute."

As to the institute's programmatic focus, the McKinsey report noted that "little was known about cochlear problems, acoustic nerve damage due to disease or degeneration, or central nervous system disorders." These should "receive the highest priorities" from the institute for continuous basic and applied research. Finally, because future expenditures of the institute in support of its applied research would be "significantly above the level of recent years, a key challenge for the Ear Research Institute's board and managers would be to secure the funds."

The trustees endorsed the McKinsey report in its entirety. Some questions not directly addressed in the report were left hanging in inference: What was to be done when the institute, while seeking an improved diagnosis and treatment of a patient's problem by means of applied clinical research, reached a point where further progress depended on basic research? What was to be done when the institute's special interests intersected with those centered in other fields and disciplines? Was the institute to maintain relations with other research centers?

Other questions would come to the front by the time a follow-up McKinsey report was made six years later. There was, however, an immediate answer to the call for more effective topside management. In October of that year the trustees secured the full-time services of Edward O. Ethell, first as a consultant and then as the new managing director of the institute.

Ethell was no "yes-man". There was a prickly quality to him and he often had the mournful look of a man wandering through a train wreck looking for relatives. But his appointment as managing director of the institute was a stroke of good luck. What he brought to his work was a darting intelligence and sound, extensive experience, first as a reporter for the Associated Press and then in the marketing field for the Rockwell Corporation. He knew how to tap or create new sources of community support for institutions. More importantly, he knew he had been engaged to develop a fund-raising plan while adhering to a conservative financial policy—to say no to demands even for worthwhile projects until funds were in hand or in sight to cover the costs.

This was not an easy thing to do. OMG surgeons such as Bill who were passionately involved in the institute's research and educational programs were not used to having a tight rein placed on the financial aspects of their work. In the test of wills that ensued, Ethell had enough toughness of spirit to withstand the momentary displeasures of the OMG doctors and to hew to a line necessary to restore the institute to financial health.

The draconian cuts that began the healing process appeared in the budget for 1975, which the trustees approved. Priorities were set for any additional funds that became available during the year. Ethell did not swerve from the terms of the bare-bone budget and the program of regrouping, which he administered, laid a solid basis on which the institute resumed its growth within a year.

Howard always proudly claimed that the institute never used its resources to construct a brick and mortar monument to itself. As it grew, its laboratories and teaching facilities were based in the surrounding homes and apartment buildings he had acquired. When discussions, however, were held among the trustees and major donors regarding long-range plans for the institute in line with the McKinsey report, it was agreed that the institute's growth would be stifled unless it had a new home.

But what kind? A new home built from the ground up was financially impossible. Expanding the current quarters had its own limitations. In fact, officials of the James E. Irvine Foundation said they would not provide further funds for electron microscopy or other equipment unless it was to be installed in fire-safe buildings.

The problem of a new home for the institute was solved as a by-product to developments in the affairs of St. Vincent Medical Center. Since community colleges were rapidly taking over the training of nurses, St. Vincent decided to close its school of nursing. At about the same time, the hospital withdrew from obstetrics leaving their medical center with a large, modern, but largely empty building that had been used as the nurses college and dormitory, while the decision to withdraw from obstetrics left the hospital with empty delivery and recovery rooms.

This set the stage for a mutually beneficial agreement between the OMG and the institute on the one side and St. Vincent Medical Center on the other. The OMG, with its ever-growing patient caseload, took over the floor with the four operating rooms for ear surgery and equipped them with closed-circuit TV for teaching purposes. The hospital granted a long-term lease to the institute for part of the six-story nurses building with the charge to the institute limited to maintenance costs such as janitorial services and utilities.

The terms were so attractive to the trustees of the institute they quickly completed a special fund-raising drive to remodel, for institute purposes, some 18,000 square feet on three floors of the building. By August 1975 new quarters were available for all components of the institute. The apartment building adjacent to the OMG that had housed the institute was reconverted into what came to be known as the "House Hilton" which provided accommodations for doctors visiting the institute for short visits. The first floor became the OMG hearing aid evaluation center. Once the institute was established in the remodeled quarters of St. Vincent's College of Nursing, a gift from Lillian Disney, Walt Disney's widow, made possible the formation of the Walt Disney Rehabilitation Center for the cochlear implant program.

True to form, Bill, while awaiting the results of the independent evaluation of his patients at Pittsburgh, implanted eight more deaf patients. Then, in collaboration with Karen Berliner, Ph.D. who was the director of clinical trials at the institute, he published the first major monograph on cochlear implant research.

When the books were closed on 1975, where the institute itself was concerned, expenses for the year were held to $696,000—or $460 under the budgeted figure—thanks to Ed Ethell's hard-nosed watchfulness. Revenues topped $1,000,000 for the first time—due in large part to the first of many major contributions by Mr. Lee Whittier. Debts were paid. Reserves were reestablished and a start was made on building a special reserve fund. The end of the watershed year found the institute in a position where it could seriously consider the terms and implications of its first long-range plan.

36

Trials, Sorrows and Recovery

Two years after HEW Secretary Casper Weinberger called for a report to be made on the cochlear implant "within four months," the assigned Pittsburgh hospital completed their paper which became the basis for the NIH policy. Noting that patients with Bill's implant did in fact hear something, it pointed out that what they heard was more than anyone could explain in the light of existing scientific knowledge. The NIH subsequently declared it would fund cochlear research involving animals, but not human beings.

In Bill's embattled view, this did not make sense. "Animal research," he said at the time, "can add very little to what we already know or can learn from patients who are now functioning with cochlear implants." Though the NIH barred the flow of federal funds in support of Bill's project, it did not amount to a legal ban on implant research on human beings. When the NIH stand was made public, however, Jack Urban's insurance company informed him it would cancel his liability insurance if he continued to take part in Bill's research.

Because he was forced to withdraw in 1976 from any direct experimental work on the implant project, the institute formed its own engineering and manufacturing facilities for cochlear implant devices. In a closely related matter, Fred Johnson was engaged to serve under Ed Ethell as the institute's first director of development to generate research funds from private sources. The research staff was expanded, and an Auditory Research Laboratory was created with Manuel Don, Ph.D. as its director.

As new types of implanted devices increasingly came into use to replace different organs of the body, the Food and Drug Administration (FDA) by an administrative order in 1976 brought all such devices, including the cochlear implant, under FDA control. With that, Bill, backed by Howard and the institute's trustees, laid the basis for a coinvestigator program involving implant patients the world over, and not merely those at the Ear Research Institute. A special group of handpicked surgeons located in different countries were trained by Bill, Jack Urban and the institute staff for adult implant work, subject to FDA guidelines.

The cochlear implant has never been a one-person operation, for it entails the work of a team—an otologist, audiologist and psychologist. Before surgery an audiological evaluation of a prospective implant candidate is conducted to determine if the hearing loss is profound sensorineural deafness which cannot be significantly helped by medical treatment or by a high-powered hearing aid.

Beyond this, no surgery is performed even in the case of a willing patient until a psychologist meets with both the patient and an "index person" (spouse, family member or friend) to be certain the patient's expectations are not unrealistic. The patient must understand what the implant entails, must want to proceed with it, and be deemed psychologically ready for its demands. Only then is surgery scheduled.

After a healing period of approximately two months, the patient returns to the clinic to be fitted with the external induction coil that is worn behind the ear, and is given the signal processor unit and transmitter. For the patient and implant team, this is a highly charged moment. Once the

FOR THE WORLD TO HEAR

signal processor is appropriately set, the patient is slowly introduced to sound.

The subsequent rehabilitation process is divided into two periods—Basic Guidance and Auditory Training. Basic Guidance lasts about a week and is used to set the internal controls on the stimulator unit. In addition, the patient is taught how to use the unit. This is followed by Auditory Training and lipreading sessions. The patient is taught to discriminate differences in everyday sounds—such as loud versus soft, long versus short, the number of syllables and the stress patterns of words. A home practice program as well as individual therapy sessions are tailored to the patient's needs.

About the time the cochlear implant coinvestigator program got under way, a crisis arose in Howard's personal life. His pride in the OMG and the institute he created had always been matched by the pleasure he found in his family—in Ken's work as a psychiatrist, in John's coming on the team as an otologist in the OMG and his activity in the institute and in Carolyn's expanding interests beyond the sphere of her home.

He recalled how the birth of Ken and Joan's first child brought out Helen's great sense of humor. While in Dallas for a medical meeting, they were awakened by a phone call at one in the morning. Howard picked up the receiver and heard Ken say, "Hi Grandpa."

A delighted Howard offered his congratulations and then handed the phone to Helen. After hanging up she peered at Howard and said, "Are you sure you want to get into a bed with a Grandma." He did, but not before he and Helen composed a telegram to their grandson, welcoming him to the "good earth"—and to his "share of the national debt."

On another occasion, Howard and Helen were asleep in a hotel room in San Francisco when they were awakened by a soft knock on the door. Helen slipped on a robe, half opened the door and saw a startled young woman. "Is this Mr. Jones' room?" she managed to ask. Helen, with a toss of her head in the direction of bed answered, "He told me his name was Smith!" The young woman wheeled around on her spiked heels and scampered down the hall.

In the passing years, Howard and Helen had traveled a great distance together since their peculiar wedding ceremony. The rocky patches of the road were now far behind them. Theirs was a solid marriage held together by mutual affection, dependence and respect. Howard in confessional moments admitted it would take a very special kind of woman such as Helen was, to "put up" with him—to subordinate everything she might otherwise want to do to his consuming drive to excel in his medical specialty.

In 1976 Helen developed a persistent cough and her health began to fail. When X-rays showed the cause was due to inoperable cancer, it fell to Howard to invent assurances that her condition would turn for the better with X-ray treatments. All the while, however, this man who had created two major medical institutions and had been singled out for honors throughout the world was reduced to virtual helplessness. He could use none of his medical expertise on Helen's behalf except to provide her with strong medication to prevent pain.

Helen was strongly attached to their home in Newport Beach and the more her physical strength ebbed, the more she preferred its informality to their formal home in Los Angeles. At Newport Beach she had only to look out of the windows and be treated to the changing panorama of maritime activity on the bay with its many boats—while overhead, sea gulls whirled and cried and came to a fluttering rest on a choice perch.

On a Sunday in 1976, as Helen and Howard were due to return to Los Angeles, she made plans to come back to their beach home the next weekend. Howard could have cursed the medical knowledge which told him this was not to be. Her cancer was so far advanced she would never be able to come back. The day before she passed away, she happily acknowledged with a faint smile the news that Carolyn had given birth to a daughter, Karen.

In the months following Helen's death, Howard tended to turn inward, much as his father had done after the death of Jesse, Howard's mother. He increased his usual heavy schedule of work on many fronts and he remained at his office well into the evening. He might then go to the California Club for supper, or in other ways delay his return to a large, empty house—visiting with his children or with his brothers Warren and Bill. But these were little more than a poultice applied to the deep wound Helen's death caused in his life. For 40 years, amid his wide wanderings, she had always been either by his side or awaiting his return home. Now she was no more.

Howard thought he might sell the Los Angeles home and move into the California Club as other widowers had done, but could not quite bring himself to such an irrevocable act—uprooting himself from a house whose rooms were crowded with memories. His indecision about what to do was resolved by a phone call from Mrs. Dorothy Smallwood, a registered nurse, herself a widow with a grown son and a patient of Howard's. Did he know of anyone who needed a house manager? He certainly did. Arrangements were quickly made for her to move into the guest cottage next to the swimming pool. The terms were acceptable to Dorothy and it was an ideal arrangement for both of them.

The emotional void in Howard's life as a widower remained unfilled until Nanette Fabray, another of Howard's patients, entered the scene. Nan's husband Randy had died of a sudden heart attack in 1974 and she had returned to the theater to provide for herself and for her son Jamie, then 15. Howard had long admired Nan, but had never seen her except in purely professional contexts—either at meetings of the foundation's trustees or when she came to his office for a scheduled checkup on her hearing.

Some months after Helen's death in 1976, he wrote Nan to ask if she would join him for lunch. In view of her own experiences as a widow in the previous two years, he wanted to talk to her about the problems of being a widower. From that lunch forward Howard began to see her socially. His children, on meeting Nan, counted it a blessing that he had found a companion in her.

37

Intersections

Other developments cut across the life of the OMG and the institute. Howard's longtime associate, Dr. Aram Glorig, who had worked with him for twelve years heading up research for the Subcommittee on Noise in Industry, in 1964 had been invited by a Dallas group "to do something about hearing in the state of Texas." More than just "something," in Dallas, Glorig created the Callier Center for Communication Disorders—now one of the finest of its kind in the world—and affiliated it with the University of Texas.

When Glorig turned 70, however, the university's retirement policy caught up with him and he was forced to retire. He then accepted a two-pronged appointment—one to serve as a consultant to the OMG specializing in industrial and forensic otology, and the other to direct the institute's research on the "aging ear" and on improved hearing aids by a magnetically driven system.

While Glorig's presence gave a new dimension to the institute's research work, Edward O. Ethell pressed on with his own responsibilities as the institute's managing director, narrowing the gap between budgeted income and expenditures to preserve the institute's fiscal health. Among other things he changed the annual reports from their earlier form as a treasurer's balance sheet to a report on all aspects of the institute's work, created a quarterly newsletter known as the *Oto Review* to keep financial contributors abreast of the institute's activities and set in place a new accounting system.

At the same time, the governing and advisory bodies of the institute were restructured. A national council was formed comprised of nationally prominent people who had been Howard's patients which initially included J. Peter Grace, William Randolph Hearst Jr., Mary Lasker and J. Willard Marriott Jr. With the enactment of California's corporation law, the number of trustees was reduced from 30 to 17 and a new board of overseers, drawn from Southern California community leaders, was formed with Justin Dart, Samuel Goldwyn Jr., Harrell J. Harrell and Mrs. Kenneth Norris as early members.

The existence of the national council and the overseers enabled the institute to retain the interest and support of those people who had formerly been members of the board of trustees. Also on Ethell's initiative, an institute annual benefit dinner was introduced in 1978 as a fund-raising device. The chair of the first event, which garnered the institute $105,000, was Leonard K. Firestone, with Bob Hope acting as master of ceremonies. Mrs. Freeman Gates and Mrs. William F. House were cochairs of the dinner committee. By the time the third annual benefit dinner was held, with Justin Dart as chair of the event and Mrs. William French Smith as chair of the dinner committee, the evening netted the institute $200,000.

Yet by 1980, the Ear Research Institute (ERI) appeared to be at a crossroads in its own history. Clearly it was one of the leading forces in the world for clinically related research in the detection, diagnosis and treatment of hearing and balance disorders, but what lay ahead? What could be done to insure its continued growth?

While these questions hung in the air, the McKinsey Corporation volunteered in 1980 to update without cost the report it had been commissioned to make several years earlier. The text of the report it produced stressed three main points as follows:

1. *Howard House's Role.* The institute remains excessively dependent for continued survival on the personal leadership, external reputation and fund-raising efforts of Howard House. . . . This suggests that a program for transitioning leadership should be considered.

2. *Board of Directors Leadership.* Partly because of the strong ongoing role Howard has been able to perform, the board of directors of ERI has not been required to exercise its normal share of strategic leadership and financial support for the institute. ERI is blessed with a strong board composed of individuals who are leaders in their own fields and are comfortable in dealing with issues of strategy and finance. . . . Yet despite this strength, the board is described by its own leaders as being relatively "passive." . . . The institute is now entering a period during which strong leadership and support from the board will be needed.

3. *Financial Support.* The present financial support for the institute is inadequate for the level of its research and teaching program. . . . There is little endowment base, and substantial longer-term grants from private or public sources have not been obtained. Unless stronger and more stable financial support is developed for the institute, the board of directors will have little choice but to eventually cut back the work of the institute.

The 1980 McKinsey report laid out certain specific proposals to strengthen the operating effectiveness of the institute and called for the addition to the institute's top management team of a full-time medical director who would work under the general supervision of Howard and Bill, to coordinate research.

At the same time, it proposed that Bill should be

appointed president of the institute so that he could increase his external representation work as well as give continued strong direction to the major research projects in which he and other OMG doctors were involved.

The report also noted that "the external image and reputation of the institute was heavily tied to the renown of the House brothers, despite the major current and past contributions of others to the institute's work."

In thinking solely of the long-term needs of the institute, therefore, it was "time for Howard to lay aside his own standing opposition to being memorialized personally." The board of trustees should include the House name when Howard House "steps up to an emeritus status, and a proposed major endowment drive is launched."

Finally, the impending retirement of Fred Johnson as the development director made it necessary to recruit and groom his successor. Total expenditures had grown from $800,000 in 1975 to $1.8 million in 1980, and the total budget for 1981 was expected to break through $2 million.

It was recognized that the steps taken to upgrade the development functions of the institute would increase development costs over the near term, but the McKinsey report concluded that only through this means could the board "expect to meet its target of providing adequate long-term support to the programs of the institute."

Most of the recommendations in the report were converted into action, some more quickly than others. Mahlon Arnett, who had been instrumental as chair of the board of trustees in stabilizing the finances of the institute with the effective assistance of Ed Ethell, had been succeeded as chair by Charles M. Hart.

Like Arnett, Hart was one of Howard's patients who had successful stapes surgery. Hart had piloted the institute through some very heavy seas, but shortly after the 1980 McKinsey report, he believed he should step down from his post while retaining his position as a board member. He was succeeded by James Ludlam, president of the California Bar Association, and a specialist in hospital law who used his expertise to reorganize the board into functioning committees.

Finances took a turn for the better when Mrs. Athalie Irvine Clarke, a gentle and loving lady in the most exact sense of the term, became an institute trustee in 1980. Years earlier on the eve of her marriage to James Irvine, an heir to the 127,000 acre Irvine Ranch in Southern California, Athalie's father, a family physician, remarked that her life "would be radically changed by her association with very great wealth." He urged her "always to keep at the forefront of her thoughts the people and institutions which were in need of the kind of help she would be able to render." Her fidelity to that reminder made her a leader in civic and philanthropic ventures around the nation.

Athalie, who bore a daughter, Joan, was widowed early in her marriage. It became necessary for her to help manage the Irvine Company properties as a member of its board of directors, a role she continued to fill even after she was married to Judge Thurmond Clarke and later when she was again widowed.

A hearing loss in one ear caused by Ménière's brought Athalie to Howard's office in the 1950s, but she did not see him again until 1978 when she attended the institute's first annual benefit dinner. Her escort, John Griffith, was Howard's patient and a trustee of the institute. As he was in declining health, he expressed the hope that Athalie would take his place on the board, which she did. With Nanette Fabray, she became the second woman to serve as a board member.

Prior to becoming a board member Athalie had only known of the OMG's work in patient care. Now as a trustee she discovered the exceptional nature of the institute's research projects and educational programs for ear specialists. On the occasion of the second board meeting she attended, she admitted previously she had not the "faintest idea" of the institute's activities. She went on to suggest that the board should have a woman's auxiliary organization to help support the institute financially and, among other things, to assume responsibility for its annual benefit dinner.

With the board's approval, she proceeded to organize an auxiliary known as The Associates. Her initial collaborators included Mrs. Will Ward, Mrs. John McClure and Mrs. Homer Toberman—the total membership soon embraced over one hundred socially prominent women in Southern California. Athalie also worked closely with a new member of the institute staff, Janet Doak, a woman with effective professional experience in fund-raising for philanthropic causes, who had been employed by Ed Ethell to succeed Fred Johnson as development director of the institute. Janet would be particularly effective in tapping private foundations as a source of financial support for the institute's work.

Meanwhile, the board at its meeting on January 10, 1981, acted on the McKinsey Report's recommendation concerning the future name of the institute and formally resolved that its name "shall henceforth be the House Ear Institute in honor and recognition of the caring devotion to the cause of the hearing impaired by Drs. Howard and William House."

President Reagan was among those who saluted that decision in a message read at the annual benefit dinner in March 1982—an affair that netted the institute $250,000 thanks in large measure to the work of the newly formed Associates.

"For 35 years," so the president's message read, "the institute has been a leader in the efforts to help the hearing handicapped and has played an essential role in the fight against disease and disability. The work of Drs. Howard and William House has gained national and international recognition. It is most fitting that your trustees pay tribute to their accomplishments in a formal manner by renaming it the House Ear Institute."

This was not the kind of pro forma "good will" note the president writes to hundreds of worthy enterprises. As he stated in his foreword, President Reagan became one of Howard's patients in late December 1980, en route to Washington for his inauguration and remained a patient and enthusiastic supporter of the institute during and after his presidency.

OMG surgeons, particularly Dr. De la Cruz, were experienced in treating presidents from other countries, but none had ever been subject to the security arrangements involving a president-elect. The White House made the appointment on Reagan's behalf and explained that the Secret Service would start work on security details two weeks before that date.

When the agents arrived they arranged for emergency care at St. Vincent Medical Center across the street from the OMG and checked surrounding buildings for the best placement of sharpshooters. They then examined the OMG building to see which rooms Reagan would use, determined how to isolate them and also supervised the laying of special lines by the telephone company.

On the day of the appointment, a swarm of Secret Service agents enveloped the OMG area. Two hours before the president-elect's arrival, all cars in the parking lot were removed and no one was allowed either to enter or leave the premises. A special area in the parking lot was roped off for the press and television. Then agents with two trained dogs searched the OMG building for explosives from top to bottom, including drawers and closets. Five minutes before Ronald Reagan was to reach the premises, traffic was stopped in all directions. His caravan included a number of motorcycle officers, two cars of Secret Service agents, two cars for members of the press corps, police cars and the macabre addition of an ambulance.

"Mr. President," Howard said in greeting, "it's nice to see you looking so well."

To which Reagan in a tone of mock severity replied, "I have something to talk to you about." He revealed what was on his mind when they were alone in Howard's office. "You called me 'Mr. President,' he said. "I want you to know this is a temporary job."

The president-elect had a mild hearing loss due to a gun that was fired close to his ear some years earlier during the filming of a western movie. The loss was in the high tones and not serious. Howard prescribed a regimen of care designed to help conserve his hearing—only decaffeinated coffee, no smoking, some tablets to increase circulation and regular exercise—which he engaged in anyway with solemn medical advice. Nancy Reagan would prove an effective aide who saw that the regimen was adhered to.

Every year the month of May is designated as Better Hearing and Speech Month and the House Ear Institute is among the members of the sponsoring council. Nanette Fabray was the first national chair of the yearly affair. To help publicize hearing problems in connection with the event, arrangements had been made for a parade in Washington, followed by President Reagan's reception at the White House of Nan, Howard, the hearing-impaired "poster child," his parents and Joe Rizzo, the executive director of the sponsoring council.

Nan had been the Reagans' neighbor in Los Angeles and her son Jamie had been school friends with Ron Jr. When the group reached the White House—against the background of the Falkland crisis—they were swept up in a series of security checks, leading to the cabinet room where a crush of people were waiting to see the president. Here they were quickly ushered into the oval office while a presidential aide sounded a reminder: "You have five minutes."

Howard recalls, "The president was gracious as always. He spoke to the parents of the 'poster child' and posed for pictures. The allotted five minutes were consumed in this way and his aide was getting nervous. As we started to leave, the president said, 'Nan, I want to talk to you and Howard.' He threw his arms around Nan and asked how her son Jamie was progressing in the USC School of Medicine. When he ushered us to a settee, he turned to me and said, 'You know, Howard, I only have trouble hearing in this office and I don't understand why.'

"I looked up and said, 'I think the problem might be the oval dome over these settees. The sound goes up and then bounces back on the settees. If you covered the dome with glass, the sound would spread better throughout the room and toward your desk.' The president seemed intrigued by the idea. 'Or,' I said, continuing, 'you could place a little microphone near the settee with a speaker on your desk. They could be concealed so that no one would know of their presence.'

"The president smiled and without any reference to President Nixon said gently but firmly, 'I don't think I want any hidden mikes around here!' "

On a subsequent occasion when President Reagan was en route from Washington to his California ranch, he stopped at the OMG clinic to be examined again by Howard. The security arrangements were even tighter, if possible, than when he first visited the clinic as president-elect. The results of the new examination were much the same as before.

A third visit was set at a time when Howard was due to be away from Los Angeles in connection with professional work that could not be rescheduled. President Reagan, therefore, became the patient of Dr. John House who fitted him with the hearing aid that was much publicized in the press.

What the press did not publicize was the way the president of United States, prior to that visit, was subject to the same reminder common among other mortals who are OMG patients. Computer-generated postcards regularly go out to OMG patients when the time comes to have their hearing checked at the clinic. One such postcard was routinely mailed to Ronald Reagan, 1600 Pennsylvania Avenue, Washington, D.C. reminding him he was due for an annual examination.

The postcard, plain as oatmeal, threaded its way through the blizzard of documents that regularly envelope the White House and landed on the desk of Nancy Reagan. In a sentence which spoke for the protective concern of a devoted wife, she wrote Howard to say simply, "*I'll* see to it that he will be there."

The publicity engendered by the president's acceptance of a hearing aid reportedly increased the sales of hearing aids nationwide by 40 percent within six months.

Bill House, meanwhile, was marching to the beat of his own drum. By the spring of 1981 he and the institute staff had trained 32 teams of coinvestigators for the adult cochlear implant program, of which 26 were based in the United States, while the rest were in England, Germany, Japan, Brazil, Argentina and the People's Republic of China. Each team regularly reported its results to the institute's computer center where the data was collected by Karen Berliner, Ph.D.

Yet even as the adult program was moving forward around the world, Bill was preparing himself to implant the cochlear device in deaf children. The mere mention of what he meant to do typically aroused an army of critics and just as typically, he ignored their outcries.

In April of 1981, he implanted his first child, Tracy Husted, an enchanting girl of three. Tracy lost her hearing due to meningitis six months before her implant and within two months her speech could not be understood. Over the next six months after receiving the implant her hearing and understanding of environmental sounds began to return. Her gains in hearing soon after receiving the implant encouraged Bill to implant seven more deaf children within the space of a few months.

At the same time, a select group of otologists who were serving as coinvestigators of the adult cochlear implant program, were chosen for training at the institute with an eye to their involvement in the children's program. To open up a new chapter in the treatment of deaf children, Bill formed within the institute a Center for Deaf Children, organized along lines that could serve as a model for other such centers elsewhere.

Bill believed that "most otologists knew very little about deafness; most audiologists knew very little about otology; and most professional teachers of the deaf, as well as regular classroom teachers, knew very little about either otology or audiology."

This being the case, deaf children were in need of the kind of rehabilitation that made a single whole out of all the specialized skills which had a bearing on deafness. Among other things, psychologists must be available to help with the emotional problems of the parents and of hearing-impaired children.

A national parent-to-parent network for better understanding of the problems of hearing-impaired children must be set in place. New research must be undertaken on how best to teach young people with an implant or hearing aid to use such sound as they actually received. All this and more like it, when taken together, might entail substantial modifications in the traditional educational programs for deaf children—a prospect that would not and did not set well with the traditionalists.

Bill found a welcome source of support for his center in Mr. and Mrs. Finn Moller who had a hearing-impaired child. No one had previously told them that their child could be helped by properly fitted hearing aids. When they came to the OMG clinic on the advice of friends, John House provided their child with suitable hearing aids, thereby enabling the youth to enter more fully into the world of sound.

Pat Moller subsequently took the lead in forming a women's auxiliary known as Sonance whose prime objective was to support the model Center for Deaf Children. Her early coworkers included Mrs. Fred C. Kemmerling, Jr., Mrs. Happy I. Franklin, Mrs. Paul B. Flynn, Mrs. Victor Rothschild, Mrs. Burke W. Francis and Mrs. Terry Hill. The full membership of Sonance is comprised of a set of young women in the greater Los Angeles area. Janet Doak has also worked closely with this Sonance group and their annual dinners have been very successful in raising funds for the Children's Center.

The institute and its Center for Deaf Children gained special attention because of a case involving Ian Patterson, a deaf child who was a suitable candidate for a cochlear implant. His final hookup of the sound was set for a day after Thanksgiving. The press was notified of that fact by the Orange County Lions Club which lent its own support to institute projects.

A *Los Angeles Times* reporter showed up at the center with a photographer and captured on film the reaction of Ian at the precise moment of the hookup when he heard sound for the first time in his life. The photograph, showing the face of the child light up in the joy of a wonderful discovery, was splashed on the front page of the metropolitan newspaper the next day.

All local and national television stations now descended on the institute to report on the cochlear implant program for children. This, however, did not sweep all obstacles before it. The program, designed to aid children in their early years when speech itself is formed through hearing and becomes indivisible with it, continued to meet with the opposition of teachers of the deaf who resisted any attempt to teach speech to the deaf in place of sign language.

38

Chairperson Emeritus and Founder

Howard, even in his early 70s, was spared the common signs of aging. His health was excellent, his hearing was normal, and he read without glasses. After he lunched at the institute, however, he noticed some pressure in his chest and shortness of breath when he walked up a slight incline en route back to his OMG office. He also noticed that he had none of these symptoms when he missed a noontime meal, so he stopped having lunch altogether. It did not occur to him that he might have inherited his father's heart ailment.

On a weekend in 1983 when Howard was alone in his beach house, he was suddenly awakened by an acute tightness and pain in his chest accompanied by shortness of breath. He was in a cold sweat, but a few minutes later the symptoms suddenly stopped and he went back to sleep. The next day he felt fine and drove back to his Los Angeles home. At four the next morning, he was again awakened by the symptoms of the previous night, except that this time they were more severe. He started to dial for the paramedics, but the symptoms again suddenly stopped and he went back to sleep.

Here was a noted figure in the medical profession showing mindless passivity in the face of clear warning signals. "How stupid can you be?" Howard later remarked. "Obviously a doctor should never be his own physician."

While making his Monday morning rounds at St. Vincent's his path crossed that of Dr. Oscar Magidson, a cardiologist. "Oscar," Howard said in cheery greeting, "you wouldn't believe what happened to me on Saturday and Sunday night. It was just amazing."

He was half way through his recital when Magidson used the hospital's loud speaker system to rasp an order. "A wheel chair for Dr. Howard House!" The chair materialized. "Sit down!"

"What do you mean?" Howard asked.

"Just sit down and don't argue!" Magidson pushed the chair to the cardiac intensive care unit where doctors surrounded Howard asking what was wrong.

"Nothing," he replied, "I've never felt better in my life." Nevertheless, he soon found himself in bed hooked up to a battery of machines.

After Magidson left, Howard unhooked himself, climbed out of bed and walked down the hall to a phone. He called Ruth Barnes, his incomparable secretary and reported that he was in St. Vincent's.

"Fine," she said, "your appointments start at nine."

"No," he answered, " *I* am in *bed* in the hospital with a heart attack. Please cancel my appointments and notify the family." Howard then called Nanette Fabray in Washington, D.C. to say he was in the hospital.

"Are you getting ready for surgery?" she asked.

"Maybe," he answered, "And it might be me."

Nanette flew back to Los Angeles and arrived in time to join the family and hear the results of the tests—which showed a 90 percent occlusion in the main coronary artery. If it were not for Howard's chance encounter with Magidson, that obstruction could have been a pistol pressed against his heart, primed to go off.

It was explained that an angioplasty would be tried, a technique where a "balloon" is inserted into the artery and "pumped up" to open the obstruction. The family, Nanette and Howard witnessed the procedure on the television monitor where they saw the blood suddenly gush through the artery. The cheers in the operating room sounded like the roar in a football stadium following a touchdown.

After a short visit, the family members and Nanette left Howard alone so he could rest. They could not be located when Howard, an hour later, had another severe attack. The balloon treatment had failed. Emergency measures were quickly applied and he was rushed to the operating room. When the family and Nanette returned to the hospital at the usual visiting hours, they were stunned to find Howard awakening from double-bypass surgery performed by Dr. Pablo Zubiate.

When Howard was due to be released from the hospital Athalie Clarke and Dolores Hope, among other friends, urged him to convalesce in their respective homes, but he declined their generous offers and convalesced in his own home in Newport Beach. Three weeks after his bypass surgery, he was strong enough to speak at the Associates annual benefit dinner for the institute.

"I'm happy to be here tonight," he said, "as a matter of fact I am very happy to be anywhere tonight." He then introduced two people who were "closer to his heart" than anyone had ever been—the surgeons who literally held his heart in their hands.

The six weeks in between Howard's heart attack and his return to his office and operating schedule was the longest period in more than a half century when he was not practicing medicine. In what became his repetitive phrase—which would kick back on him in the summer of 1987—he "never felt better in his life."

Howard, however, realized that the time had come for him to relinquish the presidency of the institute. The emotions entwined in this decision were far more complex than was the case some years previously when he relinquished the presidency of the OMG at age 65. Bill had then been elected the new president, while Dr. James Sheehy volunteered to serve as the director of administration, besides attending to both his private practice and his work at the institute. The relative ease that marked the OMG's changing of the guard had its emblem in a comic gesture where the doctors at the time elected Howard chair of the OMG Maintenance Committee, with himself as the only member.

The presidency of the House Ear Institute was another matter. It was Howard's "favorite child," the mainspring and object of much of what he had come to live for, the carrier of his hopes for the future. Now he must relinquish its direction. To whom? The question carried its answer on its face. The new president must be Bill. After all, when the board changed the name of the Ear Research Institute to the House Ear Institute, Bill's work was coupled with Howard's as the reason for identifying the institute with their family name. His extraordinary achievements in advancing the frontiers of otologic knowledge and practice had enhanced the worldwide celebrity of the institute itself and was a major contributing cause for its growth.

With Bill's election as the new president, he cut back on his private practice to devote half of his time to institute work. Howard was vested with the title of Chairman Emeritus and Founder of the Institute. In the years that followed on the heels of these changes, the institute was strengthened on a number of fronts. Athalie Clarke, for example, quietly took the initiative in a matter to which she had given much thought when Howard was recovering from his heart surgery—and decided to create an endowed chair, named in his honor, to support ear research within the institute. The necessary funds were quickly forthcoming with the help of Athalie's many friends.

Other gifts, such as the one from the estate of Harrell J. Harrell, helped bolster the general financial base of the institute. Harrell had regained his hearing after a fenestration operation Howard performed and later served on the institute's board. In his will Harrell established a 20-year testamentary trust with two pieces of property in downtown Los Angeles, the income of which the institute was to share with his widow and two daughters. Harrell's widow, Irene, and his two stepdaughters, generously modified the trust and directed the executor of the estate to make the institute the sole beneficiary.

In 1982 the institute board voted to undertake an extensive remodeling project to make room for the Children's Center with its multidisciplinary staff to be located on the first floor. St. Vincent allocated 10,000 additional square feet to enhance the laboratory space and house a library on the ground floor. Harrison Chandler provided funds to remodel the Auditory Research Laboratory.

In 1986, the institute's endowment was further augmented by a substantial bequest from the estate of Mrs. William T. Bettingen, Athalie Clarke's friend and an Associate.

By 1987 various gifts from different sources had raised the institute's total endowment to a level that could not have been imagined by Howard years earlier when the institute was brought to birth by $25,000 benefactions each from George Eccles and Jean Witter. Besides this, the funds acquired for the institute's endowment were on a plane apart from those raised later for a major building project.

The fund-raising activity of the institute not only served its clinical research work, but was itself spurred by the advances made at the institute in treating hearing and balance disorders. Bill and his coinvestigators, for example, had spent 25 years on detailed clinical research focused on 250 adults who had received cochlear implants.

In November 1984 the U.S. Food and Drug Administration finally judged the implant device to be safe for use with adults. The official announcement to that effect made front-page news around the country and stirred new hope among the deaf and their families. To Bill, personally, the announcement vindicated the massive investment of his emotions, time, mental and physical energy in pursuit of an elusive objective.

The respective talents that Howard and Bill brought to their profession had been honored over the years in different ways. In 1985, however, the pair were coupled together in the civic honors they received. In Los Angeles, for example, Mayor Bradley and the City Council proclaimed June 24, 1985, as House Day in the city. The Los Angeles County Board of Supervisors issued a proclamation in recognition of Howard and Bill's contributions to help people around the world suffering from hearing and balance disorders. The President's Committee on Employment of the Handicapped made Howard and Bill joint recipients of the Physician of the Year Award. All such civic honors entered into the fabric of public awareness about the merits of the House Ear Institute itself and thus worked in its own way to draw more private funds to its support.

Howard, as noted, never claimed personal credit for any great breakthroughs in otology. His contributions stemmed from his leadership in founding the OMG to take care of patients, in creating the institute where a select number of research scientists, OMG doctors and clinicians could carry on their studies and educational programs. He was now called upon to perform an institutional task which was not the kind that makes headlines or even the 6 o'clock TV news. What it entailed fell outside the line of vision of the public at large, but was of major concern to otologists and through them was bound to impact the public at large.

In the early days of American medicine anyone could be called "doc," so the title included patent medicine men, witch doctors and barbers who performed surgery. To protect the public against quackery, states authorized the creation of examining boards to test doctors before they were licensed to practice. This did not cover those who claimed to be "specialists," so in 1913 doctors engaged in surgery established the American College of Surgeons with a membership limited to doctors who qualified under its criteria. Two years later, doctors engaged in internal medicine similarly established the American College of Physicians.

As more knowledge was acquired, particular areas of the body became the basis for subspecialties in the practice of medicine, while proficiency in any one of them following graduation from medical school required several years of residency training. This reality led to the formation of specialty boards which administered examinations to certify doctors as specialists in a given field. The process began in 1916 when the first of such boards was formed for Ophthalmology, followed in the same year by the formation of a board in Otolaryngology (ENT). Each board that was proposed—they cover all specialties today—met with substantial resistance and opinions were sharply divided among the doctors affected by them.

Howard's own career amounted to a textbook illustration of the process of forming a specialization, followed by subspecialization. Just as at the outset of his practice he covered all phases of ear, nose and throat, he soon limited his practice only to the ear and later further limited his surgery to cases involving hearing loss due to otosclerosis.

Against the background of a continuing explosion of knowledge about the ear, the Council of American Otological Society concluded in 1986 that the time had come to upgrade the requirements of membership in its organization. The council knew that any move to that end would invite the usual resistance to change, so it put a request to Howard out of respect for his skill in the art of group diplomacy and for the fact that his career spanned more than a half century of developments in the specialty of ENT. Would Howard form and chair a committee that would propose the training requirements for future membership in the society?

This was no honorific exercise, for it would entail rounds of exhaustive meetings and arguments pro and con to arrive at a consensus where the ideal best would be brought to terms with the possible best. Accepting the challenge, Howard and the committee he chaired worked throughout 1987 forging guidelines to upgrade requirements for membership in the American Otological Society which were subsequently accepted by the council.

At that time, Dr. Brian McCabe, the president of the society, said of Howard's committee that the "report it prepared was bound to have an impact that would be felt for many years to come and would be of signal importance for patients with ear and skull-base problems in the United States. Further, the guidelines set forth in the committee's report could also be used by the American Board of ENT to certify fellowship and residency training programs in otology throughout the country."

There were national consequences from Howard's role in certification upgrade which impacted the federal government's National Institute of Health (NIH)—which is organized along lines where individual institutes—there were 13 at the time—are devoted to various specialties in medicine.

Deafness and other communication disorders are the source of the most common chronic disabilities in the nation. On this count alone, the fact that they were lumped together within the NIH as part of the Institute of

Neurology, Communicative Disorders and Stroke had long been a cause for discontent among otologists, audiologists and researchers. In the mid-1970s Howard, along with other eminent otologists such as Drs. James Snow, John Lindsay, Frank Sooy and John Boardley, had tried to mount a movement designed to establish a separate institute at the NIH for Deafness and Communicative Disorders. The timing, however, was not right and the initiative got nowhere.

The next decade saw Mrs. Geraldine D. Fox in charge of government relations for the privately endowed Deafness Research Foundation in New York. She believed, as did others, that another attempt should be made to establish a separate Institute for Deafness and other Communicative Disorders since such an institute within NIH would help focus national attention on the needs of 28 million Americans suffering from communication disorders—besides providing more funds for research. More directly, it would provide an institutional forum where a wide range of professionals could consolidate their expert knowledge.

Since three decades earlier Howard had been a founding member of the Deafness Research Foundation and served on its board of directors, it was natural for Mrs. Fox to turn to Howard and others for help in mobilizing political support for such a separate institute within the NIH.

Howard moved into action in what amounted to a protracted war of detail, starting with his patients. Starting with those patients he had treated over the years who were prominent in the world of business, government, the performing arts, athletics and the press, Howard contacted them to explain the merits of a separate institute as proposed in a bill introduced into the House by Representative Claude Pepper and in the Senate by Senator Tom Harkin.

Many of these famous patients thereupon wrote to their representatives and senators urging them to support the bill in question. Some showed up to testify before various committees of the House and Senate, as did Howard. The upshot was that the Pepper-Harkin bill was passed in the House by a vote of 409 to 2 and was unanimously approved by the Senate.

The overwhelming Congressional support for the bill did not, however, automatically insure that it would become law, for it still needed a presidential signature, so Howard contacted President Reagan and gained his personal assurance that he would sign the Pepper-Harkin Bill when it reached his desk. And so the Institute for Deafness and other Communicative disorders, which remains a component of the NIH, promises to enhance the nationwide care of patients suffering from all forms of hearing disorders.

39

On the Razor's Edge

In the spring of 1987 Howard signed up for a three-week tour of the Soviet Union sponsored by the alumni office of the University of Southern California. Aside from his general curiosity about a land he had never visited, he wanted to see firsthand the teaching and clinical work of otolaryngologists in Moscow and Leningrad.

In preparation for the trip, Howard contacted Dr. Armand Hammer, his friend and patient, who had long-standing business interests in the Soviet Union. Could he help Howard gain access to medical schools in Moscow and Leningrad? Dr. Hammer had his secretary in his Moscow office, Nina Valassova, contact the Soviet minister of health, who in turn arranged to have the door opened to places where ear work could be observed.

The departure of the USC tour group of 40 was set for mid-August and comprised, in addition to Howard, his daughter Carolyn and her husband Dick Helmuth, Nanette Fabray and several doctors and their wives who were among Howard's circle of friends. Just as they were leaving, storm clouds, long in the making, began to form over the House Ear Institute.

Years previously, soon after Bill became president, some long-term employees who had been indispensable to the institute's efficient operations were shuffled out of these positions and succeeded by various new people. A year after Ed Ethell's retirement, the board of trustees elected Janet Doak, who had been serving as the director of development, as executive vice president of the institute while she continued her previous fund-raising work.

At the same time, the institute's board agreed on the need for a research director who would work with Bill and formulate an order of priorities for the institute's various research programs. The search that followed led to Don Nielsen, Ph.D., who had extensive experience on both the substantive and administrative side of academic research. In August 1986 he joined the institute staff as executive vice president for research.

In the spring of 1987 Howard made a suggestion to the board based on his experiences as chair of the academic affairs committee at Whittier College where he was a trustee. The object of that committee was to keep other trustees abreast of problems which crop up within the college. Howard believed that a similar committee, formed from among the trustees of the institute, could serve the board as a monitoring and informational tool. When the suggestion was adopted, Charles Hart, a former chair of the board, agreed to take on responsibility for the new committee.

In the early summer of 1987, Hart's committee faced up to an uncomfortable duty. It reported to the board that the institute—despite its successful fund-raising for long range purposes—had drifted into a severe dollar overrun in its operating budget. The causes were named and some of the proposed remedies were soon put into effect. First, Brad Volkmer, an accountant with broad experience in both budget management and administration was employed to assist Janet Doak in providing the institute with more effective procedures for budget control and administration.

Other proposed remedies, however, of a sensitive personal nature led to painful discussions between Bill on the one side and the board of trustees on the other, for it was hard for the board to impose direct administrative constraints on certain expenditures which Bill from his own perspective, thought were right—and which also involved individuals of his own choice. What made the discussions all the more painful was the board's respect for Bill's authentic genius as an ear surgeon and for the way his innovative work on so many fronts had been the driving force behind the institute's rise to worldwide fame.

Bill, for his part, believed that the board's proposals regarding the necessary steps to shore up the fiscal integrity of the institute comprised an unwarranted intrusion on his presidential right of decision. The main points in contention were unresolved when Howard, along with the other members of the USC tour group, boarded a plane at the Los Angeles airport for the flight to Moscow.

Arriving in Moscow, the mid-August weather was cooler than expected but all members of the tour were impressed by what they saw in the city. The accommodations in the Cosmos Hotel were very satisfactory. The streets were clean, with no paper refuse and no graffiti on the walls. The train service in the subway system was sparkling and efficient. The waiting areas in the subway were lined with handsome statuary with spacious scenes inlaid in marble walls—all lit by sparkling chandeliers. People on the streets and in the subways were courteous and helpful in ways that transcended language barriers to communication.

On the second night in Moscow—which was cold and raining—Howard, Nanette, Carolyn and Dick arranged to see the famous Moscow Circus and went by cab to the general area which was located many miles from their hotel. They walked at least a mile through the rain before reaching the circus tent, located in a large park. Unfortunately, during this walk Howard had an angina attack, the first since his bypass surgery in 1983.

As was his wont, he kept this fact to himself so as not to mar the pleasures of the evening for the others and he controlled the attack by taking some of the nitroglycerine tablets he always carried with him. Subsequent mild attacks of angina while he was in Moscow persuaded Howard that it was best not to visit the hospital and medical schools in the city as previously planned and he informed Dr. Hammer's secretary of this decision, but added that he would visit hospitals in Leningrad after arriving there.

A pleasant three-day boat trip on the Volga River, with stops at little rural towns along the way, allowed Howard to enjoy a protracted rest, broken into only by a brief visit to a rural hospital. He did not notice any recurrence of his angina and in Leningrad, as scheduled, the tour party checked into the enormous Pribaltiiskaya Hotel. Howard spent the first day absorbing the visual feast of beauty offered to his eyes on all sides. He planned to leave the tour temporarily the next day to go to the University of Leningrad and see the kind of work being done there in his medical specialty, but his plans was derailed by what happened to him on the second day in the city.

The next morning, Howard joined Nanette, Carolyn and Dick on a cab ride from their hotel for an intended quick shopping tour in downtown Leningrad. In the course of a walk through the shopping area, Howard suddenly felt the same symptoms he had experienced prior to his heart attack four years previously—pain, tightness in the chest, shortness of breath and extreme weakness. This time he knew he was in the grip of a severe heart attack.

He slumped down on the curb with Carolyn beside him, while Dick and Nanette stopped pedestrians in an attempt to explain that Howard must get back to his hotel at once where he knew medical care was available. The attempt was in vain. The people approached could not understand what they were told and so walked on.

Nanette and Dick then stepped out into the street and tried to flag a cab. They thought rescue was at hand when one stopped, but the driver could not understand English and after no more than a moment's pause, sped on. When Nan scanned the area for possible sources of help, she saw three men standing at an intersection talking in sign language. Dashing over to them, Nan uses the signs she knew, which are quite international in nature, and got them to grasp the nature of Howard's peril and the need for immediate transportation to the Pribaltiiskaya Hotel.

One of the trio stepped into the street, stopped a sedan and used his limited speech to make the driver comprehend Howard's critical condition. With that, the driver motioned Nan and Dick into the car and then sped back to where Howard had been left with Carolyn. Picking them up, the driver took off at breakneck speed for the hotel—obviously he did not want Howard to die in *his* car.

On reaching the hotel, as Howard was being helped from his car, the driver caught his eye. He smilingly pointed to his own heart and said "OK". He then pointed toward Howard's heart and again smilingly said, "OK". He refused to accept any money for the help he had rendered, waved good-bye and drove off.

"People," Howard would later say, "are kind the world over and the Good Lord was certainly sitting on my shoulder." This certainly seemed like divine intervention, for when he considered the mathematical probability in his case, it came up miraculous. How often could one have a heart attack on the streets of a strange land and have a person with you who knew important transnational cues in sign language and then find deaf people nearby to whom that person could communicate an urgent need for medical help? Communication through sign language literally saved Howard's life.

In his hotel room, Howard picked up Dr. Hammer's recent book titled *Hammer* and began to read it—hoping it would get his mind off his physical problem—because he was still in a cold sweat. Despite the many nitroglycerine tablets he had taken, he was huffing and puffing and still had chest pain.

While Dick and Carolyn remained at Howard's side, Nanette dialed a designated number for a doctor. There was no answer. She then rushed downstairs to the reception desk where one of the clerks spoke English. She explained the urgent need for a doctor, adding that she had been unable to reach one by phone. She was told that the doctor could not be reached unless someone came to the desk and the receptionist would then secure the necessary service.

A doctor's office was just around the corner from the reception desk, but as it was known that the nurse on duty there spoke no English, the English-speaking receptionist accompanied Nanette to the office and explained the problem to her. The three soon made their way to Howard's room. What followed was a circular conversation in which questions were asked, interpreted, answered, interpreted—on a line from the nurse to the interpreter, to Howard, to the interpreter, to the nurse and back again to Howard. Name? Howard House. Address? Los Angeles. Any illnesses? Yes, open heart surgery four years ago. Any others? Yes, kidney stones removed 15 years ago. Still others? Yes, tonsillectomy as a child. What difficulties was he having at the present time? Tightness and pain in the chest, difficulty breathing, extreme weakness and perspiration.

After carefully recording all this information, the nurse took Howard's blood pressure and pulse, turned to the interpreter and said, "Tell him I think he is having a heart attack."

Howard, on being told, thanked the nurse through the interpreter. The nurse now phoned the house doctor who indicated that he would come right away. He was, however, preceded by Howard's doctor friends who were on the USC tour who immediately asked the nurse for oxygen. She informed them none was available.

When the house doctor arrived, he looked over the nurse's notes, took Howard's pulse, listened to his chest and heart and then told the interpreter to tell Howard that he was indeed having a heart attack and he would give him some helpful medicine.

The doctor reached into his bag and took from it a syringe with a needle which had been placed between two pieces of gauze—a likely sign that he did not have disposable needles and proceeded to plunge the needle into a bottle of grayish-red liquid, withdrawing some three cc's. After he had injected a slight amount of the liquid intravenously into Howard's arm, a sudden thought caused him to stop and put an imperative question to the interpreter. Ask the patient if he was allergic to anything? Both Howard and the doctor were relieved when the answer was no.

When all the fluid was injected and the needle was removed, the doctor informed Howard's family—and some added members of the tour as well as the tour guide who had crowded into the room—that it was necessary for the patient to go to a hospital. Another miracle! To Howard's astonishment, there was suddenly no more pain, no more shortness of breath, no more weakness. As the saying goes, Howard announced he "never felt better in his life" and saw no need to go to a hospital when he felt so well.

While an ambulance was called, Nan telephoned Dr. Hammer's secretary in Moscow informing her of what had happened. She, in turn, immediately contacted Dr. Hammer at his home in Los Angeles—which would be one o'clock in the morning, local time.

When the two stretcher bearers arrived they carried a military-style stretcher which they placed on the floor and then asked Howard to rise from his chair and lie down on it. In doing so, Howard remarked to others in the room—in a slurred voice—that they should all have a shot of the medicine, "It is the greatest".

The phone rang just as the stretcher was being lifted by the orderlies. Dr. Hammer's secretary called to inform Nanette that Howard should be taken to a certain hospital where a certain doctor would be waiting for him. The instructions were passed on and soon Howard found himself in a World War II-type ambulance where he was placed on the floor. Carolyn accompanied him and sat on a small seat. There was no equipment in the patient section. The street was very bumpy and the rattling within the vehicle made it difficult for Howard to converse with his daughter.

The hospital where Howard was taken presented a bleak picture—a dim hall, naked light bulbs, plaster disintegrating and paint peeling from the walls. As he was being carried on the stretcher to the designated room, he saw that a patient was being removed from the same room so that Howard would be its sole occupant. A nurse sitting at a nearby desk immediately rose to help transfer him from the stretcher to a bed whose mattress seemed to be no more than two inches thick. Howard removed his shoes and socks, but the nurse indicated that it was not necessary for him to remove his clothes. With that, she pulled the covers over him.

Soon a handsome, young man who spoke perfect English entered the room. Dr. Andrec Pulotov, the cardiologist who had been put on Howard's case by the long hand of Dr. Hammer which stretched from Los Angeles to Leningrad, examined Howard, took an EKG and told Howard he did not think his heart attack was severe or would necessarily be too damaging to him. Intravenous fluid was prescribed, together with several different tablets, of which one, so the doctor explained, was for a specific purpose.

Repeated EKGs were done and when Howard asked the reasons for so many, the cardiologist explained that the monitor on the wall was out of order but would soon be repaired and again operational. Howard's symptoms were completely alleviated by the effects of the previous injection he had received in his hotel room, but the use of a bed pan with his clothes on was not the easiest task in the world, considering that he had been told to avoid stress.

Meanwhile, Dr. Hammer had phoned Howard's son, John, informing him of Howard's heart attack. John at once contacted his Russian-speaking brother-in-law in the East and asked him to call the hospital in which Howard was a patient to find out what he could about his father's condition. In this way, he learned that Howard would have to remain in the hospital for two weeks. Moreover, because of airline regulations applicable to people who had suffered heart attacks, he would have to remain in Leningrad another week after being released from the hospital.

John reasoned that Howard would not relish remaining in Leningrad for three weeks before being able to fly home, and would no doubt prefer to be treated at the University Hospital in Helsinki—30 minutes distant by air—where he knew the doctors on the medical staff. John, who had just checked up on President Reagan's hearing, contacted the president's physician, Dr. John Hutton, to ask if there was any way to speed Howard out of Russia. This led to a call from the White House to the state department and from there to the U.S. consul general in Leningrad. In the meantime Armand Hammer, through his office, contacted the Soviet minister of health.

Hours later the U.S. consul in Leningrad appeared in Howard's room along with a Soviet assistant minister of health. There was no need to worry. To everyone's delight, Howard was told he would be able to leave the next morning for Helsinki along with other members of the USC tour.

During the three days Howard spent in the Leningrad hospital, Dr. Pulotov, the cardiologist, spent considerable time talking to Howard about the conditions in Russia as compared to those in the United States and the conversation ranged all over the landscape—from areas of medicine in which two doctors had a shared interest, to political problems common to their respective countries. Dr. Pulotov made it clear that he was an enthusiastic supporter of Gorbachev and hoped that the Russian leader and President Reagan would meet more often in order to reduce the scope of the problems that divided the Soviet Union and the United States. He cited Gorbachev's repeated statement that his first priority after reducing military expenditures and straightening out the economy was to improve health care in the Soviet Union, yet he voiced concern regarding Gorbachev's ability to cope with the entrenched interests in the Soviet Union who would not welcome any reform moves which would upset their comfortable stations.

At Howard's leave-taking from the hospital, Dr. Pulotov stopped by to wish him well and Howard, in turn, gratefully gave the cardiologist his autographed copy of Armand Hammer's book—which made a tremendous hit with the doctor. It was Howard's judgment that he had received excellent care in the Leningrad hospital and that its doctors—40 percent of whom are women—had a thorough knowledge of medicine. The drawback was that they lacked the necessary facilities and equipment to maximize the effective application of their knowledge.

The Soviet doctors not only kept abreast of general developments in U.S. medicine, but Howard was also pleasantly surprised to learn that the ENT people in Leningrad were aware of the work being done at the House Ear Institute. Those he spoke to expressed the hope that they might one day be able to visit the institute in Los Angeles. As he checked out, Howard discovered he had not been charged anything for his medical care.

The ambulance that took him to the airport was the same one that conveyed him to the hospital. En route to the airport, he heard a siren and thought he was being treated to a police escort—a nice gesture. Not so. At the airport, Howard saw that the siren was on a very modern ambulance completely equipped in much the same way as are American ambulances. It carried two doctors and two nurses, and later it was explained that this particular ambulance was continuously on call. Since it had no calls at the hospital or en route to the airport, when Howard's vehicle passed, it was free to provide Howard with escort service.

Howard was taken directly to the plane waiting on the tarmac, bypassing passport and custom officials. The stairs at the back of the plane were down, but no passengers as yet were on board. The steps were very steep and as the stretcher bearers started their ascent, Howard found himself slipping down. He grasped the stretcher as firmly as he could despite the prior admonitions to avoid stress. The lead stretcher bearer yelled in Russian to the one at the bottom to lift the stretcher higher. This was done, Howard was relieved and carried on a more even keel up the remainder of the steps. He was placed on the front seat of the plane and given an oxygen tank to use if necessary—the first he had seen since his heart attack. Soon the other members of the USC tour came aboard the plane for the short flight to Helsinki.

In Helsinki, Howard was placed in a wheel chair and then in an ambulance which took him directly to the University Hospital—which glistened with cleanliness and all staff members spoke English. In contrast to the Leningrad hospital, Howard was asked to disrobe to the buff and was given hospital pajamas. The equipment was equal to anything found in the United States, the food was excellent and the care was superb.

After examining him, the Finnish doctors made a thorough review of the records Howard had brought with him, and then confirmed the Russian findings and continued the medication he had been on. A cardiologist explained that he had had a slight obstruction of a small terminal vessel in the apex area of the heart, but the result was very little damage to the function of the heart muscle. He was also told he could be ambulatory and could walk to the bathroom and shower stalls and he could stroll down the hospital corridor to regain his strength.

Howard thought it best to wait for a nonstop flight from Helsinki to Los Angeles rather than continue with the tour group on a flight that would require an intervening stop in Seattle. However, the only nonstop flight to Los Angeles was scheduled to depart five days later. Nanette Fabray could not stay behind with Howard and so had to leave with the USC tour group to meet a commitment to perform in Hawaii. Carolyn and Dick also had to leave because of prior arrangements involving their children who were waiting in Los Angeles.

Convinced he would not need help during the nonstop flight to Los Angeles, Howard insisted he "felt absolutely wonderful." He was in that frame of mind when he received an overseas call from John's wife, Patti. It had been her intention, she said, to fly to Helsinki to accompany him on the return flight home, but she had contracted a bad cold and did not believe it wise to risk the trip. Her voice as she spoke sounded very natural, but Howard didn't think anything of it and assured her she should stay home.

Patti, however, had something more to add. Howard's two teenage grandchildren, David and Nicole—Ken and Joan House's children—had tickets to Helsinki and would be arriving to accompany his flight back to Los Angeles. Matters worked out this way to Howard's delight and to the vast enjoyment of the two grandchildren, but he had no idea of the near tragedy whose facts were being withheld from him.

Because there had been no bill when he checked out of the Leningrad hospital, Howard was surprised by the "big bill" he got as he left the Helsinki hospital. He was charged 50 marks a day—$13.50—and could not help reflect on what people are charged as heart patients in an American hospital.

The flight to Los Angeles was uneventful and marked by the pleasure Howard found in the company of his two young companions. At the Los Angeles airport he was met by his family and taken directly to St. Vincent Medical Center where his cardiologist, Dr. Magidson, was to do some tests and look over his record. All the members of his family except for his son John and his wife Patti joined Howard at dinner in the hospital—which surprised Howard, but he said nothing.

After dinner Ken came over to the bed, took Howard's hand and said, "Now, Dad, don't worry, everything is just fine. Don't worry at all, everything is fine." He paused and it seemed he was struggling for words. Finally he added, "I must tell you John has been in an accident."

Howard was relieved to learn that John "was just fine," but asked if it was an automobile accident and how it happened. Ken first hedged by saying John was in the Hoag Hospital in Newport Beach where he was doing "just fine—

just fine." At last the truth came out. John had broken his neck—which explained why Patti did not go to Helsinki.

At 5:30 on the afternoon of the same day John had set in motion the calls that led from the White House to Howard's release from the Leningrad hospital, he was body surfing with his two sons, Hans and Chris. While riding a wave—as he had been doing for over 40 years—he was suddenly thrown by the force of the wave into the sand and awakened face down with a roaring tinnitus in his ears and paralysis in both legs.

John realized at once he had fractured his sixth cervical vertebra and that his nerves had been traumatized at the point where they exited from the spinal cord into both legs. His sons carefully pulled him through the surf onto the beach and John immediately splinted his neck between his two hands, knowing he was in serious trouble.

A lifeguard several blocks away caught the picture of trouble and raced toward John in a radio-equipped jeep. John asked that a call be immediately placed to Hoag Hospital for an ambulance and John's younger son, Chris, ran to their beach house where he explained to Patti what had happened. She immediately called two doctor friends in Newport, Bill Owsley and Al Pizzo, and told them of the accident.

The ambulance arrived in ten minutes and John explained to the paramedics he had fractured his sixth cervical vertebra. They stabilized his neck with a collar brace and together with Hans, left for the hospital. When they arrived the two Newport doctor friends were waiting together with N. Edatolpour, a top neurosurgeon who had just completed a surgical case at the hospital.

Another miracle! How often would such doctors be found and be available at 5:30 on a Friday afternoon in August? Soon Drs. Bill House and Bill Hitselberger also arrived from Los Angeles to add their support.

John's diagnosis of his own case was confirmed by X-rays. Meanwhile, he could track the course of the paralysis as it moved up his body. There was no feeling in his legs, a gradual loss of feeling in his abdomen and he was developing difficulty breathing. All of this posed a critical question for the doctors. Should they operate at once? Should they instead wait to see if his condition would improve when the swelling went down? John reasoned that the paralysis creeping up his abdomen toward his chest muscles would not be happening if the cause was due only to a fracture. There had to be the complications of a hematoma (blood clot) pressing on his spinal cord.

The doctors explained there were high risks in giving him an anesthetic under conditions where he had difficulty breathing. John acknowledged that he fully understood the risks, but told the doctors to operate at once. Eight hours later John awakened from having the fracture repaired—it had pressed on the spinal cord but had not torn it. The ascending paralysis was due, as he assumed, to a hematoma.

With the correction of the fracture and the draining of the hematoma, John could now move both legs but had a slight problem with his head—which was now totally surrounded by a metal halo. In this kind of injury, such a halo is actually bolted into the skull and down onto the chest in ways which make it impossible for the wearer to move the head. While in the hospital John received a surprise telephone call from President Reagan that greatly lifted his spirit and certainly impressed the hospital staff.

The mending process that brought both Howard and John back from the edge of the abyss and into the world of health, did not, unfortunately, have a matching piece in the strained relationship between Bill House and the board of trustees of the House Ear Institute. A point was reached where anguished decisions bearing on the future of the institute had to be made. Bill relinquished the presidency of the institute and became its president emeritus, remaining a trustee and also the medical director of the Children's Center he had built. This left him in a position to devote more time to his institute research and to his OMG practice.

Bill's resignation occurred during the period Howard was felled by a heart attack in Leningrad. Howard was distressed by the circumstances which gave neither the board nor Bill any options to their disagreements aside from a resignation—though Bill's hurt on that account was naturally far more acute.

In his head and his heart, Howard endorsed every syllable in the resolution adopted by the board of trustees of the House Ear Institute at the time of Bill's resignation which read:

> Dr. William House is thanked, praised and honored for his four years as president and chief executive officer of the House Ear Institute. The growth of the institute during this period reflects his leadership, his research in so many areas, particularly the development of the cochlear implant and most importantly, his development of the Center for Deaf Children.

John House was still in intensive care when he was visited by Stafford Grady, chair of the board of the institute. who asked him if he would consider succeeding Bill and taking on other burdens of the institute as its president. John agreed, subject to his total recovery. Fears in this regard ebbed when he left the hospital wearing his halo two weeks after he was admitted. He was in due course elected to the presidency by the board and a month later assumed his new responsibilities while also seeing patients at the OMG. On Christmas he lit up his halo with lights as though it were a Christmas tree.

One evening during this period, John and neighbors were alerted to a surprise that was in store for him. Members of the USC band would be arriving in John's front yard to play and sing the school's fight song. The matter had been arranged by his oldest son, Hans, in recognition of his father's championship swimming days at USC.

There was a heartfelt thanksgiving celebration when John was at last able to remove his halo the first of January 1988 and could start to do surgery again. With the odds of one in a thousand, he had made a total recovery with no residual problems that could serve as a haunting reminder of his harrowing experience. During the first six months of John's presidency changes were made to correct the operating overrun so the institute would function within a balanced budget.

40

The Past as Prologue

It takes the passing years to reveal what the days hide. So as Howard reached his 80th birthday, vigorous in mind and active in his profession, he saw one thing more clearly than ever before—despite the "Hazards of being Howard," he had lived an almost charmed life. Physically he had been spared the consequences of perilous moments which could have cut him down—a threatened drowning as a child, polio as a medical student, rabies or tuberculosis as a resident, two heart attacks when he was in his 70s. He could thus say in the manner of a French aristocrat who was asked what he did during the French Revolution, "I survived."

Yet Howard had far more substantial grounds to count his blessings: He had been shaped by the fortunate example of his father—a person of outsized talents. He had been enveloped by the love of his Grandmother Payne and his exuberant Uncle Floyd. He was the beneficiary of an act of grace by Dean Paul S. McKibben who admitted him to medical school despite his bleak undergraduate record at three colleges. He had been subsequently aided in various ways by dominant figures at the USC medical school and Los Angeles County Hospital—J. Mackenzie Brown, "Hot Point" Percy and Simon Jesberg, among others. He had technically failed the California State Licensing Board, yet a "correction for error" after the fact by a sympathetic review board had changed a failure into a pass.

If this were not enough, backed by his father's advice and financial support, he had the good fortune after his residency to observe the clinical and research work of U.S. and foreign leaders—Dean Lierle, French Hansel, Dorothy Wolff, Vilbray Blair, Artie O. Furstenberg, James Maxwell, Chevalaire Jackson, Harris P. Mosher, Philip Meltzer, Julius Lempert, Sir Harold Gillies, Gunnar Holmgren, Hans Brunner, Ernst Fuchs and many others. In addition to the friendship he formed with all of them, he established rapport with the younger generation who would emerge as preeminent figures in their own specialties—George Shambaugh, Jr., Francis Lederer, Paul Hollinger, Claire Kos, John Lindsay, Sir Terrance Cawthorne and others. After learning the art of the practice of medicine at the prestigious Moore-White Clinic in Los Angeles, he had become nationally prominent in the surgical treatment of otosclerosis, thanks to the fortuitous early training he received in fenestration surgery from Julius Lempert, and then by an early introduction to stapes mobilization by Sam Rosen and later to the stapedectomy by his former student, John Shea.

In the most fundamental of human relationships, he had been blessed in his marriage to a woman as devoted as Helen—and in having two able sons and a lovely daughter who have presented him with seven fine grandchildren. He was lucky in the nature of the close relationships he had formed with many of his patients who became dear friends and the propitious choice of his early professional associates—Bill House, Fred Linthicum and James Sheehy— with whom he had formed the Otologic Medical Group and who with later associates had helped make possible the growth of the original Los Angeles Foundation of Otology into the House Ear Institute.

The training offered by each of these in his own specialty advanced the skills of a new generation of ear specialists and researchers. These who became OMG members were drawn into the work of the House Ear Institute and its association with the USC School of Medicine, which in turn allowed them to extend the frontiers of medical knowledge and practice still further.

Computerized records are available only from 1979 onward which compile the number of research fellows the House Ear Institute helped train, as well as the visiting U.S. and foreign doctors who took part in its various teaching programs. Yet even when the data for the previous 30 years is left out of account—an immense statistical gap—the data for this past decade alone is impressive—the institute advanced the training of 84 research fellows—18 from this country and 66 from abroad plus over 70 clinical fellows from the U.S.—all of whom teach in various medical schools, do research and practice otology. Beyond this, the institute attracted 3,798 ear specialists to its visiting doctor programs and its courses—2,522 from all 50 states and 1,276 from 68 foreign countries.

In addition the OMG members and their associates in various institute programs have produced a prodigious volume of academic articles representing contributions to scientific literature which has been published in leading scientific journals documenting the major contributions made to the fund of existing knowledge in virtually all realms of hearing and balance disorders.

Howard had long dreamed of having both the institute and the OMG (which are now a block apart) housed under one roof so that the clinicians and the full-time research personnel could work more closely together. This dream turned into an urgent cause when it became apparent that the expanding work of the institute and OMG confronted both entities with the need for expanded space to take the place of their increasingly cramped quarters. In July 1986 the institute's board voted to build the facility envisioned

and appointed James Ludlam chair of the building committee. It was agreed OMG members in turn would pay rent
to the institute for the space they would use in the new
building, so this rental income added to the institute's
endowment would make such a project feasible.

As the building project was getting underway, St. Vincent
Medical Center agreed to purchase the land owned by the
OMG and lease it to the House Ear Institute for $1 for 99
years. The Building Campaign Fund was initiated in 1986
(which continues to date) and the first substantial gift
toward the $28 million project was given by Mr. and Mrs.
Ross McCollum. Similar gifts were soon made by David
Koch, Helen McLoraine, Nanette Fabray, Dorothy Cook,
the Del Webb Foundation and Betty Hutton Williams.

On June 24, 1988, over 400 friends of the institute
gathered for the ground-breaking ceremony which coincided
with Howard's 80th birthday. At that time, over half of the
$28 million goal had been obtained in cash and pledges, but
what tipped the scale in favor of a decision to go ahead
with the building project was a substantial gift from Dolores
"Lolie" Eccles in memory of her husband, George S.
Eccles, who helped found the institute in 1946.

With history taking this full circle, it was thought to be
only right and proper to name the new structure—with
120,000 sq. ft. of internal space—in honor of George S.
Eccles, himself an outsized man. The attached Children's
Center building will bear the name of Sam and Rose Stein
in recognition of their role in providing the necessary funds
to house the institute's unique children's facility.

At the ground breaking ceremony, Nanette Fabray,
Florence Henderson and Dolores Hope led the assembled
friends of the institute in singing "Happy Birthday" to
Howard as he joined the exclusive octogenarian club in
excellent health. He was not content, however, merely to sit
in the sun and lose himself in reveries about the past. His

thoughts were of the future. What he wrote at the time was not a last will and testament, but a plan of action:

The future research and educational programs at the institute will continue to focus on the strengths provided by the close association of HEI and OMG. The new facility—when it is completed two years hence—will provide a daily interchange between science and medicine as related to the ear. The staff of researchers, audiologists, educators and clinicians will broaden the areas of basic science and applied research. The institute will contract with other ear research centers to avoid unnecessary duplication of effort and facilities and will coordinate the results of their research programs.

The enlarged Children's Center of the institute, will provide profoundly deaf children with multidisciplinary evaluation and service by otologists, audiologists, speech-pathologists, psychologists and educators of the deaf. At the other end of the human spectrum, considerable research will be directed toward the special problems of aging as the population lives longer with a consequent increase in the number of people who develop hearing impairments. In the area of applied research, the cochlear and brain stem implants pioneered at the House Ear Institute—together with hearing aids and other assistive devices—will be greatly improved through the continuous developments in space-age electronic technology.

Basic research will engender new knowledge in the areas of molecular biology, genetics, neuroanatomy, physiology, chemistry, biochemistry, histopathology and pharmacology. Cellular studies of nerve degeneration and regeneration will make great strides. Improved understanding of viral, immunologic and allergic phenomenon may evolve into vaccines and drugs that will prevent many ear problems that occur from these disorders.

Research, however, will be of little value unless it is disseminated through an educational process to others so that they, in turn, may help their patients with ear problems. The unique otologic library of the institute will be enlarged to house all types of teaching materials and these will be readily available to health professionals as well as lay persons with special interests in the field. All this will be in supplement to the hands-on training of clinicians the OMG and HEI will continue to provide in a form of educational linkage stretching from the past into the farthest future.

When he wrote this order of battle, Howard acknowledged his immense debt to the institute's board of trustees, the three auxiliaries—the Associates, Sonance and the Orange County Associates*—the foundations, corporations, friends and patients who had supported the institute throughout the years, plus the enormous gratitude owed the doctors and staffs of the OMG and institute for their continued medical research and efforts "for the world to hear."

But above all, Howard continued to hold before his eyes the model of his father, finding in him a standard for judging his own conduct plus a kind of mystic judge whose favorable opinion he must take care to earn over and over again.

---

*Recently founded by Gloria Osbrink and Athalie Clarke.

Index

Additional copies of this book may be obtained
from your local bookstore
or by sending $21.95 per copy, postpaid,
to:

Hope Publishing House
P.O.Box 60008
Pasadena, CA 91116

CA residents kindly add 6½% tax
FAX orders to: (818) 792-2121
Telephone VISA/MC orders to: (800) 326-2671